CONTENTS.

Preface,
Introduction,
Biogenesis,
Degeneration,
Growth,
Death,
Mortification,
Eternal Life,
Environment,
Conformity to Type,
Semi-Parasitism,
Parasitism,

PREFACE.

No class of works is received with more suspicion, I had almost said derision, than those which deal with Science and Religion. Science is tired of reconciliations between two things which never should have been contrasted; Religion is offended by the patronage of an ally which it professes not to need; and the critics have rightly discovered that, in most cases where Science is either pitted against Religion or fused with it, there is some fatal misconception to begin with as to the scope and province of either. But although no initial protest, probably, will save this work from the unhappy reputation of its class, the thoughtful mind will perceive that the fact of its subject-matter being Law—a property peculiar neither to Science nor to Religion—at once places it on a somewhat different footing.

The real problem I have set myself may be stated in a sentence. Is there not reason to believe that many of the Laws of the Spiritual World, hitherto regarded as occupying an entirely separate province, are simply the Laws of the Natural World? Can we identify the Natural Laws, or any one of them, in the Spiritual sphere? That vague lines everywhere run through the Spiritual World is already beginning to be recognized. Is it possible to link them with those great lines running through the visible universe which we call the Natural Laws, or are they fundamentally distinct? In a word, Is the Supernatural natural or unnatural?

I may, perhaps, be allowed to answer these questions in the form in which they have answered themselves to myself. And I must apologize at the outset for personal references which, but for the clearness they may lend to the statement, I would surely avoid.

It has been my privilege for some years to address regularly two very different audiences on two very different themes. On week days I have lectured to a class of students on the Natural Sciences, and on Sundays to an audience consisting for the most part of working men on subjects of a moral and religious character. I cannot say that this collocation ever appeared as a difficulty to myself, but to certain of my friends it was more than a problem.

It was solved to me, however, at first, by what then seemed the necessities of the case—I must keep the two departments entirely by themselves. They lay at opposite poles of thought; and for a time I succeeded in keeping the Science and the Religion shut off from one another in two separate compartments of my mind. But gradually the wall of partition showed symptoms of giving way. The two fountains of knowledge also slowly began to overflow, and finally their waters met and mingled. The great change was in the compartment which held the Religion. It was not that the well there was dried; still less that the fermenting waters were washed away by the flood of Science. The actual contents remained the same. But the crystals of former doctrine were dissolved; and as they precipitated themselves once more in definite forms, I observed that the Crystalline System was changed. New channels also for outward expression opened, and some of the old closed up; and I found the truth running out to my audience on the Sundays by the week-day outlets. In other words, the subject-matter Religion had taken on the method of expression of Science, and I discovered myself enunciating Spiritual Law in the exact terms of Biology and Physics.

Now this was not simply a scientific coloring given to Religion, the mere freshening of the theological air with natural facts and illustrations. It was an entire re-casting of truth. And when I came seriously to consider what it involved, I saw, or seemed to see, that it meant essentially the introduction of Natural Law into the Spiritual World. It was not, I repeat, that new and detailed analogies of *Phenomena* rose into view—although material for Parable lies unnoticed and unused on the field of recent Science in inexhaustible profusion. But Law has a still grander function to discharge toward Religion than Parable. There is a deeper unity between the two Kingdoms than the analogy of their Phenomena—a unity which the poet's vision, more quick than the theologian's, has already dimly seen:—

> "And verily many thinkers of this age,
> Aye, many Christian teachers, half in heaven,
> Are wrong in just my sense, who understood
> Our natural world too insularly, as if
> No spiritual counterpart completed it,
> Consummating its meaning, rounding all
> To justice and perfection, *line by line,*

> *Form by form, nothing single nor alone,*
> The great below clenched by the great above."[1]

The function of Parable in religion is to exhibit "form by form." Law undertakes the profounder task of comparing "line by line." Thus Natural Phenomena serve mainly an illustrative function in Religion. Natural Law, on the other hand, could it be traced in the Spiritual World, would have an important scientific value—it would offer Religion a new credential. The effect of the introduction of Law among the scattered Phenomena of Nature has simply been to make Science, to transform knowledge into eternal truth. The same crystallizing touch is needed in Religion. Can it be said that the Phenomena of the Spiritual World are other than scattered? Can we shut our eyes to the fact that the religious opinions of mankind are in a state of flux? And when we regard the uncertainty of current beliefs, the war of creeds, the havoc of inevitable as well as of idle doubt, the reluctant abandonment of early faith by those who would cherish it longer if they could, is it not plain that the one thing thinking men are waiting for is the introduction of Law among the Phenomena of the Spiritual World? When that comes we shall offer to such men a truly scientific theology. And the Reign of Law will transform the whole Spiritual World as it has already transformed the Natural World.

I confess that even when in the first dim vision, the organizing hand of Law moved among the unordered truths of my Spiritual World, poor and scantily-furnished as it was, there seemed to come over it the beauty of a transfiguration. The change was as great as from the old chaotic world of Pythagoras to the symmetrical and harmonious universe of Newton. My Spiritual World before was a chaos of facts; my Theology, a Pythagorean system trying to make the best of Phenomena apart from the idea of Law. I make no charge against Theology in general. I speak of my own. And I say that I saw it to be in many essential respects centuries behind every department of Science I knew. It was the one region still unpossessed by Law. I saw then why men of Science distrust Theology; why those who have learned to look upon Law as Authority grow cold to it—it was the Great Exception.

I have alluded to the genesis of the idea in my own mind partly for another reason—to show its naturalness. Certainly I never premeditated anything to myself so objectionable and so unwarrantable in itself, as either to read Theology into Science or Science into Theology. Nothing could be more artificial than to attempt this on the speculative side; and it has been a substantial relief to me throughout that the idea rose up thus in the course of practical work and shaped itself day by day unconsciously. It might be charged, nevertheless, that I was all the time, whether consciously or unconsciously, simply reading my Theology into my Science. And as this would hopelessly vitiate the conclusions arrived at, I must acquit myself at least of the intention. Of nothing have I been more fearful throughout than of making Nature parallel with my own or with any creed. The only legitimate questions one dare put to Nature are those which concern universal human good and the Divine interpretation of things. These I conceive may be there actually studied at first-hand, and before their purity is soiled by human touch. We have Truth in Nature as it came from God. And it has to be read with the same unbiased mind, the same open eye, the same faith, and the same reverence as all other Revelation. All that is found there, whatever its place in Theology, whatever its orthodoxy or heterodoxy, whatever its narrowness or its breadth, we are bound to accept as Doctrine from which on the lines of Science there is no escape.

When this presented itself to me as a method, I felt it to be due to it—were it only to secure, so far as that was possible, that no former bias should interfere with the integrity of the results—to begin again at the beginning and reconstruct my Spiritual World step by step. The result of that inquiry, so far as its expression in systematic form is concerned, I have not given in this book. To reconstruct a Spiritual Religion, or a department of Spiritual Religion—for this is all the method can pretend to—on the lines of Nature would be an attempt from which one better equipped in both directions might well be pardoned if he shrank. My object at present is the humbler one of venturing a simple contribution to practical Religion along the lines indicated. What Bacon predicates of the Natural World, *Natura enim non nisi parendo vincitur*, is also true, as Christ had already told us, of the Spiritual World. And I present a few samples of the religious teaching referred to formerly as having been prepared under the influence of scientific ideas in the hope that they may be useful first of all in this direction.

I would, however, carefully point out that though their unsystematic arrangement here may create the impression that these papers are merely isolated readings in Religion pointed by casual scientific truths, they are organically connected by a single principle. Nothing could be more false both to Science and to Religion than attempts to adjust the two spheres by making out ingenious points of contact in detail. The solution of this great question of conciliation, if one may still refer to a problem so gratuitous, must be general rather than particular. The basis in a common principle—the Continuity of Law—can alone save specific applications from ranking as mere coincidences, or exempt them from the reproach of being a hybrid between two things which must be related by the deepest affinities or remain forever separate.

To the objection that even a basis in Law is no warrant for so great a trespass as the intrusion into another field of thought of the principles of Natural Science, I would reply that in this I find I am following a lead which in other departments has not only been allowed but has achieved results as rich as they were unexpected. What is the Physical Politic of Mr. Walter Bagehot but the extension of Natural Law to the Political World? What is the Biological Sociology of Mr. Herbert Spencer but the application of Natural Law to the Social World? Will it be charged that the splendid achievements of such thinkers are hybrids between things which Nature has meant to remain apart? Nature usually solves such problems for herself. Inappropriate hybridism is checked by the Law of Sterility. Judged by this great Law these modern developments of our knowledge stand uncondemned. Within their own sphere the results of Mr. Herbert Spencer are far from sterile—the application of Biology to Political Economy is already revolutionizing the Science. If the introduction of Natural Law into the Social sphere is no violent contradiction but a genuine and permanent contribution, shall its further extension to the Spiritual sphere be counted an extravagance? Does not the Principle of Continuity demand its application in every direction? To carry it as a working principle into so lofty a region may appear impracticable. Difficulties lie on the threshold which may seem, at first sight, insurmountable. But obstacles to a true method only test its validity. And he who honestly faces the task may find relief in feeling that whatever else of crudeness and imperfection mar it, the attempt is at least in harmony with the thought and movement of his time.

That these papers were not designed to appear in a collective form, or indeed to court the more public light at all, needs no disclosure. They are published out of regard to the wish of known and unknown friends by whom, when in a fugitive form, they were received with so curious an interest as to make one feel already that there are minds which such forms of truth may touch. In making the present selection, partly from manuscript, and partly from articles already published, I have been guided less by the wish to constitute the papers a connected series than to exhibit the application of the principle in various directions. They will be found, therefore, of unequal interest and value, according to the standpoint from which they are regarded. Thus some are designed with a directly practical and popular bearing, others being more expository, and slightly apologetic in tone. The risk of combining two objects so very different is somewhat serious. But, for the reason named, having taken this responsibility, the only compensation I can offer is to indicate which of the papers incline to the one side or to the other. "Degeneration," "Growth," "Mortification," "Conformity to Type," "Semi-Parasitism," and "Parasitism" belong to the more practical order; and while one or two are intermediate, "Biogenesis," "Death," and "Eternal Life" may be offered to those who find the atmosphere of the former uncongenial. It will not disguise itself, however, that, owing to the circumstances in which they were prepared, all the papers are more or less practical in their aim; so that to the merely philosophical reader there is little to be offered except—and that only with the greatest diffidence—the Introductory chapter.

In the Introduction, which the general reader may do well to ignore, I have briefly stated the case for Natural Law in the Spiritual World. The extension of Analogy to Laws, or rather the extension of the Laws themselves so far as known to me, is new; and I cannot hope to have escaped the mistakes and misadventures of a first exploration in an unsurveyed land. So general has been the survey that I have not even paused to define specially to what departments of the Spiritual World exclusively the principle is to be applied. The danger of making a new principle apply too widely inculcates here the utmost caution. One thing is certain, and I state it pointedly, the application of Natural Law to the Spiritual World has decided and necessary limits. And if elsewhere with undue enthusiasm I seem to magnify the principle at stake, the exaggeration—like the extreme amplification of the moon's disc when near the horizon—must be charged to that almost necessary aberration of light which distorts every new idea while it is yet slowly climbing to its zenith.

In what follows the Introduction, except in the setting there is nothing new. I trust there is nothing new. When I began to follow out these lines, I had no idea where they would lead me. I was prepared, nevertheless, at least for the time, to be loyal to the method throughout, and share with nature whatever consequences might ensue. But in almost every case, after stating what appeared to be the truth in words gathered directly from the lips of Nature, I was sooner or later startled by a certain similarity in the general idea to something I had heard before, and this often developed in a moment, and when I was least expecting it, into recognition of some familiar article of faith. I was not watching for this result. I did not begin by tabulating the doctrines, as I did the Laws of Nature, and then proceed with the attempt to pair them. The majority of them seemed at first too far removed from the natural world even to suggest this. Still less did I begin with doctrines and work downward to find their relations in the natural sphere. It was the opposite process entirely. I ran up the Natural Law as far as it would go, and the appropriate doctrine seldom even loomed in sight till I had reached the top. Then it burst into view in a single moment.

I can scarcely now say whether in those moments I was more overcome with thankfulness that Nature was so like Revelation, or more filled with wonder that Revelation was so like Nature. Nature, it is true, is a part of Revelation—a much greater part doubtless than is yet believed—and one could have anticipated nothing but harmony here. But that a derived Theology, in spite of the venerable verbiage which has gathered round it, should be at bottom and in all cardinal respects so faithful a transcript of "the truth as it is in Nature" came as a surprise and to me at least as a rebuke. How, under the rigid necessity of incorporating in its system much that seemed nearly unintelligible, and much that was barely credible, Theology has succeeded so perfectly in adhering through good report and ill to what in the main are truly the lines of Nature, awakens a new admiration for those who constructed and kept this faith. But however nobly it has held its ground, Theology must feel to-day that the modern world calls for a further proof. Nor will the best Theology resent this demand; it also demands it. Theology is searching on every hand for another echo of the

Voice of which Revelation also is the echo, that out of the mouths of two witnesses its truths should be established. That other echo can only come from Nature. Hitherto its voice has been muffled. But now that Science has made the world around articulate, it speaks to Religion with a twofold purpose. In the first place it offers to corroborate Theology, in the second to purify it.

If the removal of suspicion from Theology is of urgent moment, not less important is the removal of its adulterations. These suspicions, many of them at least, are new; in a sense they mark progress. But the adulterations are the artificial accumulations of centuries of uncontrolled speculation. They are the necessary result of the old method and the warrant for its revision—they mark the impossibility of progress without the guiding and restraining hand of Law. The felt exhaustion of the former method, the want of corroboration for the old evidence, the protest of reason against the monstrous overgrowths which conceal the real lines of truth, these summon us to the search for a surer and more scientific system. With truths of the theological order, with dogmas which often depend for their existence on a particular exegesis, with propositions which rest for their evidence upon a balance of probabilities, or upon the weight of authority; with doctrines which every age and nation may make or unmake, which each sect may tamper with, and which even the individual may modify for himself, a second court of appeal has become an imperative necessity.

Science, therefore, may yet have to be called upon to arbitrate at some points between conflicting creeds. And while there are some departments of Theology where its jurisdiction cannot be sought, there are others in which Nature may yet have to define the contents as well as the limits of belief.

What I would desire especially is a thoughtful consideration of the method. The applications ventured upon here may be successful or unsuccessful. But they would more than satisfy me if they suggested a method to others whose less clumsy hands might work it out more profitably. For I am convinced of the fertility of such a method at the present time. It is recognized by all that the younger and abler minds of this age find the most serious difficulty in accepting or retaining the ordinary forms or belief. Especially is this true of those whose culture is scientific. And the reason is palpable. No man can study modern Science without a change coming over his view of truth. What impresses him about Nature is its solidity. He is there standing upon actual things, among fixed laws. And the integrity of the scientific method so seizes him that all other forms of truth begins to appear comparatively unstable. He did not know before that any form of truth could so hold him; and the immediate effect is to lessen his interest in all that stands on other bases. This he feels in spite of himself; he struggles against it in vain; and he finds perhaps to his alarm that he is drifting fast into what looks at first like pure Positivism. This is an inevitable result of the scientific training. It is quite erroneous to suppose that science ever overthrows Faith, if by that is implied that any natural truth can oppose successfully any single spiritual truth. Science cannot overthrow Faith; but it shakes it. Its own doctrines, grounded in Nature, are so certain, that the truths of Religion, resting to most men on Authority, are felt to be strangely insecure. The difficulty, therefore, which men of Science feel about Religion is real and inevitable, and in so far as Doubt is a conscientious tribute to the inviolability of Nature it is entitled to respect.

None but those who have passed through it can appreciate the radical nature of the change wrought by Science in the whole mental attitude of its disciples. What they really cry out for in Religion is a new standpoint—a standpoint like their own. The one hope, therefore, for Science is more Science. Again, to quote Bacon—we shall hear enough from the moderns by-and-by—"This I dare affirm in knowledge of Nature, that a little natural philosophy, and the first entrance into it, doth dispose the opinion to atheism; but, on the other side, much natural philosophy, and wading deep into it, will bring about men's minds to religion."[2]

The application of *similia similibus curantur* was never more in point. If this is a disease, it is the disease of Nature, and the cure is more Nature. For what is this disquiet in the breasts of men but the loyal fear that Nature is being violated? Men must oppose with every energy they possess what seems to them to oppose the eternal course of things. And the first step in their deliverance must be not to "reconcile" Nature and Religion, but to exhibit Nature in Religion. Even to convince them that there is no controversy between Religion and Science is insufficient. A mere flag of truce, in the nature of the case, is here impossible; at least, it is only possible so long as neither party is sincere. No man who knows the splendor of scientific achievement or cares for it, no man who feels the solidity of its method or works with it, can remain neutral with regard to Religion. He must either extend his method into it, or, if that is impossible, oppose it to the knife. On the other hand, no one who knows the content of Christianity, or feels the universal need of a Religion, can stand idly by while the intellect of his age is slowly divorcing itself from it. What is required, therefore, to draw Science and Religion together again—for they began the centuries hand in hand—is the disclosure of the naturalness of the supernatural. Then, and not till then, will men see how true it is, that to be loyal to all of Nature, they must be loyal to the part defined as Spiritual. No science contributes to another without receiving a reciprocal benefit. And even as the contribution of Science to Religion is the vindication of the naturalness of the Supernatural, so the gift of Religion to Science is the demonstration of the supernaturalness of the Natural. Thus, as the Supernatural becomes slowly Natural, will also the Natural become slowly Supernatural, until in the impersonal authority of Law men everywhere recognize the Authority of God.

To those who already find themselves fully nourished on the older forms of truth, I do not commend these pages. They will find them superfluous. Nor is there any reason why they should mingle with light which is already clear the distorting rays of a foreign expression.

But to those who are feeling their way to a Christian life, haunted now by a sense of instability in the foundation of their faith, now brought to bay by specific doubt at one point raising, as all doubt does, the question for the whole, I would hold up a light which has often been kind to me. There is a sense of solidity about a Law of Nature which belongs to nothing else in the world. Here, at last, amid all that is shifting, is one thing sure; one thing outside ourselves, unbiased, unprejudiced, uninfluenced by like or dislike, by doubt or fear; one thing that holds on its way to me eternally, incorruptible, and undefiled. This more than anything else, makes one eager to see the Reign of Law traced in the Spiritual Sphere. And should this seem to some to offer only a surer, but not a higher Faith; should the better ordering of the Spiritual World appear to satisfy the intellect at the sacrifice of reverence, simplicity, or love; especially should it seem to substitute a Reign of Law and a Lawgiver for a Kingdom of Grace and a Personal God, I will say, with Browning,—

> "I spoke as I saw.
> I report, as a man may of God's work—*all's love, yet all's Law.*
> Now I lay down the judgeship He lent me. Each faculty tasked,
> To perceive Him, has gained an abyss where a dewdrop was asked."

FOOTNOTES:

[1] Aurora Leigh.

[2] "Meditationes Sacræ," x.

ANALYSIS OF INTRODUCTION.

[For the sake of the general reader who may desire to pass at once to the practical applications, the following outline of the Introduction—devoted rather to general principles—is here presented.]

PART I.

NATURAL LAW IN THE SPIRITUAL SPHERE.

1. The growth of the Idea of Law.

2. Its gradual extension throughout every department of Knowledge.

3. Except one. Religion hitherto the Great Exception. Why so?

4. Previous attempts to trace analogies between the Natural and Spiritual spheres. These have been limited to analogies between *Phenomena*; and are useful mainly as illustrations. Analogies of *Law* would also have a Scientific value.

5. Wherein that value would consist. (1) The Scientific demand of the age would be met; (2) Greater clearness would be introduced into Religion practically; (3) Theology, instead of resting on Authority, would rest equally on Nature.

PART II.

THE LAW OF CONTINUITY.

A priori argument for Natural Law in the spiritual world.

1. The Law Discovered.

2.   "   Defined.

3.   "   Applied.

4. The objection answered that the *material* of the Natural and Spiritual worlds being different they must be under different Laws.

5. The existence of Laws in the Spiritual world other than the Natural Laws (1) improbable, (2) unnecessary, (3) unknown. Qualification.

6. The Spiritual not the projection upward of the Natural; but the Natural the projection downward of the Spiritual.

INTRODUCTION.

"This method turns aside from hypotheses not to be tested by any known logical canon familiar to science, whether the hypothesis claims support from intuition, aspiration or general plausibility. And, again, this method turns aside from ideal standards which avow themselves to be lawless, which profess to transcend the field of law. We say, life and conduct shall stand for us wholly on a basis of law, and must rest entirely in that region of science (not physical, but moral and social science), where we are free to use our intelligence in the methods known to us as intelligible logic, methods which the intellect can analyze. When you confront us with hypotheses, however sublime and however affecting, if they cannot be stated in terms of the rest of our knowledge, if they are disparate to that world of sequence and sensation which to us is the ultimate base of all our real knowledge, then we shake our heads and turn aside."—*Frederick Harrison.*

"Ethical science is already forever completed, so far as her general outline and main principles are concerned, and has been, as it were, waiting for physical science to come up with her."—*Paradoxical Philosophy.*

PART I.

Natural Law is a new word. It is the last and the most magnificent discovery of science. No more telling proof is open to the modern world of the greatness of the idea than the greatness of the attempts which have always been made to justify it. In the earlier centuries, before the birth of science, Phenomena were studied alone. The world then was a chaos, a collection of single, isolated, and independent facts. Deeper thinkers saw, indeed, that relations must subsist between these facts, but the Reign of Law was never more to the ancients than a far-off vision. Their philosophies, conspicuously those of the Stoics and Pythagoreans, heroically sought to marshal the discrete materials of the universe into thinkable form, but from these artificial and fantastic systems nothing remains to us now but an ancient testimony to the grandeur of that harmony which they failed to reach.

With Copernicus, Galileo, and Kepler the first regular lines of the universe began to be discerned. When Nature yielded to Newton her great secret, Gravitation was felt to be not greater as a fact in itself than as a revelation that Law was fact. And thenceforth the search for individual Phenomena gave way before the larger study of their relations. The pursuit of Law became the passion of science.

What that discovery of Law has done for Nature, it is impossible to estimate. As a mere spectacle the universe to-day discloses a beauty so transcendent that he who disciplines himself by scientific work finds it an overwhelming reward simply to behold it. In these Laws one stands face to face with truth, solid and unchangeable. Each single Law is an instrument of scientific research, simple in its adjustments, universal in its application, infallible in its results. And despite the limitations of its sphere on every side Law is still the largest, richest, and surest source of human knowledge.

It is not necessary for the present to more than lightly touch on definitions of Natural Law. The Duke of Argyll[3] indicates five senses in which the word is used, but we may content ourselves here by taking it in its most simple and obvious significance. The fundamental conception of Law is an ascertained working sequence or constant order among the Phenomena of Nature. This impression of Law as order it is important to receive in its simplicity, for the idea is often corrupted by having attached to it erroneous views of cause and effect. In its true sense Natural Law predicates nothing of causes. The Laws of Nature are simply statements of the orderly condition of things in Nature, what is found in Nature by a sufficient number of competent observers. What these Laws are in themselves is not agreed. That they have any absolute existence even is far from certain. They are relative to man in his many limitations, and represent for him the constant expression of what he may always expect to find in the world around him. But that they have any causal connection with the things around him is not to be conceived. The Natural Laws originate nothing, sustain nothing; they are merely responsible for uniformity in sustaining what has been originated and what is being sustained. They are modes of operation, therefore, not operators; processes, not powers. The Law of Gravitation, for instance, speaks to science only of process. It has no light to offer as to itself. Newton did not discover Gravity—that is not discovered yet. He discovered its Law, which is Gravitation, but tells us nothing of its origin, of its nature or of its cause.

The Natural Laws then are great lines running not only through the world, but, as we now know, through the universe, reducing it like parallels of latitude to intelligent order. In themselves, be it once more repeated, they may have no more absolute existence than parallels of latitude. But they exist for us. They are drawn for us to understand the part by some Hand that drew the whole; so drawn, perhaps, that, understanding the part, we too in time may learn to understand the whole. Now the inquiry we propose to ourselves resolves itself into the simple question, Do these lines stop with what we call the Natural sphere? Is it not possible that they may lead further? Is it probable that the Hand which ruled them gave up the work where most of all they were required? Did that Hand divide the world into two, a cosmos and a chaos, the higher being the chaos? With Nature as the symbol of all of harmony and beauty that is known to man, must we still talk of the super-natural, not as a convenient word, but as a different order of world, an unintelligible world, where the Reign of Mystery supersedes the Reign of Law?

This question, let it be carefully observed, applies to Laws not to Phenomena. That the Phenomena of the Spiritual World are in analogy with the Phenomena of the Natural World requires no restatement. Since Plato enunciated his doctrine of the Cave or of the twice-divided line; since Christ spake in parables; since Plotinus wrote of the world as an image; since the mysticism of Swedenborg; since Bacon and Pascal; since "Sartor Resartus" and "In Memoriam," it has been all but a commonplace with thinkers that "the invisible things of God from the creation of the world are clearly seen, being understood by the things that are made." Milton's question—

> "What if earth
> Be but the shadow of heaven, and things therein
> Each to other like more than on earth is thought?"

is now superfluous. "In our doctrine of representations and correspondences," says Swedenborg, "we shall treat of both these symbolical and typical resemblances, and of the astonishing things that occur, I will not say in the living body only, but throughout Nature, and which correspond so entirely to supreme and spiritual things, that one would swear that the physical world was purely symbolical of the spiritual world."[4] And Carlyle: "All visible things are emblems. What thou seest is not there on its own account; strictly speaking is not there at all. Matter exists only spiritually, and to represent some idea and body it forth."[5]

But the analogies of Law are a totally different thing from the analogies of Phenomena and have a very different value. To say generally, with Pascal, that—"La nature est une image de la grace," is merely to be poetical. The function of Hervey's "Meditations in a Flower Garden," or, Flavel's "Husbandry Spiritualized," is mainly homiletical. That such works have an interest is not to be denied. The place of parable in teaching, and especially after the sanction of the greatest of Teachers, must always be recognized. The very necessities of language indeed demand this method of presenting truth. The temporal is the husk and framework of the eternal, and thoughts can be uttered only through things.[6]

But analogies between Phenomena bear the same relation to analogies of Law that Phenomena themselves bear to Law. The light of Law on truth, as we have seen, is an immense advance upon the light of Phenomena. The discovery of Law is simply the discovery of Science. And if the analogies of Natural Law can be extended to the Spiritual World, that whole region at once falls within the domain of science and secures a basis as well as an illumination in the constitution and course of Nature. All, therefore, that has been claimed for parable can be predicated *a fortiori* of this—with the addition that a proof on the basis of Law would want no criterion possessed by the most advanced science.

That the validity of analogy generally has been seriously questioned one must frankly own. Doubtless there is much difficulty and even liability to gross error in attempting to establish analogy in specific cases. The value of the likeness appears differently to different minds, and in discussing an individual instance questions of relevancy will invariably crop up. Of course, in the language of John Stuart Mill, "when the analogy can be proved, the argument founded upon it cannot be resisted."[7] But so great is the difficulty of proof that many are compelled to attach the most inferior weight to analogy as a method of reasoning. "Analogical evidence is generally more successful in silencing objections than in evincing truth. Though it rarely refutes it frequently repels refutation; like those weapons which though they cannot kill the enemy, will ward his blows.... It must be allowed that analogical evidence is at least but a feeble support, and is hardly ever honored with the name of proof."[8] Other authorities on the other hand, such as Sir William Hamilton, admit analogy to a primary place in logic and regard it as the very basis of induction.

But, fortunately, we are spared all discussion on this worn subject, for two cogent reasons. For one thing, we do not demand of Nature directly to prove Religion. That was never its function. Its function is to interpret. And this, after all, is possibly the most fruitful proof. The best proof of a thing is that we *see* it; if we do not see it, perhaps proof will not convince us of it. It is the want of the discerning faculty, the clairvoyant power of seeing the eternal in the temporal, rather than the failure of the reason, that begets the sceptic. But secondly, and more particularly, a significant circumstance has to be taken into account, which, though it will appear more clearly afterward, may be stated here at once. The position we have been led to take up is not that the Spiritual Laws are analogous to the Natural Laws, but that *they are the same Laws*. It is not a question of analogy but of *Identity*. The Natural Laws are not the shadows or images of the Spiritual in the same sense as autumn is emblematical of Decay, or the falling leaf of Death. The Natural Laws, as the Law of Continuity might well warn us, do not stop with the visible and then give place to a new set of Laws bearing a strong similitude to them. The Laws of the invisible are the same Laws, projections of the natural not supernatural. Analogous Phenomena are not the fruit of parallel Laws, but of the same Laws—Laws which at one end, as it were, may be dealing with Matter, at the other end with Spirit. As there will be some inconvenience, however, in dispensing with the word analogy, we shall continue occasionally to employ it. Those who apprehend the real relation will mentally substitute the larger term.

Let us now look for a moment at the present state of the question. Can it be said that the Laws of the Spiritual World are in any sense considered even to have analogies with the Natural World? Here and there certainly one finds an attempt, and a successful attempt, to exhibit on a rational basis one or two of the great Moral Principles of the Spiritual World. But the Physical World has not been appealed to. Its magnificent system of Laws remains outside, and its contribution meanwhile is either silently ignored or purposely set aside. The Physical, it is said, is too remote from the Spiritual. The Moral World may afford a basis for religious truth, but even this is often the baldest concession; while the appeal to the Physical universe is everywhere dismissed as, on the face of it, irrelevant and unfruitful. From the scientific side, again, nothing has been done to court a closer fellowship. Science has taken theology at its own estimate. It is a thing apart. The Spiritual World is not only a different world, but a different kind of world, a world arranged on a totally different principle, under a different governmental scheme.

The Reign of Law has gradually crept into every department of Nature, transforming knowledge everywhere into Science. The process goes on, and Nature slowly appears to us as one great unity, until the borders of the Spiritual World are reached. There the Law of Continuity ceases, and the harmony breaks down. And men who have learned their elementary lessons truly from the alphabet of the lower Laws, going on to seek a higher knowledge, are suddenly confronted with the Great Exception.

Even those who have examined most carefully the relations of the Natural and the Spiritual, seem to have committed themselves deliberately to a final separation in matters of Law. It is a surprise to find such a writer as Horace Bushnell, for instance, describing the Spiritual World as "another system of nature incommunicably separate from ours," and further defining it thus: "God has, in fact, erected another and higher system, that of spiritual being and government for which nature exists; a system not under the law of cause and effect, but ruled and marshaled under other kinds of laws."[9] Few men have shown more insight than Bushnell in illustrating Spiritual truth from the Natural World; but he has not only failed to perceive the analogy with regard to Law, but emphatically denies it.

In the recent literature of this whole region there nowhere seems any advance upon the position of "Nature and the Supernatural." All are agreed in speaking of Nature *and* the Supernatural. Nature *in* the Supernatural, so far as Laws are concerned, is still an unknown truth.

"The Scientific Basis of Faith" is a suggestive title. The accomplished author announces that the object of his investigation is to show that "the world of nature and mind, as made known by science, constitute a basis and a preparation for that highest moral and spiritual life of man, which is evoked by the self-revelation of God."[10] On the whole, Mr. Murphy seems to be more philosophical and more profound in his view of the relation of science and religion than any writer of modern times. His conception of religion is broad and lofty, his acquaintance with science adequate.

He makes constant, admirable, and often original use of analogy; and yet, in spite of the promise of this quotation, he has failed to find any analogy in that department of Law where surely, of all others, it might most reasonably be looked for. In the broad subject even of the analogies of what he defines as "evangelical religion" with Nature, Mr. Murphy discovers nothing. Nor can this be traced either to short-sight or over-sight. The subject occurs to him more than once, and he deliberately dismisses it—dismisses it not merely as unfruitful, but with a distinct denial of its relevancy. The memorable paragraph from Origen which forms the text of Butler's "Analogy," he calls "this shallow and false saying."[11] He says: "The designation of Butler's scheme of religious philosophy ought then to be *the analogy of religion, legal and evangelical, to the constitution of nature.* But does this give altogether a true meaning? Does this double analogy really exist? If justice is natural law among beings having a moral nature, there is the closest analogy between the constitution of nature and merely legal religion. Legal religion is only the extension of natural justice into a future life.... But is this true of evangelical religion? Have the doctrines of Divine grace any similar support in the analogies of nature? I trow not."[12] And with reference to a specific question, speaking of immortality, he asserts that "the analogies of mere nature are opposed to the doctrine of immortality."[13]

With regard to Butler's great work in this department, it is needless at this time of day to point out that his aims did not lie exactly in this direction. He did not seek to indicate analogies *between* religion and the constitution and course of Nature. His theme was, "The Analogy *of* Religion *to* the constitution and course of Nature." And although he pointed out direct analogies of Phenomena, such as those between the metamorphoses of insects and the doctrine of a future state; and although he showed that "the natural and moral constitution and government of the world are so connected as to make up together but one scheme,"[14] his real intention was not so much to construct arguments as to repel objections. His emphasis accordingly was laid upon the difficulties of the two schemes rather than on their positive lines; and so thoroughly has he made out this point that as is well known, the effect upon many has been, not to lead them to accept the

Spiritual World on the ground of the Natural, but to make them despair of both. Butler lived at a time when defence was more necessary than construction, when the materials for construction were scarce and insecure, and when, besides, some of the things to be defended were quite incapable of defence. Notwithstanding this, his influence over the whole field since has been unparalleled.

After all, then, the Spiritual World, as it appears at this moment, is outside Natural Law. Theology continues to be considered, as it has always been, a thing apart. It remains still a stupendous and splendid construction, but on lines altogether its own. Nor is Theology to be blamed for this. Nature has been long in speaking; even yet its voice is low, sometimes inaudible. Science is the true defaulter, for Theology had to wait patiently for its development. As the highest of the sciences, Theology in the order of evolution should be the last to fall into rank. It is reserved for it to perfect the final harmony. Still, if it continues longer to remain a thing apart, with increasing reason will be such protests as this of the "Unseen Universe," when, in speaking of a view of miracles held by an older Theology, it declares:—"If he submits to be guided by such interpreters, each intelligent being will forever continue to be baffled in any attempt to explain these phenomena, because they are said to have no physical relation to anything that went before or that followed after; in fine, they are made to form a universe within a universe, a portion cut off by an insurmountable barrier from the domain of scientific inquiry."[15]

This is the secret of the present decadence of Religion in the world of Science. For Science can hear nothing of a Great Exception. Constructions on unique lines, "portions cut off by an insurmountable barrier from the domain of scientific inquiry," it dare not recognize. Nature has taught it this lesson, and Nature is right. It is the province of Science to vindicate Nature here at any hazard. But in blaming Theology for its intolerance, it has been betrayed into an intolerance less excusable. It has pronounced upon it too soon. What if Religion be yet brought within the sphere of Law? Law is the revelation of time. One by one slowly through the centuries the Sciences have crystallized into geometrical form, each form not only perfect in itself, but perfect in its relation to all other forms. Many forms had to be perfected before the form of the Spiritual. The Inorganic has to be worked out before the Organic, the Natural before the Spiritual. Theology at present has merely an ancient and provisional philosophic form. By-and-by it will be seen whether it be not susceptible of another. For Theology must pass through the necessary stages of progress, like any other science. The method of science-making is now fully established. In almost all cases the natural history and development are the same. Take, for example, the case of Geology. A century ago there was none. Science went out to look for it, and brought back a Geology which, if Nature were a harmony, had falsehood written almost on its face. It was the Geology of Catastrophism, a Geology so out of line with Nature as revealed by the other sciences, that on *a priori* grounds a thoughtful mind might have been justified in dismissing it as a final form of any science. And its fallacy was soon and thoroughly exposed. The advent of modified uniformitarian principles all but banished the word catastrophe from science, and marked the birth of Geology as we know it now. Geology, that is to say, had fallen at last into the great scheme of Law. Religious doctrines, many of them at least, have been up to this time all but as *catastrophic* as the old Geology. They are not on the lines of Nature as we have learned to decipher her. If any one feel, as Science complains that it feels, that the lie of things in the Spiritual World as arranged by Theology is not in harmony with the world around, is not, in short, scientific, he is entitled to raise the question whether this be really the final form of those departments of Theology to which his complaint refers. He is justified, moreover, in demanding a new investigation with all modern methods and resources; and Science is bound by its principles not less than by the lessons of its own past, to suspend judgment till the last attempt is made. The success of such an attempt will be looked forward to with hopefulness or fearfulness just in proportion to one's confidence in Nature —in proportion to one's belief in the divinity of man and in the divinity of things. If there is any truth in the unity of Nature, in that supreme principle of Continuity which is growing in splendor with every discovery of science, the conclusion is foregone. If there is any foundation for Theology, if the phenomena of the Spiritual World are real, in the nature of things they ought to come into the sphere of Law. Such is at once the demand of Science upon Religion and the prophecy that it can and shall be fulfilled.

The Botany of Linnæus, a purely artificial system, was a splendid contribution to human knowledge, and did more in its day to enlarge the view of the vegetable kingdom than all that had gone before. But all artificial systems must pass away. None knew better than the great Swedish naturalist himself that his system, being artificial, was but provisional. Nature must be read in its own light. And as the botanical field became more luminous, the system of Jussieu and De Candolle slowly emerged as a native growth, unfolded itself as naturally as the petals of one of its own flowers, and forcing itself upon men's intelligence as the very voice of Nature, banished the Linnæan system forever. It were unjust to say that the present Theology is as artificial as the system of Linnæus; in many particulars it wants but a fresh expression to make it in the most modern sense scientific. But if it has a basis in the constitution and course of Nature, that basis has never been adequately shown. It has depended on Authority rather than on Law; and a new basis must be sought and found if it is to be presented to those with whom Law alone is Authority.

It is not of course to be inferred that the scientific method will ever abolish the radical distinctions of the Spiritual World. True science proposes to itself no such general leveling in any department. Within the unity of the whole there must always be room for the characteristic differences of the parts, and those tendencies of thought at the present time which ignore such distinctions, in their zeal for simplicity really create confusion. As has been well said by Mr. Hutton: "Any attempt to merge the distinctive characteristic of a higher science in a lower—of chemical changes in mechanical—of physiological in chemical—above all, of mental changes in physiological—is a neglect of the radical assumption of all science, because it is an attempt to deduce representations—or rather misrepresentations—of one kind of phenomena from a conception of another kind which does not contain it, and must have it implicitly and illicitly smuggled in before it can be extracted out of it. Hence, instead of increasing our means of representing the universe to ourselves without the detailed examination of particulars, such a procedure leads to misconstructions of fact on the basis of an imported theory, and generally ends in forcibly perverting the least-known science to the type of the better known."[16]

What is wanted is simply a unity of conception, but not such a unity of conception as should be founded on an absolute identity of phenomena. This latter might indeed be a unity, but it would be a very tame one. The perfection of unity is attained where there is infinite variety of phenomena, infinite complexity of relation, but great simplicity of Law. Science will be complete when all known phenomena can be arranged in one vast circle in which a few well known Laws shall form the radii—these radii at once separating and uniting, separating into particular groups, yet uniting all to a common center. To show that the radii for some of the most characteristic phenomena of the Spiritual World are already drawn within that circle by science is the main object of the papers which follow. There will be found an attempt to restate a few of the more elementary facts of the Spiritual Life in terms of Biology. Any argument for Natural Law in the Spiritual World may be best tested in the *a posteriori* form. And although the succeeding pages are not designed in the first instance to prove a principle, they may yet be entered here as evidence. The practical test is a severe one, but on that account all the more satisfactory.

And what will be gained if the point be made out? Not a few things. For one, as partly indicated already, the scientific demand of the age will be satisfied. That demand is that all that concerns life and conduct shall be placed on a scientific basis. The only great attempt to meet that at present is Positivism.

But what again is a scientific basis? What exactly is this demand of the age? "By Science I understand," says Huxley, "all knowledge which rests upon evidence and reasoning of a like character to that which claims our assent to ordinary scientific propositions; and if any one is able to make good the assertion that his theology rests upon valid evidence and sound reasoning, then it appears to me that such theology must take its place as a part of science." That the assertion has been already made good is claimed by many who deserve to be heard on questions of scientific evidence. But if more is wanted by some minds, more not perhaps of a higher kind but of a different kind, at least the attempt can be made to gratify them. Mr. Frederick Harrison,[17] in name of the Positive method of thought, "turns aside from ideal standards which avow themselves to be *lawless* [the italics are Mr. Harrison's], which profess to transcend the field of law. We say, life and conduct shall stand for us wholly on a basis of law, and must rest entirely in that region of science (not physical, but moral and social science) where we are free to use our intelligence, in the methods known to us as intelligible logic, methods which the intellect can analyze. When you confront us with hypotheses, however sublime and however affecting, if they cannot be stated in terms of the rest of our knowledge, if they are disparate to that world of sequence and sensation which to us is the ultimate base of all our real knowledge, then we shake our heads and turn aside." This is a most reasonable demand, and we humbly accept the challenge. We think religious truth, or at all events certain of the largest facts of the Spiritual Life, can be stated "in terms of the rest of our knowledge."

We do not say, as already hinted, that the proposal includes an attempt to prove the existence of the Spiritual World. Does that need proof? And if so, what sort of evidence would be considered in court? The facts of the Spiritual World are as real to thousands as the facts of the Natural World—and more real to hundreds. But were one asked to prove that the Spiritual World can be discerned by the appropriate faculties, one would do it precisely as one would attempt to prove the Natural World to be an object of recognition to the senses—and with as much or as little success. In either instance probably the fact would be found incapable of demonstration, but not more in the one case than in the other. Were one asked to prove the existence of Spiritual Life, one would also do it exactly as one would seek to prove Natural Life. And this perhaps might be attempted with more hope. But this is not on the immediate programme. Science deals with known facts; and accepting certain known facts in the Spiritual World we proceed to arrange them, to discover their Laws, to inquire if they can be stated "in terms of the rest of our knowledge."

At the same time, although attempting no philosophical proof of the existence of a Spiritual Life and a Spiritual World, we are not without hope that the general line of thought here may be useful to some who are honestly inquiring in these directions. The stumbling-block to most minds is perhaps less the mere existence of the unseen than the want of definition, the apparently hopeless vagueness, and not least, the delight in this vagueness as mere vagueness by some who look upon this as the mark of quality in Spiritual things. It will be at least something to tell earnest seekers that the Spiritual World is not a castle in the air, of an architecture unknown to earth or heaven, but a fair ordered realm furnished with many familiar things and ruled by well-remembered Laws.

It is scarcely necessary to emphasize under a second head the gain in clearness. The Spiritual World as it stands is full of perplexity. One can escape doubt only by escaping thought. With regard to many important articles of religion perhaps the best and the worst course at present open to a doubter is simple credulity. Who is to answer for this state of things? It comes as a necessary tax for improvement on the age in which we live. The old ground of faith, Authority, is given up; the new, Science, has not yet taken its place. Men did not require to *see* truth before; they only needed to believe it. Truth, therefore, had not been put by Theology in a seeing form—which, however, was its original form. But now they ask to see it. And when it is shown them they start back in despair. We shall not say what they see. But we shall say what they might see. If the Natural Laws were run through the Spiritual World, they might see the great lines of religious truth as clearly and simply as the broad lines of science. As they gazed into that Natural-Spiritual World they would say to themselves, "We have seen something like this before. This order is known to us. It is not arbitrary. This Law here is that old Law there, and this Phenomenon here, what can it be but that which stood in precisely the same relation to that Law yonder?" And so gradually from the new form everything assumes new meaning. So the Spiritual World becomes slowly Natural; and, what is of all but equal moment, the Natural World becomes slowly Spiritual. Nature is not a mere image or emblem of the Spiritual. It is a working model of the Spiritual. In the Spiritual World the same wheels revolve—but without the iron. The same figures flit across the stage, the same processes of growth go on, the same functions are discharged, the same biological laws prevail—only with a different quality of βιος. Plato's prisoner, if not out of the Cave, has at least his face to the light.

> "The earth is cram'd with heaven,
> And every common bush afire with God."

How much of the Spiritual World is covered by Natural law we do not propose at present to inquire. It is certain, at least, that the whole is not covered. And nothing more lends confidence to the method than this. For one thing, room is still left for mystery. Had no place remained for mystery it had proved itself both unscientific and irreligious. A Science without mystery is unknown; a Religion without mystery is absurd. This is no attempt to reduce Religion to a question of mathematics, or demonstrate God in biological formulæ. The elimination of mystery from the universe is the elimination of Religion. However far the scientific method may penetrate the Spiritual World, there will always remain a region to be explored by a scientific faith. "I shall never rise to the point of view which wishes to 'raise' faith to knowledge. To me, the way of truth is to come through the knowledge of my ignorance to the submissiveness of faith, and then, making that my starting place, to raise my knowledge into faith."[18]

Lest this proclamation of mystery should seem alarming, let us add that this mystery also is scientific. The one subject on which all scientific men are agreed, the one theme on which all alike become eloquent, the one strain of pathos in all their writing and speaking and thinking, concerns that final uncertainty, that utter blackness of darkness bounding their work on every side. If the light of Nature is to illuminate for us the Spiritual Sphere, there may well be a black Unknown, corresponding, at least at some points, to this zone of darkness round the Natural World.

But the final gain would appear in the department of Theology. The establishment of the Spiritual Laws on "the solid ground of Nature," to which the mind trusts "which builds for aye," would offer a new basis for certainty in Religion. It has been indicated that the authority of Authority is waning. This is a plain fact. And it was inevitable. Authority—man's Authority, that is—is for children. And there necessarily comes a time when they add to the question, What shall I do? or, What shall I believe? the adult's interrogation—Why? Now this question is sacred, and must be answered.

"How truly its central position is impregnable," Herbert Spencer has well discerned, "religion has never adequately realized. In the devoutest faith, as we habitually see it, there lies hidden an innermost core of scepticism; and it is this scepticism which causes that dread of inquiry displayed by religion when face to face with science."[19]

True indeed; Religion has never realized how impregnable are many of its positions. It has not yet been placed on that basis which would make them impregnable. And in a transition period like the present, holding Authority with one hand, the other feeling all around in the darkness for some strong new support, Theology is surely to be pitied. Whence this dread when brought face to face with Science? It cannot be dread of scientific fact. No single fact in Science has ever discredited a fact in Religion. The theologian knows that, and admits that he has no fear of facts. What then has Science done to make Theology tremble? It is its method. It is its system. It is its Reign of Law. It is its harmony and continuity. The attack is not specific. No one point is assailed. It is the whole system which when compared with the other and weighed in its balance is found wanting. An eye which has looked at the first cannot look upon this. To do that, and rest in the contemplation, it has first to uncentury itself.

Herbert Spencer points out further, with how much truth need not now be discussed, that the purification of Religion has always come from Science. It is very apparent at all events that an immense debt must soon be contracted. The shifting of the furnishings will be a work of time. But it must be accomplished. And not the least result of the process will be the effect upon Science itself. No department of knowledge ever contributes to another without receiving its own again with usury—witness the reciprocal favors of Biology and Sociology. From the time that Comte defined the analogy between the phenomena exhibited by aggregations of associated men and those of animal colonies, the Science of Life and the Science of Society have been so contributing to one another that their progress since has been all but hand-in-hand. A conception borrowed by the one has been observed in time finding its way back, and always in an enlarged form, to further illuminate and enrich the field it left. So must it be with Science and Religion. If the purification of Religion comes from Science, the purification of Science, in a deeper sense, shall come from Religion. The true ministry of Nature must at last be honored, and Science take its place as the great expositor. To Men of Science, not less than to Theologians,

> "Science then
> Shall be a precious visitant; and then,
> And only then, be worthy of her name;
> For then her heart shall kindle, her dull eye,
> Dull and inanimate, no more shall hang
> Chained to its object in brute slavery;
> But taught with patient interest to watch
> The process of things, and serve the cause
> Of order and distinctness, not for this
> Shall it forget that its most noble use,
> Its most illustrious province, must be found
> In furnishing clear guidance, a support,
> Not treacherous, to the mind's *excursive* power."[20]

But the gift of Science to Theology shall be not less rich. With the inspiration of Nature to illuminate what the inspiration of Revelation has left obscure, heresy in certain whole departments shall become impossible. With the demonstration of the naturalness of the supernatural, scepticism even may come to be regarded as unscientific. And those who have wrestled long for a few bare truths to ennoble life and rest their souls in thinking of the future will not be left in doubt.

It is impossible to believe that the amazing succession of revelations in the domain of Nature during the last few centuries, at which the world has all but grown tired wondering, are to yield nothing for the higher life. If the development of doctrine is to have any meaning for the future, Theology must draw upon the further revelation of the seen for the further revelation of the unseen. It need, and can, add nothing to fact; but as the vision of Newton rested on a clearer and richer world than that of Plato, so, though seeing the same things in the Spiritual World as our fathers, we may see them clearer and richer. With the work of the centuries upon it, the mental eye is a finer instrument, and demands a more ordered world. Had the revelation of Law been given sooner, it had been unintelligible. Revelation never volunteers anything that man could discover for himself—on the principle, probably, that it is only when he is capable of discovering it that he is capable of appreciating it. Besides, children do not need Laws, except Laws in the sense of commandments. They repose with simplicity on authority, and ask no questions. But there comes a time, as the world reaches its manhood, when they will ask questions, and stake, moreover, everything on the answers. That time is now. Hence we must exhibit our doctrines, not lying athwart the lines of the world's thinking, in a place reserved, and therefore shunned, for the Great Exception; but in their kinship to all truth and in their Law-relation to the whole of Nature. This is, indeed, simply following out the system of teaching begun by Christ Himself. And what is the search for spiritual truth in the Laws of Nature but an attempt to utter the parables which have been hid so long in the world around without a preacher, and to tell men at once more that the Kingdom of Heaven is like unto this and to that?

PART II.

The Law of Continuity having been referred to already as a prominent factor in this inquiry, it may not be out of place to sustain the plea for Natural Law in the Spiritual Sphere by a brief statement and application of this great principle. The Law of Continuity furnishes an *a priori* argument for the position we are attempting to establish of the most convincing kind —of such a kind, indeed, as to seem to our mind final. Briefly indicated, the ground taken up is this, that if Nature be a harmony, Man in all his relations —physical, mental, moral, and spiritual—falls to be included within its circle. It is altogether unlikely that man spiritual should be violently separated in all the conditions of growth, development, and life, from man physical. It is indeed difficult to conceive that one set of principles should guide the natural life, and these at a certain period—the very point where they are needed—suddenly give place to another set of principles altogether new and unrelated. Nature has never taught us to expect such a catastrophe. She has nowhere prepared us for it. And Man cannot in the nature of things, in the nature of thought, in the nature of language, be separated into two such incoherent halves.

The spiritual man, it is true, is to be studied in a different department of science from the natural man. But the harmony established by science is not a harmony within specific departments. It is the universe that is the harmony, the universe of which these are but parts. And the harmonies of the parts depend for all their weight and interest on the harmony of the whole. While, therefore, there are many harmonies, there is but one harmony. The breaking up of the phenomena of the universe into carefully guarded groups, and the allocation of certain prominent Laws to each, it must never be forgotten, and however much Nature lends herself to it, are artificial. We find an evolution in Botany, another in Geology, and another in Astronomy, and the effect is to lead one insensibly to look upon these as three distinct evolutions. But these sciences, of course, are mere departments created by ourselves to facilitate knowledge—reductions of Nature to the scale of our own intelligence. And we must beware of breaking up Nature except for this purpose. Science has so dissected everything, that it becomes a mental difficulty to put the puzzle together again; and we must keep ourselves in practice by constantly thinking of Nature as a whole, if science is not to be spoiled by its own refinements. Evolution being found in so many different sciences, the likelihood is that it is a universal principle. And there is no presumption whatever against this Law and many others being excluded from the domain of the spiritual life. On the other hand, there are very convincing reasons why the Natural Laws should be continuous through the Spiritual Sphere—not changed in any way to meet the new circumstances, but continuous as they stand.

But to the exposition. One of the most striking generalizations of recent science is that even Laws have their Law. Phenomena first, in the progress of knowledge, were grouped together, and Nature shortly presented the spectacle of a cosmos, the lines of beauty being the great Natural Laws. So long, however, as these Laws were merely great lines running through Nature, so long as they remained isolated from one another, the system of Nature was still incomplete. The principle which sought Law among phenomena had to go further and seek a Law among the Laws. Laws themselves accordingly came to be treated as they treated phenomena, and found themselves finally grouped in a still narrower circle. That inmost circle is governed by one great Law, the Law of Continuity. It is the Law for Laws.

It is perhaps significant that few exact definitions of Continuity are to be found. Even in Sir W. R. Grove's famous paper,[21] the fountain-head of the modern form of this far from modern truth, there is no attempt at definition.

In point of fact, its sweep is so magnificent, it appeals so much more to the imagination than to the reason, that men have preferred to exhibit rather than to define it. Its true greatness consists in the final impression it leaves on the mind with regard to the uniformity of Nature. For it was reserved for the Law of Continuity to put the finishing touch to the harmony of the universe.

Probably the most satisfactory way to secure for one's self a just appreciation of the Principle of Continuity is to try to conceive the universe without it. The opposite of a continuous universe would be a discontinuous universe, an incoherent and irrelevant universe—as irrelevant in all its ways of doing things as an irrelevant person. In effect, to withdraw Continuity from the universe would be the same as to withdraw reason from an individual. The universe would run deranged; the world would be a mad world.

There used to be a children's book which bore the fascinating title of "The Chance World." It described a world in which everything happened by chance. The sun might rise or it might not; or it might appear at any hour, or the moon might come up instead. When children were born they might have one head or a dozen heads, and those heads might not be on their shoulders —there might be no shoulders—but arranged about the limbs. If one jumped up in the air it was impossible to predict whether he would ever come down again. That he came down yesterday was no guarantee that he would do it next time. For every day antecedent and consequent varied, and gravitation and everything else changed from hour to hour. To-day a child's body might be so light that it was impossible for it to descend from its chair to the floor; but to-morrow, in attempting the experiment again, the impetus might drive it through a three-story house and dash it to pieces somewhere near the center of the earth. In this chance world cause and effect were abolished. Law was annihilated. And the result to the inhabitants of such a world could only be that reason would be impossible. It would be a lunatic world with a population of lunatics.

Now this is no more than a real picture of what the world would be without Law, or the universe without Continuity. And hence we come in sight of the necessity of some principle of Law according to which Laws shall be, and be "continuous" throughout the system. Man as a rational and moral being demands a pledge that if he depends on Nature for any given result on the ground that Nature has previously led him to expect such a result, his intellect shall not be insulted, nor his confidence in her abused. If he is to trust Nature, in short, it must be guaranteed to him that in doing so he will "never be put to confusion." The authors of the *Unseen Universe* conclude their examination of this principle by saying that "assuming the existence of a supreme Governor of the universe, the Principle of Continuity may be said to be the definite expression in words of our trust that He will not put us to permanent intellectual confusion, and we can easily conceive similar expressions of trust with reference to the other faculties of man."[22] Or, as it has been well put elsewhere, Continuity is the expression of "the Divine Veracity in Nature."[23] The most striking examples of the continuousness of Law are perhaps those furnished by Astronomy, especially in connection with the more recent applications of spectrum analysis. But even in the case of the simpler Laws the demonstration is complete. There is no reason apart from Continuity to expect that gravitation for instance should prevail outside our world. But wherever matter has been detected throughout the entire universe, whether in the form of star or planet, comet or meteorite, it is found to obey that Law. "If there were no other indication of unity than this, it would be almost enough. For the unity which is implied in the mechanism of the heavens is indeed a unity which is all-embracing and complete. The structure of our own bodies, with all that depends upon it, is a structure governed by, and therefore adapted to, the same force of gravitation which has determined the form and the movements of myriads of worlds. Every part of the human organism is fitted to conditions which would all be destroyed in a moment if the forces of gravitation were to change or fail."[24]

But it is unnecessary to multiply illustrations. Having defined the principle we may proceed at once to apply it. And the argument may be summed up in a sentence. As the Natural Laws are continuous through the universe of matter and of space, so will they be continuous through the universe of spirit.

If this be denied, what then? Those who deny it must furnish the disproof. The argument is founded on a principle which is now acknowledged to be universal; and the *onus* of disproof must lie with those who may be bold enough to take up the position that a region exists where at last the Principle of Continuity fails. To do this one would first have to overturn Nature, then science, and last, the human mind.

It may seem an obvious objection that many of the Natural Laws have no connection whatever with the Spiritual World, and as a matter of fact are not continued through it. Gravitation for instance—what direct application has that in the Spiritual World? The reply is threefold. First, there is no proof that it does not hold there. If the spirit be in any sense material it certainly must hold. In the second place, gravitation may hold for the Spiritual Sphere although it cannot be directly proved. The spirit may be armed with powers which enable it to rise superior to gravity. During the action of these powers gravity need be no more suspended than in the case of a plant which rises in the air during the process of growth. It does this in virtue of a higher Law and in apparent defiance of the lower. Thirdly, if the spiritual be not material it still cannot be said that gravitation ceases at that point to be continuous. It is not gravitation that ceases—it is matter.

This point, however, will require development for another reason. In the case of the plant just referred to, there is a principle of growth or vitality at work superseding the attraction of gravity. Why is there no trace of that Law in the Inorganic world? Is not this another instance of the discontinuousness of Law? If the Law of vitality has so little connection with the Inorganic kingdom—less even than gravitation with the Spiritual, what becomes of Continuity? Is it not evident that each kingdom of Nature has its own set of Laws which continue possibly untouched for the specific kingdom but never extend beyond it?

It is quite true that when we pass from the Inorganic to the Organic, we come upon a new set of Laws. But the reason why the lower set do not seem to act in the higher sphere is not that they are annihilated, but that they are overruled. And the reason why the higher Laws are not found operating in the lower is not because they are not continuous downward, but because there is nothing for them there to act upon. It is not Law that fails, but opportunity. The biological Laws are continuous for life. Wherever there is life, that is to say, they will be found acting, just as gravitation acts wherever there is matter.

We have purposely, in the last paragraph, indulged in a fallacy. We have said that the biological Laws would certainly be continuous in the lower or mineral sphere were there anything there for them to act upon. Now Laws do not act upon anything. It has been stated already, although apparently it cannot be too abundantly emphasized, that Laws are only modes of operation, not themselves operators. The accurate statement, therefore, would be that the biological Laws would be continuous in the lower sphere were there anything there for them, not to act upon, but to keep in order. If there is no acting going on, if there is nothing being kept in order, the responsibility does not lie with Continuity. The Law will always be at its post, not only when its services are required, but wherever they are possible.

Attention is drawn to this, for it is a correction one will find one's self compelled often to make in his thinking. It is so difficult to keep out of mind the idea of substance in connection with the Natural Laws, the idea that they are the movers, the essences, the energies, that one is constantly on the verge of falling into false conclusions. Thus a hasty glance at the present argument on the part of any one ill-furnished enough to confound Law with substance or with cause would probably lead to its immediate rejection. For, to continue the same line of illustration, it might next be urged that such a Law as Biogenesis, which, as we hope to show afterward, is the fundamental Law of life for both the natural and spiritual worlds, can have no application whatsoever in the latter sphere. The *life* with which it deals in the Natural World does not enter at all into the Spiritual World, and therefore, it might be argued, the Law of Biogenesis cannot be capable of extension into it. The Law of Continuity seems to be snapped at the point where the natural passes into the spiritual. The vital principle of the body is a different thing from the vital principle of the spiritual life. Biogenesis deals with βιος, with the natural life, with cells and germs, and as there are no exactly similar cells and germs in the Spiritual World, the Law cannot therefore apply. All which is as true as if one were to say that the fifth proposition of the First Book of Euclid applies when the figures are drawn with chalk upon a blackboard, but fails with regard to structures of wood or stone.

The proposition is continuous for the whole world, and, doubtless, likewise for the sun and moon and stars. The same universality may be predicated likewise for the Law of life. Wherever there is life we may expect to find it arranged, ordered, governed according to the same Law. At the beginning of the natural life we find the Law that natural life can only come from preëxisting natural life; and at the beginning of the spiritual life we find that the spiritual life can only come from preëxisting spiritual life. But there are not two Laws; there is one—Biogenesis. At one end the Law is dealing with matter, at the other with spirit. The qualitative terms natural and spiritual make no difference. Biogenesis is the Law for all life and for all kinds of life, and the particular substance with which it is associated is as indifferent to Biogenesis as it is to Gravitation. Gravitation will act whether the substance be suns and stars, or grains of sand, or raindrops. Biogenesis, in like manner, will act wherever there is life.

The conclusion finally is, that from the nature of Law in general, and from the scope of the Principle of Continuity in particular, the Laws of the natural life must be those of the spiritual life. This does not exclude, observe, the possibility of there being new Laws in addition within the Spiritual Sphere; nor does it even include the supposition that the old Laws will be the conspicuous Laws of the Spiritual World, both which points will be dealt with presently. It simply asserts that whatever else may be found, these must be found there; that they must be there though they may not be seen there; and that they must project beyond there if there be anything beyond there. If the Law of Continuity is true, the only way to escape the conclusion that the Laws of the natural life are the Laws, or at least are Laws, of the spiritual life, is to say that there is no spiritual life. It is really easier to give up the phenomena than to give up the Law.

Two questions now remain for further consideration—one bearing on the possibility of new Law in the spiritual; the other, on the assumed invisibility or inconspicuousness of the old Laws on account of their subordination to the new.

Let us begin by conceding that there may be new Laws. The argument might then be advanced that since, in Nature generally, we come upon new Laws as we pass from lower to higher kingdoms, the old still remaining in force, the newer Laws which one would expect to meet in the Spiritual World would so transcend and overwhelm the older as to make the analogy or identity, even if traced, of no practical use. The new Laws would represent operations and energies so different, and so much more elevated, that they would afford the true keys to the Spiritual World. As Gravitation is practically lost sight of when we pass into the domain of life, so Biogenesis would be lost sight of as we enter the Spiritual Sphere.

We must first separate in this statement the old confusion of Law and energy. Gravitation is not lost sight of in the organic world. Gravity may be, to a certain extent, but not Gravitation; and gravity only where a higher power counteracts its action. At the same time it is not to be denied that the conspicuous thing in Organic Nature is not the great Inorganic Law.

But the objection turns upon the statement that reasoning from analogy we should expect, in turn, to lose sight of Biogenesis as we enter the Spiritual Sphere. One answer to which is that, as a matter of fact, we do not lose sight of it. So far from being invisible, it lies across the very threshold of the Spiritual World, and, as we shall see, pervades it everywhere. What we lose sight of, to a certain extent, is the natural βιος. In the Spiritual World that is not the conspicuous thing, and it is obscure there just as gravity becomes obscure in the Organic, because something higher, more potent, more characteristic of the higher plane, comes in. That there are higher energies, so to speak, in the Spiritual World is, of course, to be affirmed alike on the ground of analogy and of experience; but it does not follow that these necessitate other Laws. A Law has nothing to do with potency. We may lose sight of a substance, or of an energy, but it is an abuse of language to talk of losing sight of Laws.

Are there, then, no other Laws in the Spiritual World except those which are the projections or extensions of Natural Laws? From the number of Natural Laws which are found in the higher sphere, from the large territory actually embraced by them, and from their special prominence throughout the whole region, it may at least be answered that the margin left for them is small. But if the objection is pressed that it is contrary to the analogy, and unreasonable in itself, that there should not be new Laws for this higher sphere, the reply is obvious. Let these Laws be produced. If the spiritual nature, in inception, growth, and development, does not follow natural principles, let the true principles be stated and explained. We have not denied that there may be new Laws. One would almost be surprised if there were not. The mass of material handed over from the natural to the spiritual, continuous, apparently, from the natural to the spiritual, is so great that till that is worked out it will be impossible to say what space is still left unembraced by Laws that are known. At present it is impossible even approximately to estimate the size of that supposed *terra incognita*. From one point of view it ought to be vast, from another extremely small. But however large the region governed by the suspected new Laws may be that cannot diminish by a hair's-breadth the size of the territory where the old Laws still prevail. That territory itself, relatively to us though perhaps not absolutely, must be of great extent. The size of the key which is to open it, that is, the size of all the Natural Laws which can be found to apply, is a guarantee that the region of the knowable in the Spiritual World is at least as wide as these regions of the Natural World which by the help of these Laws have been explored. No doubt also there yet remain some Natural Laws to be discovered, and these in time may have a further light to shed on the spiritual field. Then we may know all that is? By no means. We may only know all that may be known. And that may be very little. The Sovereign Will which sways the scepter of that invisible empire must be granted a right of freedom—that freedom which by putting it into our wills He surely teaches us to honor in His. In much of His dealing with us also, in what may be called the paternal relation, there may seem no special Law—no Law except the highest of all, that Law of which all other Laws are parts, that Law which neither Nature can wholly reflect nor the mind begin to fathom—the Law of Love. He adds nothing to that, however, who loses sight of all other Laws in that, nor does he take from it who finds specific Laws everywhere radiating from it.

With regard to the supposed new Laws of the Spiritual World—those Laws, that is, which are found for the first time in the Spiritual World, and have no analogies lower down—there is this to be said, that there is one strong reason against exaggerating either their number or importance—their importance at least for our immediate needs. The connection between language and the Law of Continuity has been referred to incidentally already. It is clear that we can only express the Spiritual Laws in language borrowed from the visible universe. Being dependent for our vocabulary on images, if an altogether new and foreign set of Laws existed in the Spiritual World, they could never take shape as definite ideas from mere want of words. The hypothetical new Laws which may remain to be discovered in the domain of Natural or Mental Science may afford some index of these hypothetical higher Laws, but this would of course mean that the latter were no longer foreign but in analogy, or, likelier still, identical. If, on the other hand, the Natural Laws of the future have nothing to say of these higher Laws, what can be said of them? Where is the language to come from in which to frame them? If their disclosure could be of any practical use to us, we may be sure the clue to them, the revelation of them, in some way would have been put into Nature. If, on the contrary, they are not to be of immediate use to man, it is better they should not embarrass him. After all, then, our knowledge of higher Law must be limited by our knowledge of the lower. The Natural Laws as at present known, whatever additions may yet be made to them, give a fair rendering of the facts of Nature. And their analogies or their projections in the Spiritual sphere may also be said to offer a fair account of that sphere, or of one or two conspicuous departments of it. The time has come for that account to be given. The greatest among the theological Laws are the Laws of Nature in disguise. It will be the splendid task of the theology of the future to take off the mask and disclose to a waning scepticism the naturalness of the supernatural.

It is almost singular that the identification of the Laws of the Spiritual World with the Laws of Nature should so long have escaped recognition. For apart from the probability on *a priori* grounds, it is involved in the whole structure of Parable. When any two Phenomena in the two spheres are seen to be analogous, the parallelism must depend upon the fact that the Laws governing them are not analogous but identical. And yet this basis for Parable seems to have been overlooked. Thus Principal Shairp:—"This seeing of Spiritual truths mirrored in the face of Nature rests not on any fancied, but in a real analogy between the natural and the spiritual worlds. They are *in some sense which science has not ascertained,* but which the vital and religious imagination can perceive, counterparts one of the other." [25] But is not this the explanation, that parallel Phenomena depend upon identical Laws? It is a question indeed whether one can speak of Laws at all as being analogous. Phenomena are parallel, Laws which make them so are themselves one.

In discussing the relations of the Natural and Spiritual kingdom, it has been all but implied hitherto that the Spiritual Laws were framed originally on the plan of the Natural; and the impression one might receive in studying the two worlds for the first time from the side of analogy would naturally be that the lower world was formed first, as a kind of scaffolding on which the higher and Spiritual should be afterward raised. Now the exact opposite has been the case. The first in the field was the Spiritual World.

It is not necessary to reproduce here in detail the argument which has been stated recently with so much force in the "Unseen Universe." The conclusion of that work remains still unassailed, that the visible universe has been developed from the unseen. Apart from the general proof from the Law of Continuity, the more special grounds of such a conclusion are, first, the fact insisted upon by Herschel and Clerk-Maxwell that the atoms of which the visible universe is built up bear distinct marks of being manufactured articles; and, secondly, the origin in time of the visible universe is implied from known facts with regard to the dissipation of energy. With the gradual aggregation of mass the energy of the universe has been slowly disappearing, and this loss of energy must go on until none remains. There is, therefore, a point in time when the energy of the universe must come to an end; and that which has its end in time cannot be infinite, it must also have had a beginning in time. Hence the unseen existed before the seen.

There is nothing so especially exalted therefore in the Natural Laws in themselves as to make one anxious to find them blood relations of the Spiritual. It is not only because these Laws are on the ground, more accessible therefore to us who are but groundlings; not only, as the "Unseen Universe" points out in another connection, "because they are at the bottom of the list—are in fact the simplest and lowest—that they are capable of being most readily grasped by the finite intelligences of the universe."[26] But their true significance lies in the fact that they are on the list at all, and especially in that the list is the same list. Their dignity is not as Natural Laws, but as Spiritual Laws, Laws which, as already said, at one end are dealing with Matter, and at the other with Spirit. "The physical properties of matter form the alphabet which is put into our hands by God, the study of which, if properly conducted, will enable us more perfectly to read that great book which we call the 'Universe.'"[27] But, over and above this, the Natural Laws will enable us to read that great duplicate which we call the "Unseen Universe," and to think and live in fuller harmony with it. After all, the true greatness of Law lies in its vision of the Unseen. Law in the visible is the Invisible in the visible. And to speak of Laws as Natural is to define them in their application to a part of the universe, the sense-part, whereas a wider survey would lead us to regard all Law as essentially Spiritual. To magnify the Laws of Nature, as Laws of this small world of ours, is to take a provincial view of the universe. Law is great not because the phenomenal world is great, but because these vanishing lines are the avenues into the eternal Order. "It is less reverent to regard the universe as an illimitable avenue which leads up to God, than to look upon it as a limited area bounded by an impenetrable wall, which, if we could only pierce it would admit us at once into the presence of the Eternal?"[28] Indeed the authors of the "Unseen Universe" demur even to the expression *material universe,* since, as they tell us "Matter is (though it may seem paradoxical to say so) the less important half of the material of the physical universe."[29] And even Mr. Huxley, though in a different sense, assures us, with Descartes, "that we know more of mind than we do of body; that the immaterial world is a firmer reality than the material."[30]

How the priority of the Spiritual improves the strength and meaning of the whole argument will be seen at once. The lines of the Spiritual existed first, and it was natural to expect that when the "Intelligence resident in the 'Unseen'" proceeded to frame the material universe He should go upon the lines already laid down. He would, in short, simply project the higher Laws downward, so that the Natural World would become an incarnation, a visible representation, a working model of the spiritual. The whole function of the material world lies here. The world is only a thing that is; it is not. It is a thing that teaches, yet not even a thing—a show that shows, a teaching shadow. However useless the demonstration otherwise, philosophy does well in proving that matter is a non-entity. We work with it as the mathematician with an x. The reality is alone the Spiritual. "It is very well for physicists to speak of 'matter,' but for men generally to call this 'a material world' is an absurdity. Should we call it an x-world it would mean as much, viz., that we do not know what it is."[31] When shall we learn the true mysticism of one who was yet far from being a mystic—"We look not at the things which are seen, but at the things which are not seen; for the things which are seen are temporal, but the things which are not seen are eternal?"[32] The visible is the ladder up to the invisible; the temporal is but the scaffolding of the eternal. And when the last immaterial souls have climbed through this material to God, the scaffolding shall be taken down, and the earth dissolved with fervent heat—not because it was base, but because its work is done.

FOOTNOTES:

[3] "Reign of Law," chap. ii.

[4] "Animal Kingdom."

[5] "Sartor Resartus," 1858 Ed., p. 43.

[6] Even parable, however, has always been considered to have attached to it a measure of evidential as well as of illustrative value. Thus: "The parable or other analogy to spiritual truth appropriated from the world of nature or man, is not merely illustrative, but also in some sort proof. It is not merely that these analogies assist to make the truth intelligible or, if intelligible before, present it more vividly to the mind, which is all that some will allow them. Their power lies deeper than this, in the harmony unconsciously felt by all men, and which all deeper minds have delighted to trace, between the natural and spiritual worlds, so that analogies from the first are felt to be something more than illustrations happily but yet arbitrarily chosen. They are arguments, and may be alleged as witnesses; the world of nature being throughout a witness for the world of spirit, proceeding from the same hand, growing out of the same root, and being constituted for that very end."—(Archbishop Trench: "Parables," pp. 12, 13.)

[7] Mill's "Logic," vol. ii. p. 96.

[8] Campbell's "Rhetoric," vol. i. p. 114.

[9] "Nature and the Supernatural," p. 19.

[10] "The Scientific Basis of Faith." By J. J. Murphy, p. 466.

[11] Op. cit., p. 333.

[12] *Ibid.*, p. 333.

[13] *Ibid.*, p. 331.

[14] "Analogy," chap. vii.

[15] "Unseen Universe," 6th Ed., pp. 89, 90.

[16] "Essays," vol. i. p. 40.

[17] "A Modern Symposium."—*Nineteenth Century*, vol. i. p. 625.

[18] Beck: "Bib. Psychol.," Clark's Tr., Pref., 2d Ed., p. xiii.

[19] "First Principles," p. 161.

[20] Wordsworth's *Excursion*, Book iv.

[21] "The Correlation of Physical Forces," 6th Ed., p. 181 *et seq.*

[22] "Unseen Universe," 6th Ed., p. 88.

[23] "Old Faiths in New Light," by Newman Smith. Unwin's English edition, p. 252.

[24] The Duke of Argyll: *Contemporary Review*, Sept., 1880, p. 358.

[25] "Poetic Interpretation of Nature," p. 115.

[26] 6th edition, p. 235.

[27] *Ibid.*, p. 286.

[28] "Unseen Universe," p. 96.

[29] "Unseen Universe," p. 100.

[30] "Science and Culture," p. 259.

[31] Hinton's "Philosophy and Religion," p. 40.

[32] 2 Cor. iv. 18.

> "What we require is no new Revelation, but simply an adequate conception of the true essence of Christianity. And I believe that, as time goes on, the work of the Holy Spirit will be continuously shown in the gradual insight which the human race will attain into the true essence of the Christian religion. I am thus of opinion that a standing miracle exists, and that it has ever existed—a direct and continued influence exerted by the supernatural on the natural."—*Paradoxical Philosophy.*
>
> "He that hath the Son hath Life, and he that hath not the Son of God hath not Life."—*John.*
>
> "Omne vivum ex vivo."—*Harvey.*

For two hundred years the scientific world has been rent with discussions upon the Origin of Life. Two great schools have defended exactly opposite views—one that matter can spontaneously generate life, the other that life can only come from preëxisting life. The doctrine of Spontaneous Generation, as the first is called, has been revived within recent years by Dr. Bastian, after a series of elaborate experiments on the Beginnings of Life. Stated in his own words, his conclusion is this: "Both observation and experiment unmistakably testify to the fact that living matter is constantly being formed *de novo,* in obedience to the same laws and tendencies which determined all the more simple chemical combinations."[33] Life, that is to say, is not the Gift of Life. It is capable of springing into being of itself. It can be Spontaneously Generated.

This announcement called into the field a phalanx of observers, and the highest authorities in biological science engaged themselves afresh upon the problem. The experiments necessary to test the matter can be followed or repeated by any one possessing the slightest manipulative skill. Glass vessels are three-parts filled with infusions of hay or any organic matter. They are boiled to kill all germs of life, and hermetically sealed to exclude the outer air. The air inside, having been exposed to the boiling temperature for many hours, is supposed to be likewise dead; so that any life which may subsequently appear in the closed flasks must have sprung into being of itself. In Bastian's experiments, after every expedient to secure sterility, life did appear inside in myriad quantity. Therefore, he argued, it was spontaneously generated.

But the phalanx of observers found two errors in this calculation. Professor Tyndall repeated the same experiment, only with a precaution to insure absolute sterility suggested by the most recent science—a discovery of his own. After every care, he conceived there might still be undestroyed germs in the air inside the flasks. If the air were absolutely germless and pure, would the myriad-life appear? He manipulated his experimental vessels in an atmosphere which under the high test of optical purity—the most delicate known test—was absolutely germless. Here not a vestige of life appeared. He varied the experiment in every direction, but matter in the germless air never yielded life.

The other error was detected by Mr. Dallinger. He found among the lower forms of life the most surprising and indestructible vitality. Many animals could survive much higher temperatures than Dr. Bastian had applied to annihilate them. Some germs almost refused to be annihilated—they were all but fire-proof.

These experiments have practically closed the question. A decided and authoritative conclusion has now taken its place in science. So far as science can settle anything, this question is settled. The attempt to get the living out of the dead has failed. Spontaneous Generation has had to be given up. And it is now recognized on every hand that Life can only come from the touch of Life. Huxley categorically announces that the doctrine of Biogenesis, or life only from life, is "victorious along the whole line at the present day."[34] And even while confessing that he wishes the evidence were the other way, Tyndall is compelled to say, "I affirm that no shred of trustworthy experimental testimony exists to prove that life in our day has ever appeared independently of antecedent life."[35]

For much more than two hundred years a similar discussion has dragged its length through the religious world. Two great schools here also have defended exactly opposite views—one that the Spiritual Life in man can only come from preëxisting Life, the other that it can Spontaneously Generate itself. Taking its stand upon the initial statement of the Author of the Spiritual Life, one small school, in the face of derision and opposition, has persistently maintained the doctrine of Biogenesis. Another, larger and with greater pretension to philosophic form, has defended Spontaneous Generation. The weakness of the former school consists—though this has been much exaggerated—in its more or less general adherence to the extreme view that religion had nothing to do with the natural life; the weakness of the latter lay in yielding to the more fatal extreme that it had nothing to do with anything else. That man, being a worshiping animal by nature, ought to maintain certain relations to the Supreme Being, was indeed to some extent conceded by the naturalistic school, but religion itself we looked upon as a thing to be spontaneously generated by the evolution of character in the laboratory of common life.

The difference between the two positions is radical. Translating from the language of Science into that of Religion, the theory of Spontaneous Generation is simply that a man may become gradually better and better until in course of the process he reaches that quantity of religious nature known as Spiritual Life. This Life is not something added *ab extra* to the natural man; it is the normal and appropriate development of the natural man. Biogenesis opposes to this the whole doctrine of Regeneration. The Spiritual Life is the gift of the Living Spirit. The spiritual man is no mere development of the natural man. He is a New Creation born from Above. As well expect a hay infusion to become gradually more and more living until in course of the process it reached Vitality, as expect a man by becoming better and better to attain the Eternal Life.

The advocates of Biogenesis in Religion have founded their argument hitherto all but exclusively on Scripture. The relation of the doctrine to the constitution and course of Nature was not disclosed. Its importance, therefore, was solely as a dogma; and being directly concerned with the Supernatural, it was valid for those alone who chose to accept the Supernatural.

Yet it has been keenly felt by those who attempt to defend this doctrine of the origin of the Spiritual Life, that they have nothing more to oppose to the rationalistic view than the *ipse dixit* of Revelation. The argument from experience, in the nature of the case, is seldom easy to apply, and Christianity has always found at this point a genuine difficulty in meeting the challenge of Natural Religions. The direct authority of Nature, using Nature in its limited sense, was not here to be sought for. On such a question its voice was necessarily silent; and all that the apologist could look for lower down was a distant echo or analogy. All that is really possible, indeed, is such an analogy; and if that can now be found in Biogenesis, Christianity in its most central position secures at length a support and basis in the Laws of Nature.

Up to the present time the analogy required has not been forthcoming. There was no known parallel in Nature for the spiritual phenomena in question. But now the case is altered. With the elevation of Biogenesis to the rank of a scientific fact, all problems concerning the Origin of Life are placed on a different footing. And it remains to be seen whether Religion cannot at once reaffirm and re-shape its argument in the light of this modern truth.

If the doctrine of the Spontaneous Generation of Spiritual Life can be met on scientific grounds, it will mean the removal of the most serious enemy Christianity has to deal with, and especially within its own borders, at the present day. The religion of Jesus has probably always suffered more from those who have misunderstood than from those who have opposed it. Of the multitudes who confess Christianity at this hour how many have clear in their minds the cardinal distinction established by its Founder between "born of the flesh" and "born of the Spirit?" By how many teachers of Christianity even is not this fundamental postulate persistently ignored? A thousand modern pulpits every seventh day are preaching the doctrine of Spontaneous Generation. The finest and best of recent poetry is colored with this same error. Spontaneous Generation is the leading theology of the modern religious or irreligious novel; and much of the most serious and cultured writing of the day devotes itself to earnest preaching of this impossible gospel. The current conception of the Christian religion in short —the conception which is held not only popularly but by men of culture— is founded upon a view of its origin which, if it were true, would render the whole scheme abortive.

Let us first place vividly in our imagination the picture of the two great Kingdoms of Nature, the inorganic and organic, as these now stand in the light of the Law of Biogenesis. What essentially is involved in saying that there is no Spontaneous Generation of Life? It is meant that the passage from the mineral world to the plant or animal world is hermetically sealed on the mineral side. This inorganic world is staked off from the living world by barriers which have never yet been crossed from within. No change of substance, no modification of environment, no chemistry, no electricity, nor any form of energy, nor any evolution can endow any single atom of the mineral world with the attribute of Life. Only by the bending down into this dead world of some living form can these dead atoms be gifted with the properties of vitality, without this preliminary contact with Life they remain fixed in the inorganic sphere forever. It is a very mysterious Law which guards in this way the portals of the living world. And if there is one thing in Nature more worth pondering for its strangeness it is the spectacle of this vast helpless world of the dead cut off from the living by the Law of Biogenesis and denied forever the possibility of resurrection within itself. So very strange a thing, indeed, is this broad line in Nature, that Science has long and urgently sought to obliterate it. Biogenesis stands in the way of some forms of Evolution with such stern persistency that the assaults upon this Law for number and thoroughness have been unparalleled. But, as we have seen, it has stood the test. Nature, to the modern eye, stands broken in two. The physical Laws may explain the inorganic world; the biological Laws may account for the development of the organic. But of the point where they meet, of that strange borderland between the dead and the living, Science is silent. It is as if God had placed everything in earth and heaven in the hands of Nature, but reserved a point at the genesis of Life for His direct appearing.

The power of the analogy, for which we are laying the foundations, to seize and impress the mind, will largely depend on the vividness with which one realizes the gulf which Nature places between the living and the dead.[36] But those who, in contemplating Nature, have found their attention arrested by this extraordinary dividing-line severing the visible universe eternally into two; those who in watching the progress of science have seen barrier after barrier disappear—barrier between plant and plant, between animal and animal, and even between animal and plant—but this gulf yawn more hopelessly wide with every advance of knowledge, will be prepared to attach a significance to the Law of Biogenesis and its analogies more profound perhaps than to any other fact or law in Nature. If, as Pascal says, Nature is an image of grace; if the things that are seen are in any sense the images of the unseen, there must lie in this great gulf fixed, this most unique and startling of all natural phenomena, a meaning of peculiar moment.

Where now in the Spiritual spheres shall we meet a companion phenomena to this? What in the Unseen shall be likened to this deep dividing-line, or where in human experience is another barrier which never can be crossed?

There is such a barrier. In the dim but not inadequate vision of the Spiritual World presented in the Word of God, the first thing that strikes the eye is a great gulf fixed. The passage from the Natural World to the Spiritual World is hermetically sealed on the natural side. The door from the inorganic to the organic is shut, no mineral can open it; so the door from the natural to the spiritual is shut, and no man can open it. This world of natural men is staked off from the Spiritual World by barriers which have never yet been crossed from within. No organic change, no modification of environment, no mental energy, no moral effort, no evolution of character, no progress of civilization can endow any single human soul with the attribute of Spiritual Life. The Spiritual World is guarded from the world next in order beneath it by a law of Biogenesis—*except a man be born again ... except a man be born of water and of the Spirit, he cannot enter the Kingdom of God.*

It is not said, in this enunciation of the law, that if the condition be not fulfilled the natural man *will not* enter the Kingdom of God. The word is *cannot*. For the exclusion of the spiritually inorganic from the Kingdom of the spiritually organic is not arbitrary. Nor is the natural man refused admission on unexplained grounds. His admission is a scientific impossibility. Except a mineral be born "from above"—from the Kingdom just *above* it—it cannot enter the Kingdom just above it. And except a man be born "from above," by the same law, he cannot enter the Kingdom just above him. There being no passage from one Kingdom to another, whether from inorganic to organic, or from organic to spiritual, the intervention of Life is a scientific necessity if a stone or a plant or an animal or a man is to pass from a lower to a higher sphere. The plant stretches down to the dead world beneath it, touches its minerals and gases with its mystery of Life, and brings them up ennobled and transformed to the living sphere. The breath of God, blowing where it listeth, touches with its mystery of Life the dead souls of men, bears them across the bridgeless gulf between the natural and the spiritual, between the spiritually inorganic and the spiritually organic, endows them with its own high qualities, and develops within them these new and secret faculties, by which those who are born again are said to *see the Kingdom of God.*

What is the evidence for this great gulf fixed at the portals of the Spiritual World? Does Science close this gate, or Reason, or Experience, or Revelation? We reply, all four. The initial statement, it is not to be denied, reaches us from Revelation. But is not this evidence here in court? Or shall it be said that any argument deduced from this is a transparent circle—that after all we simply come back to the unsubstantiality of the *ipse dixit*? Not altogether, for the analogy lends an altogether new authority to the *ipse dixit*. How substantial that argument really is, is seldom realized. We yield the point here much too easily. The right of the Spiritual World to speak of its own phenomena is as secure as the right of the Natural World to speak of itself. What is Science but what the Natural World has said to natural men? What is Revelation but what the Spiritual World has said to Spiritual men? Let us at least ask what Revelation has announced with reference to this Spiritual Law of Biogenesis; afterward we shall inquire whether Science, while indorsing the verdict, may not also have some further vindication of its title to be heard.

The words of Scripture which preface this inquiry contain an explicit and original statement of the Law of Biogenesis for the Spiritual Life. "He that hath the Son hath Life, and he that hath not the Son of God hath not Life." Life, that is to say, depends upon contact with Life. It cannot spring up of itself. It cannot develop out of anything that is not Life. There is no Spontaneous Generation in religion any more than in Nature. Christ is the source of Life in the Spiritual World; and he that hath the Son hath Life, and he that hath not the Son, whatever else he may have, hath not Life. Here, in short, is the categorical denial of Abiogenesis and the establishment in this high field of the classical formula *Omne vivum ex vivo*—no Life without antecedent Life. In this mystical theory of the Origin of Life the whole of the New Testament writers are agreed. And, as we have already seen, Christ Himself founds Christianity upon Biogenesis stated in its most literal form. "Except a man be born of water and of the Spirit he cannot enter into the Kingdom of God. That which is born of the flesh is flesh; and that which is born of the Spirit is Spirit. Marvel not that I said unto you, ye must be born again."[37] Why did He add *Marvel not*? Did He seek to allay the fear in the bewildered ruler's mind that there was more in this novel doctrine than a simple analogy from the first to the second birth?

The attitude of the natural man, again, with reference to the Spiritual, is a subject on which the New Testament is equally pronounced. Not only in his relation to the spiritual man, but to the whole Spiritual World, the natural man is regarded as *dead*. He is as a crystal to an organism. The natural world is to the Spiritual as the inorganic to the organic. "To be carnally minded is *Death*."[38] "Thou hast a name to live, but art *Dead*."[39] "She that liveth in pleasure is *Dead* while she liveth."[40] "To you he Hath given Life which were *Dead* in trespasses and sins."[41]

It is clear that a remarkable harmony exists here between the Organic World as arranged by Science and the Spiritual World as arranged by Scripture. We find one great Law guarding the thresholds of both worlds, securing that entrance from a lower sphere shall only take place by a direct regenerating act, and that emanating from the world next in order above. There are not two laws of Biogenesis, one for the natural, the other for the Spiritual; one law is for both. Wherever there is Life, Life of any kind, this same law holds. The analogy, therefore, is only among the phenomena; between laws there is no analogy—there is Continuity. In either case, the first step in peopling these worlds with the appropriate living forms is virtually miracle. Nor in one case is there less of mystery in the act than in the other. The second birth is scarcely less perplexing to the theologian than the first to the embryologist.

A moment's reflection ought now to make it clear why in the Spiritual World there had to be added to this mystery the further mystery of its proclamation through the medium of Revelation. This is the point at which the scientific man is apt to part company with the theologian. He insists on having all things materialized before his eyes in Nature. If Nature cannot discuss this with him, there is nothing to discuss. But Nature can discuss this with him—only she cannot open the discussion or supply all the material to begin with. If Science averred that she could do this, the theologian this time must part company with such Science. For any Science which makes such a demand is false to the doctrines of Biogenesis. What is this but the demand that a lower world, hermetically sealed against all communication with a world above it, should have a mature and intelligent acquaintance with its phenomena and laws? Can the mineral discourse to me of animal Life? Can it tell me what lies beyond the narrow boundary of its inert being? Knowing nothing of other than the chemical and physical laws, what is its criticism worth of the principles of Biology? And even when some visitor from the upper world, for example some root from a living tree, penetrating its dark recess, honors it with a touch, will it presume to define the form and purpose of its patron, or until the bioplasm has done its gracious work can it even know that it is being touched? The barrier which separates Kingdoms from one another restricts mind not less than matter. Any information of the Kingdoms above it that could come to the mineral world could only come by a communication from above. An analogy from the lower world might make such communication intelligible as well as credible, but the information in the first instance must be vouchsafed as a *revelation*. Similarly if those in the organic Kingdom are to know anything of the Spiritual World, that knowledge must at least begin as Revelation. Men who reject this source of information, by the Law of Biogenesis, can have no other. It is no spell of ignorance arbitrarily laid upon certain members of the Organic Kingdom that prevents them reading the secrets of the Spiritual World. It is a scientific necessity. No exposition of the case could be more truly scientific than this: "The natural man receiveth not the things of the Spirit of God; for they are foolishness unto him: *neither can he know them,* because they are spiritually discerned."[42] The verb here, it will be again observed, is potential. This is not a dogma of theology, but a necessity of Science. And Science, for the most part, has consistently accepted the situation. It has always proclaimed its ignorance of the Spiritual World. When Mr. Herbert Spencer affirms, "Regarding Science as a gradually increasing sphere we may say that every addition to its surface does but bring it into wider contact with surrounding nescience," [43] from his standpoint he is quite correct. The endeavors of well-meaning persons to show that the Agnostic's position, when he asserts his ignorance of the Spiritual World, is only a pretence; the attempts to prove that he really knows a great deal about it if he would only admit it, are quite misplaced. He really does not know. The verdict that the natural man receiveth not the things of the Spirit of God, that they are foolishness unto him, that *neither can he* know them, is final as a statement of scientific truth —a statement on which the entire Agnostic literature is simply one long commentary.

We are now in a better position to follow out the more practical bearings of Biogenesis. There is an immense region surrounding Regeneration, a dark and perplexing region where men would be thankful for any light. It may well be that Biogenesis in its many ramifications may yet reach down to some of the deeper mysteries of the Spiritual Life. But meantime there is much to define even on the surface. And for the present we shall content ourselves by turning its light upon one or two points of current interest.

It must long ago have appeared how decisive is the answer of Science to the practical question with which we set out as to the possibility of a Spontaneous Development of Spiritual Life in the individual soul. The inquiry into the Origin of Life is the fundamental question alike of Biology and Christianity. We can afford to enlarge upon it, therefore, even at the risk of repetition. When men are offering us a Christianity without a living Spirit, and a personal religion without *conversion*, no emphasis or reiteration can be extreme. Besides, the clearness as well as the definiteness of the Testimony of Nature to any Spiritual truth is of immense importance. Regeneration has not merely been an outstanding difficulty, but an overwhelming obscurity. Even to earnest minds the difficulty of grasping the truth at all has always proved extreme. Philosophically one scarcely sees either the necessity or the possibility of being born again. Why a virtuous man should not simply grow better and better until in his own right he enter the Kingdom of God is what thousands honestly and seriously fail to understand. Now Philosophy cannot help us here. Her arguments are, if anything, against us. But Science answers to the appeal at once. If it be simply pointed out that this is the same absurdity as to ask why a stone should not grow more and more living till it enters the Organic World, the point is clear in an instant.

What now, let us ask specifically, distinguishes a Christian man from a non-Christian man? Is it that he has certain mental characteristics not possessed by the other? Is it that certain faculties have been trained in him, that morality assumes special and higher manifestations, and character a nobler form? Is the Christian merely an ordinary man who happens from birth to have been surrounded with a peculiar set of ideas? Is his religion merely that peculiar quality of the moral life defined by Mr. Matthew Arnold as "morality touched by emotion?" And does the possession of a high ideal, benevolent sympathies, a reverent spirit, and a favorable environment account for what men call his Spiritual Life?

The distinction between them is the same as that between the Organic and the Inorganic, the living and the dead. What is the difference between a crystal and an organism, a stone and a plant? They have much in common. Both are made of the same atoms. Both display the same properties of matter. Both are subject to the Physical Laws. Both may be very beautiful. But besides possessing all that the crystal has, the plant possesses something more—a mysterious something called Life. This Life is not something which existed in the crystal only in a less developed form. There is nothing at all like it in the crystal. There is nothing like the first beginning of it in the crystal, not a trace or symptom of it. This plant is tenanted by something new, an original and unique possession added over and above all the properties common to both. When from vegetable Life we rise to animal Life, here again we find something original and unique— unique at least as compared with the mineral. From animal Life we ascend again to Spiritual Life. And here also is something new, something still more unique. He who lives the Spiritual Life has a distinct kind of Life added to all the other phases of Life which he manifests—a kind of Life infinitely more distinct than is the active Life of a plant from the inertia of a stone. The Spiritual man is more distinct in point of fact than is the plant from the stone. This is the one possible comparison in Nature, for it is the widest distinction in Nature; but compared with the difference between the Natural and the Spiritual the gulf which divides the organic from the inorganic is a hair's-breadth. The natural man belongs essentially to this present order of things. He is endowed simply with a high quality of the natural animal Life. But it is Life of so poor a quality that it is not Life at all. He that hath not the Son *hath not Life*; but he that hath the Son hath Life —a new and distinct and supernatural endowment. He is not of this world. He is of the timeless state, of Eternity. *It doth not yet appear what he shall be.*

The difference between the Spiritual man and the Natural man is not a difference of development, but of generation. It is a distinction of quality not of quantity. A man cannot rise by any natural development from "morality touched by emotion," to "morality touched by Life." Were we to construct a scientific classification, Science would compel us to arrange all natural men, moral or immoral, educated or vulgar, as one family. One might be high in the family group, another low; yet, practically, they are marked by the same set of characteristics—they eat, sleep, work, think, live, die. But the Spiritual man is removed from this family so utterly by the possession of an additional characteristic that a biologist, fully informed of the whole circumstances, would not hesitate a moment to classify him elsewhere. And if he really entered into these circumstances it would not be in another family but in another Kingdom. It is an old-fashioned theology which divides the world in this way—which speaks of men as Living and Dead, Lost and Saved—a stern theology all but fallen into disuse. This difference between the Living and the Dead in souls is so unproved by casual observation, so impalpable in itself, so startling as a doctrine, that schools of culture have ridiculed or denied the grim distinction. Nevertheless the grim distinction must be retained. It is a scientific distinction. "He that hath not the Son hath not Life."

Now it is this great Law which finally distinguishes Christianity from all other religions. It places the religion of Christ upon a footing altogether unique. There is no analogy between the Christian religion and, say, Buddhism or the Mohammedan religion. There is no true sense in which a man can say, He that hath Buddha hath Life. Buddha has nothing to do with Life. He may have something to do with morality. He may stimulate, impress, teach, guide, but there is no distinct new thing added to the souls of those who profess Buddhism. These religions *may* be developments of the natural, mental, or moral man. But Christianity professes to be more. It is the mental or moral man *plus* something else or some One else. It is the infusion into the Spiritual man of a New Life, of a quality unlike anything else in Nature. This constitutes the separate Kingdom of Christ, and gives to Christianity alone of all the religions of mankind the strange mark of Divinity.

Shall we next inquire more precisely what is this something extra which constitutes Spiritual Life? What is this strange and new endowment in its nature and vital essence? And the answer is brief—it is Christ. He that hath *the Son* hath Life.

Are we forsaking the lines of Science in saying so? Yes and No. Science has drawn for us the distinction. It has no voice as to the nature of the distinction except this—that the new endowment is a something different from anything else with which it deals. It is not ordinary Vitality, it is not intellectual, it is not moral, but something beyond. And Revelation steps in and names what it is—it is Christ. Out of the multitude of sentences where this announcement is made, these few may be selected: "Know ye not your own selves how that *Jesus Christ is in you*?"[44] "Your bodies are the members of Christ."[45] "At that day ye shall know that I am in the Father, and ye in Me, and I in you."[46] "We will come unto him and make our abode with him."[47] "I am the Vine, ye are the branches."[48] "I am crucified with Christ, nevertheless I live, yet not I, but Christ liveth in me."[49]

Three things are clear from these statements: First, they are not mere figures of rhetoric. They are explicit declarations. If language means anything these words announce a literal fact. In some of Christ's own statements the literalism is if possible still more impressive. For instance, "Except ye eat the flesh of the Son of man and drink His blood, ye have no life in you. Whoso eateth My flesh and drinketh My blood hath eternal life; and I will raise him up at the last day. For My flesh is meat indeed, and My blood is drink indeed. He that eateth My flesh and drinketh My blood *dwelleth in Me and I in him*."

In the second place, Spiritual Life is not something outside ourselves. The idea is not that Christ is in heaven and that we can stretch out some mysterious faculty and deal with Him there. This is the vague form in which many conceive the truth, but it is contrary to Christ's teaching and to the analogy of nature. Vegetable Life is not contained in a reservoir somewhere in the skies, and measured out spasmodically at certain seasons. The Life is *in* every plant and tree, inside its own substance and tissue, and continues there until it dies. This localization of Life in the individual is precisely the point where Vitality differs from the other forces of nature, such as magnetism and electricity. Vitality has much in common with such forces as magnetism and electricity, but there is one inviolable distinction between them—that Life is permanently fixed and rooted in the organism. The doctrines of conservation and transformation of energy, that is to say, do not hold for Vitality. The electrician can demagnetize a bar of iron, that is, he can transform its energy of magnetism into something else—heat, or motion, or light—and then re-form these back into magnetism. For magnetism has no root, no individuality, no fixed indwelling. But the biologist cannot devitalize a plant or an animal and revivify it again.[50] Life is not one of the homeless forces which promiscuously inhabit space, or which can be gathered like electricity from the clouds and dissipated back again into space. Life is definite and resident; and Spiritual Life is not a visit from a force, but a resident tenant in the soul.

This is, however, to formulate the statement of the third point, that Spiritual Life is not an ordinary form of energy or force. The analogy from Nature indorses this, but here Nature stops. It cannot say what Spiritual Life is. Indeed what natural Life is remains unknown, and the word Life still wanders through Science without a definition. Nature is silent, therefore, and must be as to Spiritual Life. But in the absence of natural light we fall back upon that complementary revelation which always shines, when truth is necessary and where Nature fails. We ask with Paul when this Life first visited him on the Damascus road, What is this? "Who art Thou, Lord?" And we hear, "I am Jesus."[51]

We must expect to find this denied. Besides a proof from Revelation, this is an argument from experience. And yet we shall still be told that this Spiritual Life is a force. But let it be remembered what this means in Science, it means the heresy of confounding Force with Vitality. We must also expect to be told that this Spiritual Life is simply a development of ordinary Life—just as Dr. Bastian tells us that natural Life is formed according to the same laws which determine the more simple chemical combinations. But remember what this means in Science. It is the heresy of Spontaneous Generation, a heresy so thoroughly discredited now that scarcely an authority in Europe will lend his name to it. Who art Thou, Lord? Unless we are to be allowed to hold Spontaneous Generation there is no alternative: Life can only come from Life: "I am Jesus."

A hundred other questions now rush into the mind about this Life: How does it come? Why does it come? How is it manifested? What faculty does it employ? Where does it reside? Is it communicable? What are its conditions? One or two of these questions may be vaguely answered, the rest bring us face to face with mystery. Let it not be thought that the scientific treatment of a Spiritual subject has reduced religion to a problem of physics, or demonstrated God by the laws of biology. A religion without mystery is an absurdity. Even Science has its mysteries, none more inscrutable than around this Science of Life. It taught us sooner or later to expect mystery, and now we enter its domain. Let it be carefully marked, however, that the cloud does not fall and cover us till we have ascertained the most momentous truth of Religion—that Christ is in the Christian.

Not that there is anything new in this. The Churches have always held that Christ was the source of Life. No spiritual man ever claims that his spirituality is his own. "I live," he will tell you; "nevertheless it is not I, but Christ liveth in me." Christ our Life has indeed been the only doctrine in the Christian Church from Paul to Augustine, from Calvin to Newman. Yet, when the Spiritual man is cross-examined upon this confession it is astonishing to find what uncertain hold it has upon his mind. Doctrinally he states it adequately and holds it unhesitatingly. But when pressed with the literal question he shrinks from the answer. We do not really believe that the Living Christ has touched us, that He makes His abode in us. Spiritual Life is not as real to us as natural Life. And we cover our retreat into unbelieving vagueness with a plea of reverence, justified, as we think, by the "Thus far and no farther" of ancient Scriptures. There is often a great deal of intellectual sin concealed under this old aphorism. When men do not really wish to go farther they find it an honorable convenience sometimes to sit down on the outermost edge of the Holy Ground on the pretext of taking off their shoes. Yet we must be certain that, making a virtue of reverence, we are not merely excusing ignorance; or, under the plea of mystery, evading a truth which has been stated in the New Testament a hundred times, in the most literal form, and with all but monotonous repetition. The greatest truths are always the most loosely held. And not the least of the advantages of taking up this question from the present standpoint is that we may see how a confused doctrine can really bear the luminous definition of Science and force itself upon us with all the weight of Natural Law.

What is mystery to many men, what feeds their worship, and at the same time spoils it, is that area round all great truth which is really capable of illumination, and into which every earnest mind is permitted and commanded to go with a light. We cry mystery long before the region of mystery comes. True mystery casts no shadows around. It is a sudden and awful gulf yawning across the field of knowledge; its form is irregular, but its lips are clean cut and sharp, and the mind can go to the very verge and look down the precipice into the dim abyss—

> "Where writhing clouds unroll,
> Striving to utter themselves in shapes."

We have gone with a light to the very verge of this truth. We have seen that the Spiritual Life is an endowment from the Spiritual World, and that the Living Spirit of Christ dwells in the Christian. But now the gulf yawns black before us. What more does Science know of life? Nothing. It knows nothing further about its origin in detail. It knows nothing about its ultimate nature. It cannot even define it. There is a helplessness in scientific books here, and a continual confession of it which to thoughtful minds is almost touching. Science, therefore, has not eliminated the true mysteries from our faith, but only the false. And it has done more. It has made true mystery scientific. Religion in having mystery is in analogy with all around it. Where there is exceptional mystery in the Spiritual world it will generally be found that there is a corresponding mystery in the natural world. And, as Origen centuries ago insisted, the difficulties of Religion are simply the difficulties of Nature.

One question more we may look at for a moment. What can be gathered on the surface as to the process of Regeneration in the individual soul? From the analogies of Biology we should expect three things: First, that the New Life should dawn suddenly; Second, that it should come "without observation;" Third, that it should develop gradually. On two of these points there can be little controversy. The gradualness of growth is a characteristic which strikes the simplest observer. Long before the word Evolution was coined Christ applied it in this very connection—"First the blade, then the ear, then the full corn in the ear." It is well known also to those who study the parables of Nature that there is an ascending scale of slowness as we rise in the scale of Life. Growth is most gradual in the highest forms. Man attains his maturity after a score of years; the monad completes its humble cycle in a day. What wonder if development be tardy in the Creature of Eternity? A Christian's sun has sometimes set, and a critical world has seen as yet no corn in the ear. As yet? "As yet," in this long Life, has not begun. Grant him the years proportionate to his place in the scale of Life. "The time of harvest is *not yet*."

Again, in addition to being slow, the phenomena of growth are secret. Life is invisible. When the New Life manifests itself it is a surprise. *Thou canst not tell whence it cometh or whither it goeth.* When the plant lives whence has the Life come? When it dies whither has it gone? *Thou canst not tell ... so is every one that is born of the Spirit. For the kingdom of God cometh without observation.*

Yet once more—and this is a point of strange and frivolous dispute—this Life comes suddenly. This is the only way in which Life can come. Life cannot come gradually—health can, structure can, but not Life. A new theology has laughed at the Doctrine of Conversion. Sudden Conversion especially has been ridiculed as untrue to philosophy and impossible to human nature. We may not be concerned in buttressing any theology because it is old. But we find that this old theology is scientific. There may be cases—they are probably in the majority—where the moment of contact with the Living Spirit though sudden has been obscure. But the real moment and the conscious moment are two different things. Science pronounces nothing as to the conscious moment. If it did it would probably say that that was seldom the real moment—just as in the natural Life the conscious moment is not the real moment. The moment of birth in the natural world is not a conscious moment—we do not know we are born till long afterward. Yet there are men to whom the Origin of the New Life in time has been no difficulty. To Paul, for instance, Christ seems to have come at a definite period of time, the exact moment and second of which could have been known. And this is certainly, in theory at least, the normal Origin of Life, according to the principles of Biology. The line between the living and the dead is a sharp line. When the dead atoms of Carbon, Hydrogen, Oxygen, Nitrogen, are seized upon by Life, the organism at first is very lowly. It possesses few functions. It has little beauty. Growth is the work of time. But Life is not. That comes in a moment. At one moment it was dead; the next it lived. This is conversion, the "passing," as the Bible calls it, "from Death unto Life." Those who have stood by another's side at the solemn hour of this dread possession have been conscious sometimes of an experience which words are not allowed to utter—a something like the sudden snapping of a chain, the waking from a dream.

FOOTNOTES:

[33] "Beginnings of Life." By H. C. Bastian, M.A., M.D., F.R.S. Macmillan, vol. ii. p. 633.

[34] "Critiques and Addresses." T. H. Huxley. F.R.S., p. 239.

[35] *Nineteenth Century*, 1878, p. 507.

[36] This being the crucial point it may not be inappropriate to supplement the quotations already given in the text with the following:—

"We are in the presence of the one incommunicable gulf—the gulf of all gulfs—that gulf which Mr. Huxley's protoplasm is as powerless to efface as any other material expedient that has ever been suggested since the eyes of men first looked into it—the mighty gulf between death and life."—"As Regards Protoplasm." By J. Hutchinson Stirling, LL.D., p. 42.

"The present state of knowledge furnishes us with no link between the living and the not-living."—Huxley, "Encyclopædia Britannica" (new Ed.). Art. "Biology."

"Whoever recalls to mind the lamentable failure of all the attempts made very recently to discover a decided support for the *generatio æquivoca* in the lower forms of transition from the inorganic to the organic world, will feel it doubly serious to demand that this theory, so utterly discredited, should be in any way accepted as the basis of all our views of life."—Virchow: "The Freedom of Science in the Modern State."

"All really scientific experience tells us that life can be produced from a living antecedent only."—"The Unseen Universe," 6th Ed., p. 229.

[37] John iii.

[38] Rom. viii. 6.

[39] Rev. iii. 1.

[40] 1 Tim. v. 6.

[41] Eph. ii. 1, 5.

[42] 1 Cor. ii. 14.

[43] "First Principles," 2d Ed., p. 17.

[44] 2 Cor. xii. 5.

[45] 1 Cor. vi. 15.

[46] John xiv. 20.

[47] John xiv. 21-23.

[48] John xv. 4.

[49] Gal. ii. 20.

[50] One must not be misled by popular statements in this connection, such as this of Professor Owen's: "There are organisms which we can devitalize and

revitalize—devive and revive—many times." (*Monthly Microscopical Journal*, May, 1869, p. 294.) The reference is of course to the extraordinary capacity for *resuscitation* possessed by many of the Protozoa and other low forms of life.

[51] Acts ix. 5.

> "I went by the field of the slothful, and by the vineyard of the man void of understanding; and lo, it was all grown over with thorns, and nettles had covered the face thereof, and the stone wall thereof was broken down. Then I saw and considered it well; I looked upon it and received instruction."—*Solomon.*
>
> "How shall we escape if we neglect so great salvation?"—*Hebrews.*
>
> "We have as possibilities either Balance, or Elaboration, or Degeneration."—*E. Ray Lankester.*

In one of his best known books, Mr. Darwin brings out a fact which may be illustrated in some such way as this: Suppose a bird fancier collects a flock of tame pigeons distinguished by all the infinite ornamentations of their race. They are of all kinds, of every shade of color, and adorned with every variety of marking. He takes them to an uninhabited island and allows them to fly off wild into the woods. They found a colony there, and after the lapse of many years the owner returns to the spot. He will find that a remarkable change has taken place in the interval. The birds, or their descendants rather, have all become changed into the same color. The black, the white and the dun, the striped, the spotted, and the ringed, are all metamorphosed into one—a dark slaty blue. Two plain black bands monotonously repeat themselves upon the wings of each, and the loins beneath are white; but all the variety, all the beautiful colors, all the old graces of form it may be, have disappeared. These improvements were the result of care and nature, of domestication, of civilization; and now that these influences are removed, the birds themselves undo the past and lose what they had gained. The attempt to elevate the race has been mysteriously thwarted. It is as if the original bird, the far remote ancestor of all doves, had been blue, and these had been compelled by some strange law to discard the badges of their civilization and conform to the ruder image of the first. The natural law by which such a change occurs is called *The Principle of Reversion to Type.*

It is a proof of the universality of this law that the same thing will happen with a plant. A garden is planted, let us say, with strawberries and roses, and for a number of years is left alone. In process of time it will run to waste. But this does not mean that the plants will really waste away, but that they will change into something else, and, as it invariably appears, into something worse; in the one case, namely, into the small, wild strawberry of the woods, and in the other into the primitive dog-rose of the hedges.

If we neglect a garden plant, then, a natural principle of deterioration comes in, and changes it into a worse plant. And if we neglect a bird, by the same imperious law it will be gradually changed into an uglier bird. Or if we neglect almost any of the domestic animals, they will rapidly revert to wild and worthless forms again.

Now the same thing exactly would happen in the case of you or me. Why should Man be an exception to any of the laws of Nature? Nature knows him simply as an animal—Sub-kingdom *Vertebrata*, Class *Mammalia*, Order *Bimana*. And the law of Reversion to Type runs through all creation. If a man neglect himself for a few years he will change into a worse man and a lower man. If it is his body that he neglects, he will deteriorate into a wild and bestial savage—like the de-humanized men who are discovered sometimes upon desert islands. If it is his mind, it will degenerate into imbecility and madness—solitary confinement has the power to unmake men's minds and leave them idiots. If he neglect his conscience, it will run off into lawlessness and vice. Or, lastly, if it is his soul, it must inevitably atrophy, drop off in ruin and decay.

We have here, then, a thoroughly natural basis for the question before us. If we neglect, with this universal principle staring us in the face, how shall we escape? If we neglect the ordinary means of keeping a garden in order, how shall it escape running to weeds and waste? Or, if we neglect the opportunities for cultivating the mind, how shall it escape ignorance and feebleness? So, if we neglect the soul, how shall it escape the natural retrograde movement, the inevitable relapse into barrenness and death?

It is not necessary, surely, to pause for proof that there is such a retrograde principle in the being of every man. It is demonstrated by facts, and by the analogy of all Nature. Three possibilities of life, according to Science, are open to all living organisms—Balance, Evolution, and Degeneration. The first denotes the precarious persistence of a life along what looks like a level path, a character which seems to hold its own alike against the attacks of evil and the appeals of good. It implies a set of circumstances so balanced by choice or fortune that they neither influence for better nor for worse. But except in theory this state of equilibrium, normal in the inorganic kingdom, is really foreign to the world of life; and what seems inertia may be a true Evolution unnoticed from its slowness, or likelier still a movement of Degeneration subtly obliterating as it falls the very traces of its former height. From this state of apparent Balance, Evolution is the escape in the upward direction, Degeneration in the lower. But Degeneration, rather than Balance or Elaboration, is the possibility of life embraced by the majority of mankind. And the choice is determined by man's own nature. The life of Balance is difficult. It lies on the verge of continual temptation, its perpetual adjustments become fatiguing, its measured virtue is monotonous and uninspiring. More difficult still, apparently, is the life of ever upward growth. Most men attempt it for a time, but growth is slow; and despair overtakes them while the goal is far away. Yet none of these reasons fully explains the fact that the alternative which remains is adopted by the majority of men. That Degeneration is easy only half accounts for it. Why is it easy? Why but that already in each man's very nature this principle is supreme? He feels within his soul a silent drifting motion impelling him downward with irresistible force. Instead of aspiring to Conversion to a higher Type he submits by a law of his nature to Reversion to a lower. This is Degeneration—that principle by which the organism, failing to develop itself, failing even to keep what it has got, deteriorates, and becomes more and more adapted to a degraded form of life.

All men who know themselves are conscious that this tendency, deep-rooted and active, exists within their nature. Theologically it is described as a gravitation, a bias toward evil. The Bible view is that man is conceived in sin and shapen in iniquity. And experience tells him that he will shape himself into further sin and ever deepening iniquity without the smallest effort, without in the least intending it, and in the most natural way in the world if he simply let his life run. It is on this principle that, completing the conception, the wicked are said further in the Bible to be lost. They are not really lost as yet, but they are on the sure way to it. The bias of their lives is in full action. There is no drag on anywhere. The natural tendencies are having it all their own way; and although the victims may be quite unconscious that all this is going on, it is patent to every one who considers even the natural bearings of the case that "the end of these things is Death."

When we see a man fall from the top of a five-story house, we say the man is lost. We say that before he has fallen a foot; for the same principle that made him fall the one foot will undoubtedly make him complete the descent by falling another eighty or ninety feet. So that he is a dead man, or a lost man from the very first. The gravitation of sin in a human soul acts precisely in the same way. Gradually, with gathering momentum it sinks a man further and further from God and righteousness, and lands him, by the sheer action of a natural law, in the hell of a neglected life.

But the lesson is not less clear from analogy. Apart even from the law of Degeneration, apart from Reversion to Type, there is in every living organism a law of Death. We are wont to imagine that Nature is full of Life. In reality it is full of Death. One cannot say it is natural for a plant to live. Examine its nature fully, and you have to admit that its natural tendency is to die. It is kept from dying by a mere temporary endowment which gives it an ephemeral dominion over the elements—gives it power to utilize for a brief span the rain, the sunshine, and the air. Withdraw this temporary endowment for a moment and its true nature is revealed. Instead of overcoming Nature it is overcome. The very things which appeared to minister to its growth and beauty now turn against it and make it decay and die. The sun which warmed it, withers it; the air and rain which nourished it, rot it. It is the very forces which we associate with life which, when their true nature appears, are discovered to be really the ministers of death.

This law, which is true for the whole plant-world, is also valid for the animal and for man. Air is not life, but corruption—so literally corruption that the only way to keep out corruption, when life has ebbed, is to keep out air. Life is merely a temporary suspension of these destructive powers; and this is truly one of the most accurate definitions of life we have yet received —"the sum total of the functions which resist death."

Spiritual life, in like manner, is the sum total of the functions which resist sin. The soul's atmosphere is the daily trial, circumstance, and temptation of the world. And as it is life alone which gives the plant power to utilize the elements, and as, without it, they utilize it, so it is the spiritual life alone which gives the soul power to utilize temptation and trial; and without it they destroy the soul. How shall we escape if we refuse to exercise these functions—in other words, if we neglect?

This destroying process, observe, goes on quite independently of God's judgment on sin. God's judgment on sin is another and a more awful fact of which this may be a part. But it is a distinct fact by itself, which we can hold and examine separately, that on purely natural principles the soul that is left to itself unwatched, uncultivated, unredeemed, must fall away into death by its own nature. The soul that sinneth "it shall die." It shall die, not necessarily because God passes sentence of death upon it, but because it cannot help dying. It has neglected "the functions which resist death" and has always been dying. The punishment is in its very nature, and the sentence is being gradually carried out all along the path of life by ordinary processes which enforce the verdict with the appalling faithfulness of law.

There is an affectation that religious truths lie beyond the sphere of the comprehension which serves men in ordinary things. This question at least must be an exception. It lies as near the natural as the spiritual. If it makes no impression on a man to know that God will visit his iniquities upon him, he cannot blind himself to the fact that Nature will. Do we not all know what it is to be punished by Nature for disobeying her? We have looked round the wards of a hospital, a prison, or a madhouse, and seen there Nature at work squaring her accounts with sin. And we knew as we looked that if no Judge sat on the throne of heaven at all there was a Judgment there, where an inexorable Nature was crying aloud for justice, and carrying out her heavy sentences for violated laws.

When God gave Nature the law into her own hands in this way, He seems to have given her two rules upon which her sentences were to be based. The one is formally enunciated in this sentence, "WHATSOEVER A MAN SOWETH THAT SHALL HE ALSO REAP." The other is informally expressed in this, "IF WE NEGLECT HOW SHALL WE ESCAPE?"

The first is the positive law, and deals with sins of commission. The other, which we are now discussing, is the negative, and deals with sins of omission. It does not say anything about sowing but about not sowing. It takes up the case of souls which are lying fallow. It does not say, if we sow corruption we shall reap corruption. Perhaps we would not be so unwise, so regardless of ourselves, of public opinion, as to sow corruption. It does not say, if we sow tares we shall reap tares. We might never do anything so foolish as sow tares. But if we sow nothing, it says, we shall reap nothing. If we put nothing into the field, we shall take nothing out. If we neglect to cultivate in summer, how shall we escape starving in winter?

Now the Bible raises this question, but does not answer it—because it is too obvious to need answering. How shall we escape if we neglect? The answer is, we cannot. In the nature of things we cannot. We cannot escape any more than a man can escape drowning who falls into the sea and has neglected to learn to swim. In the nature of things he cannot escape—nor can he escape who has neglected the great salvation.

Now why should such fatal consequences follow a simple process like neglect? The popular impression is that a man, to be what is called lost, must be an open and notorious sinner. He must be one who has abandoned all that is good and pure in life, and sown to the flesh with all his might and main. But this principle goes further. It says simply, "If we neglect." Any one may see the reason why a notoriously wicked person should not escape; but why should not all the rest of us escape? What is to hinder people who are not notoriously wicked escaping—people who never sowed anything in particular? Why is it such a sin to sow nothing in particular?

There must be some hidden and vital relation between these three words, Salvation, Neglect, and Escape—some reasonable, essential, and indissoluble connection. Why are these words so linked together as to weight this clause with all the authority and solemnity of a sentence of death?

The explanation has partly been given already. It lies still further, however, in the meaning of the word Salvation. And this, of course, is not at all Salvation in the ordinary sense of forgiveness of sin. This is one great meaning of Salvation, the first and the greatest. But this is spoken to people who are supposed to have had this. It is the broader word, therefore, and includes not only forgiveness of sin but salvation or deliverance from the downward bias of the soul. It takes in that whole process of rescue from the power of sin and selfishness that should be going on from day to day in every human life. We have seen that there is a natural principle in man lowering him, deadening him, pulling him down by inches to the mere animal plane, blinding reason, searing conscience, paralyzing will. This is the active destroying principle, or Sin. Now to counteract this, God has discovered to us another principle which will stop this drifting process in the soul, steer it round, and make it drift the other way. This is the active saving principle, or Salvation. If a man find the first of these powers furiously at work within him, dragging his whole life downward to destruction, there is only one way to escape his fate—to take resolute hold of the upward power, and be borne by it to the opposite goal. And as this second power is the only one in the universe which has the slightest real effect upon the first, how shall a man escape if he neglect it? To neglect it is to cut off the only possible chance of escape. In declining this he is simply abandoning himself with his eyes open to that other and terrible energy which is already there, and which, in the natural course of things, is bearing him every moment further and further from escape.

From the very nature of Salvation, therefore, it is plain that the only thing necessary to make it of no effect is neglect. Hence the Bible could not fail to lay strong emphasis on a word so vital. It was not necessary for it to say, how shall we escape if we trample upon the great salvation, or doubt, or despise, or reject it. A man who has been poisoned only need neglect the antidote and he will die. It makes no difference whether he dashes it on the ground, or pours it out of the window, or sets it down by his bedside, and stares at it all the time he is dying. He will die just the same, whether he destroys it in a passion, or coolly refuses to have anything to do with it. And as a matter of fact probably most deaths, spiritually, are gradual dissolutions of the last class rather than rash suicides of the first.

This, then, is the effect of neglecting salvation from the side of salvation itself; and the conclusion is that from the very nature of salvation escape is out of the question. Salvation is a definite process. If a man refuse to submit himself to that process, clearly he cannot have the benefits of it. *As many as received Him to them gave He* power *to become the sons of God.* He does not avail himself of this power. It may be mere carelessness or apathy. Nevertheless the neglect is fatal. He cannot escape because he will not.

Turn now to another aspect of the case—to the effect upon the soul itself. Neglect does more for the soul than make it miss salvation. It despoils it of its capacity for salvation. Degeneration in the spiritual sphere involves primarily the impairing of the faculties of salvation and ultimately the loss of them. It really means that the very soul itself becomes piecemeal destroyed until the very capacity for God and righteousness is gone.

The soul, in its highest sense, is a vast capacity for God. It is like a curious chamber added on to being, and somehow involving being, a chamber with elastic and contractile walls, which can be expanded, with God as its guest, illimitably, but which without God shrinks and shrivels until every vestige of the Divine is gone, and God's image is left without God's Spirit. One cannot call what is left a soul; it is a shrunken, useless organ, a capacity sentenced to death by disuse, which droops as a withered hand by the side, and cumbers nature like a rotted branch. Nature has her revenge upon neglect as well as upon extravagance. Misuse, with her, is as mortal a sin as abuse.

There are certain burrowing animals—the mole for instance—which have taken to spending their lives beneath the surface of the ground. And Nature has taken her revenge upon them in a thoroughly natural way—she has closed up their eyes. If they mean to live in darkness, she argues, eyes are obviously a superfluous function. By neglecting them these animals made it clear they do not want them. And as one of Nature's fixed principles is that nothing shall exist in vain, the eyes are presently taken away, or reduced to a rudimentary state. There are fishes also which have had to pay the same terrible forfeit for having made their abode in dark caverns where eyes can never be required. And in exactly the same way the spiritual eye must die and lose its power by purely natural law if the soul choose to walk in darkness rather than in light.

This is the meaning of the favorite paradox of Christ, "From him that hath not shall be taken away even that which he hath;" "take therefore the talent from him." The religious faculty is a talent, the most splendid and sacred talent we possess. Yet it is subject to the natural conditions and laws. If any man take his talent and hide it in a napkin, although it is doing him neither harm nor good apparently, God will not allow him to have it. Although it is lying there rolled up in the darkness, not conspicuously affecting any one, still God will not allow him to keep it. He will not allow him to keep it any more than Nature would allow the fish to keep their eyes. Therefore, He says, "take the talent from him." And Nature does it.

This man's crime was simply neglect—"thou wicked and *slothful* servant." It was a wasted life—a life which failed in the holy stewardship of itself. Such a life is a peril to all who cross its path. Degeneration compasses Degeneration. It is only a character which is itself developing that can aid the Evolution of the world and so fulfill the end of life. For this high usury each of our lives, however small may seem our capital, was given us by God. And it is just the men whose capital seems small who need to choose the best investments. It is significant that it was the man who had only one talent who was guilty of neglecting it. Men with ten talents, men of large gifts and burning energies, either direct their powers nobly and usefully, or misdirect them irretrievably. It is those who belong to the rank and file of life who need this warning most. Others have an abundant store and sow to the spirit or the flesh with a lavish hand. But we, with our small gift, what boots our sowing? Our temptation as ordinary men is to neglect to sow at all. The interest on our talent would be so small that we excuse ourselves with the reflection that it is not worth while.

It is no objection to all this to say that we are unconscious of this neglect or misdirection of our powers. That is the darkest feature in the case. If there were uneasiness there might be hope. If there were, somewhere about our soul, a something which was not gone to sleep like all the rest; if there were a contending force anywhere; if we would let even that work instead of neglecting it, it would gain strength from hour to hour, and waken up one at a time each torpid and dishonored faculty till our whole nature became alive with strivings against self, and every avenue was open wide for God. But the apathy, the numbness of the soul, what can be said of such a symptom but that it means the creeping on of death? There are accidents in which the victims feel no pain. They are well and strong they think. But they are dying. And if you ask the surgeon by their side what makes him give this verdict, he will say it is this numbness over the frame which tells how some of the parts have lost already the very capacity for life.

Nor is it the least tragic accompaniment of this process that its effects may even be concealed from others. The soul undergoing Degeneration, surely by some arrangement with Temptation planned in the uttermost hell, possesses the power of absolute secrecy. When all within is festering decay and rottenness, a Judas, without anomaly, may kiss his Lord. This invisible consumption, like its fell analogue in the natural world, may even keep its victim beautiful while slowly slaying it. When one examines the little *Crustacea* which have inhabited for centuries the lakes of the Mammoth Cave of Kentucky, one is at first astonished to find these animals apparently endowed with perfect eyes. The pallor of the head is broken by two black pigment specks, conspicuous indeed as the only bits of color on the whole blanched body; and these, even to the casual observer, certainly represent well-defined organs of vision. But what do they with eyes in these Stygian waters? There reigns an everlasting night. Is the law for once at fault? A swift incision with the scalpel, a glance with a lens, and their secret is betrayed. The eyes are a mockery. Externally they are organs of vision—the front of the eye is perfect; behind, there is nothing but a mass of ruins. The optic nerve is a shrunken, atrophied and insensate thread. These animals have organs of vision, and yet they have no vision. They have eyes, but they see not.

Exactly what Christ said of men: They had eyes, but no vision. And the reason is the same. It is the simplest problem of natural history. The *Crustacea* of the Mammoth Cave have chosen to abide in darkness. Therefore they have become fitted for it. By refusing to see they have waived the right to see. And Nature has grimly humored them. Nature had to do it by her very constitution. It is her defence against waste that decay of faculty should immediately follow disuse of function. He that hath ears to hear, he whose ears have not degenerated, let him hear.

Men tell us sometimes there is no such thing as an atheist. There must be. There are some men to whom it is true that there is no God. They cannot see God because they have no eye. They have only an abortive organ, atrophied by neglect.

All this, it is commonplace again to insist, is not the effect of neglect when we die, but while we live. The process is in full career and operation now. It is useless projecting consequences into the future when the effects may be measured now. We are always practicing these little deceptions upon ourselves, postponing the consequences of our misdeeds as if they were to culminate some other day about the time of death. It makes us sin with a lighter hand to run an account with retribution, as it were, and delay the reckoning time with God. But every day is a reckoning day. Every soul is a Book of Judgment and Nature, as a recording angel, marks there every sin.

As all will be judged by the great Judge some day, all are judged by Nature now. The sin of yesterday, as part of its penalty, has the sin of to-day. All follow us in silent retribution on our past, and go with us to the grave. We cannot cheat Nature. No sleight-of-heart can rob religion of *a present*, the immortal nature of a *now*. The poet sings—

> "I looked behind to find my past,
> And lo, it had gone before."

But no, not all. The unforgiven sins are not away in keeping somewhere to be let loose upon us when we die; they are here, within us, now. To-day brings the resurrection of their past, to-morrow of to-day. And the powers of sin, to the exact strength that we have developed them, nearing their dreadful culmination with every breath we draw, are here, within us, now. The souls of some men are already honey-combed through and through with the eternal consequences of neglect, so that taking the natural and rational view of their case *just now,* it is simply inconceivable that there is any escape *just now*. What a fearful thing it is to fall into the hands of the living God! A fearful thing even if, as the philosopher tells us, "the hands of the Living God are the Laws of Nature."

Whatever hopes of a "heaven" a neglected soul may have, can be shown to be an ignorant and delusive dream. How is the soul to escape to heaven if it has neglected for a lifetime the means of escape from the world and self? And where is the capacity for heaven to come from if it be not developed on earth? Where, indeed, is even the smallest spiritual appreciation of God and heaven to come from when so little of spirituality has ever been known or manifested here? If every Godward aspiration of the soul has been allowed to become extinct, and every inlet that was open to heaven to be choked, and every talent for religious love and trust to have been persistently neglected and ignored, where are the faculties to come from that would ever find the faintest relish in such things as God and heaven give?

These three words, Salvation, Escape, and Neglect, then, are not casually, but organically and necessarily connected. Their doctrine is scientific, not arbitrary. Escape means nothing more than the gradual emergence of the higher being from the lower, and nothing less. It means the gradual putting off of all that cannot enter the higher state, or heaven, and simultaneously the putting on of Christ. It involves the slow completing of the soul and the development of the capacity for God.

Should any one object that from this scientific standpoint the opposite of salvation is annihilation, the answer is at hand. From this standpoint there is no such word.

If, then, escape is to be open to us, it is not to come to us somehow, vaguely. We are not to hope for anything startling or mysterious. It is a definite opening along certain lines which are definitely marked by God, which begin at the Cross of Christ, and lead direct to Him. Each man in the silence of his own soul must work out this salvation for himself with fear and trembling—with fear, realizing the momentous issues of his task; with trembling, lest before the tardy work be done the voice of Death should summon him to stop.

What these lines are may, in closing, be indicated in a word. The true problem of the spiritual life may be said to be, do the opposite of Neglect. Whatever this is, do it, and you shall escape. It will just mean that you are so to cultivate the soul that all its powers will open out to God, and in beholding God be drawn away from sin. The idea really is to develop among the ruins of the old a new "creature"—a new creature which, while the old is suffering Degeneration from Neglect, is gradually to unfold, to escape away and develop on spiritual lines to spiritual beauty and strength. And as our conception of spiritual being must be taken simply from natural being, our ideas of the lines along which the new religious nature is to run must be borrowed from the known lines of the old.

There is, for example, a Sense of Sight in the religious nature. Neglect this, leave it undeveloped and you never miss it. You simply see nothing. But develop it and you see God. And the line along which to develop it is known to us. Become pure in heart. The pure in heart shall see God. Here, then, is one opening for soul-culture—the avenue through purity of heart to the spiritual seeing of God.

Then there is a Sense of Sound. Neglect this, leave it undeveloped, and you never miss it. You simply hear nothing. Develop it, and you hear God. And the line along which to develop it is known to us. Obey Christ. Become one of Christ's flock. "The sheep hear His voice, and He calleth them by name."

Here, then, is another opportunity for the culture of the soul—a gateway through the Shepherd's fold to hear the Shepherd's voice.

And there is a Sense of Touch to be acquired—such a sense as the woman had who touched the hem of Christ's garment, that wonderful electric touch called faith, which moves the very heart of God.

And there is a Sense of Taste—a spiritual hunger after God; a something within which tastes and sees that He is good. And there is the Talent for Inspiration. Neglect that, and all the scenery of the spiritual world is flat and frozen. But cultivate it, and it penetrates the whole soul with sacred fire, and illuminates creation with God. And last of all there is the great capacity for Love, even for the love of God—the expanding capacity for feeling more and more its height and depth, its length and breadth. Till that is felt no man can really understand that word, "so great salvation," for what is its measure but that other "so" of Christ—God so loved the world that He gave His only begotten Son? Verily, how shall we escape if we neglect that?[52]

FOOTNOTES:

[52] For the scientific basis of this spiritual law the following works may be consulted:—

"The Origin of Species." By Charles Darwin, F.R.S. London: John Murray. 1872.

"Degeneration." By E. Ray Lankester, F.R.S. London: Macmillan. 1880.

"Der Ursprung der Wirbelthiere und das Princip des Functions Wechsels." Dr. A. Dorhn. Leipzig: 1875.

"Lessons from Nature." By St. George Mivart, F.R.S. London: John Murray. 1876.

"The Natural Conditions of Existence as they Affect Animal Life." Karl Semper. London: C. Kegan Paul & Co. 1881.

GROWTH.

"Is not the evidence of Ease on the very front of all the greatest works in existence? Do they not say plainly to us, not 'there has been a great *effort* here,' but 'there has been a great *power* here?' It is not the weariness of mortality but the strength of divinity, which we have to recognize in all mighty things; and that is just what we now never recognize, but think that we are to do great things by help of iron bars and perspiration; alas! we shall do nothing that way, but lose some pounds of our own weight."—*Ruskin.*

"Consider the lilies of the field how they grow."—*The Sermon on the Mount.*

"Nunquam aliud natura, aliud sapientia dicit."—*Juvenal.*

What gives the peculiar point to this object-lesson from the lips of Jesus is, that He not only made the illustration, but made the lilies. It is like an inventor describing his own machine. He made the lilies and He made me—both on the same broad principle. Both together, man and flower, He planted deep in the Providence of God; but as men are dull at studying themselves He points to this companion-phenomenon to teach us how to live a free and natural life, a life which God will unfold for us, without our anxiety, as He unfolds the flower. For Christ's words are not a general appeal to consider nature. Men are not to consider the lilies simply to admire their beauty, to dream over the delicate strength and grace of stem and leaf. The point they were to consider was *how they grew*—how without anxiety or care the flower woke into loveliness, how without weaving these leaves were woven, how without toiling these complex tissues spun themselves, and how without any effort or friction the whole slowly came ready-made from the loom of God in its more than Solomon-like glory. "So," He says, making the application beyond dispute, "you care-worn, anxious men must grow. You, too, need take no thought for your life, what ye shall eat or what ye shall drink or what ye shall put on. For if God so clothe the grass of the field, which to-day is, and to-morrow is cast into the oven, shall He not much more clothe you, O ye of little faith?"

This nature-lesson was a great novelty in its day; but all men now who have even a "little faith" have learned this Christian secret of a composed life. Apart even from the parable of the lily, the failures of the past have taught most of us the folly of disquieting ourselves in vain, and we have given up the idea that by taking thought we can add a cubit to our stature.

But no sooner has our life settled down to this calm trust in God than a new and graver anxiety begins. This time it is not for the body we are in travail, but for the soul. For the temporal life we have considered the lilies, but how is the spiritual life to grow. How are we to become better men? How are we to grow in grace? By what thought shall we add the cubits to the spiritual stature and reach the fullness of the Perfect Man? And because we know ill how to do this, the old anxiety comes back again and our inner life is once more an agony of conflict and remorse. After all, we have but transferred our anxious thoughts from the body to the soul. Our efforts after Christian growth seem only a succession of failures, and instead of rising into the beauty of holiness our life is a daily heartbreak and humiliation.

Now the reason of this is very plain. We have forgotten the parable of the lily. Violent efforts to grow are right in earnestness, but wholly wrong in principle. There is but one principle of growth both for the natural and spiritual, for animal and plant, for body and soul. For all growth is an organic thing. And the principle of growing in grace is once more this, "Consider the lilies *how they grow*."

In seeking to extend the analogy from the body to the soul there are two things about the lilies' growth, two characteristics of all growth, on which one must fix attention. These are—

First, Spontaneousness.

Second, Mysteriousness.

I. Spontaneousness. There are three lines along which one may seek for evidence of the spontaneousness of growth. The first is Science. And the argument here could not be summed up better than in the words of Jesus. The lilies grow, He says, of themselves; they toil not, neither do they spin. They grow, that is, automatically, spontaneously, without trying, without fretting, without thinking. Applied in any direction, to plant, to animal, to the body or to the soul this law holds. A boy grows, for example, without trying. One or two simple conditions are fulfilled, and the growth goes on. He thinks probably as little about the condition as about the result; he fulfills the conditions by habit, the result follows by nature. Both processes go steadily on from year to year apart from himself and all but in spite of himself. One would never think of *telling* a boy to grow. A doctor has no prescription for growth. He can tell me how growth may be stunted or impaired, but the process itself is recognized as beyond control—one of the few, and therefore very significant, things which Nature keeps in her own hands. No physician of souls, in like manner, has any prescription for spiritual growth. It is the question he is most often asked and most often answers wrongly. He may prescribe more earnestness, more prayer, more self-denial, or more Christian work. These are prescriptions for something, but not for growth. Not that they may not encourage growth; but the soul grows as the lily grows, without trying, without fretting, without ever thinking. Manuals of devotion, with complicated rules for getting on in the Christian life, would do well sometimes to return to the simplicity of nature; and earnest souls who are attempting sanctification by struggle instead of sanctification by faith might be spared much humiliation by learning the botany of the Sermon on the Mount. There *can* indeed be no other principle of growth than this. It is a vital act. And to try to *make* a thing grow is as absurd as to help the tide to come in or the sun rise.

Another argument for the spontaneousness of growth is universal experience. A boy not only grows without trying, but he cannot grow if he tries. No man by taking thought has ever added a cubit to his stature; nor has any man by mere working at his soul ever approached nearer to the stature of the Lord Jesus. The stature of the Lord Jesus was not itself reached by work, and he who thinks to approach its mystical height by anxious effort is really receding from it. Christ's life unfolded itself from a divine germ, planted centrally in His nature, which grew as naturally as a flower from a bud. This flower may be imitated; but one can always tell an artificial flower. The human form may be copied in wax, yet somehow one never fails to detect the difference. And this precisely is the difference between a native growth of Christian principle and the moral copy of it. The one is natural, the other mechanical. The one is a growth, the other an accretion. Now this, according to modern biology, is the fundamental distinction between the living and the not living, between an organism and a crystal. The living organism grows, the dead crystal increases. The first grows vitally from within, the last adds new particles from the outside. The whole difference between the Christian and the moralist lies here. The Christian works from the center, the moralist from the circumference. The one is an organism, in the center of which is planted by the living God a living germ. The other is a crystal, very beautiful it may be; but only a crystal—it wants the vital principle of growth.

And one sees here also, what is sometimes very difficult to see, why salvation in the first instance is never connected directly with morality. The reason is not that salvation does not demand morality, but that it demands so much of it that the moralist can never reach up to it. The end of Salvation is perfection, the Christ-like mind, character and life. Morality is on the way to this perfection; it may go a considerable distance toward it, but it can never reach it. Only Life can do that. It requires something with enormous power of movement, of growth, of overcoming obstacles, to attain the perfect. Therefore the man who has within himself this great formative agent, Life, is nearer the end than the man who has morality alone. The latter can never reach perfection; the former *must*. For the Life must develop out according to its type; and being a germ of the Christ-life, it must unfold into *a Christ*. Morality, at the utmost, only develops the character in one or two directions. It may perfect a single virtue here and there, but it cannot perfect all. And especially it fails always to give that rounded harmony of parts, that perfect tune to the whole orchestra, which is the marked characteristic of life. Perfect life is not merely the possessing of perfect functions, but of perfect functions perfectly adjusted to each other and all conspiring to a single result, the perfect working of the whole organism. It is not said that the character will develop in all its fullness in this life. That were a time too short for an Evolution so magnificent. In this world only the cornless ear is seen; sometimes only the small yet still prophetic blade. The sneer at the godly man for his imperfections is ill-judged. A blade is a small thing. At first it grows very near the earth. It is often soiled and crushed and downtrodden. But it is a living thing. That great dead stone beside it is more imposing; only it will never be anything else than a stone. But this small blade—*it doth not yet appear what it shall be.*

Seeing now that Growth can only be synonymous with a living automatic process, it is all but superfluous to seek a third line of argument from Scripture. Growth there is always described in the language of physiology.

The regenerate soul is a new creature. The Christian is a new man in Christ Jesus. He adds the cubits to his stature just as the old man does. He is rooted and built up in Christ; he abides in the vine, and so abiding, not toiling or spinning, brings forth fruit. The Christian in short, like the poet, is born not made; and the fruits of his character are not manufactured things but living things, things which have grown from the secret germ, the fruits of the living Spirit. They are not the produce of this climate, but exotics from a sunnier land.

II. But, secondly, besides this Spontaneousness there is this other great characteristic of Growth—Mysteriousness. Upon this quality depends the fact, probably, that so few men ever fathom its real character. We are most unspiritual always in dealing with the simplest spiritual things. A lily grows mysteriously, pushing up its solid weight of stem and leaf in the teeth of gravity. Shaped into beauty by secret and invisible fingers, the flower develops we know not how. But we do not wonder at it. Every day the thing is done; it is Nature, it is God. We are spiritual enough at least to understand that. But when the soul rises slowly above the world, pushing up its delicate virtues in the teeth of sin, shaping itself mysteriously into the image of Christ, we deny that the power is not of man. A strong will, we say, a high ideal, the reward of virtue, Christian influence—these will account for it. Spiritual character is merely the product of anxious work, self-command, and self-denial. We allow, that is to say, a miracle to the lily, but none to the man. The lily may grow; the man must fret and toil and spin.

Now grant for a moment that by hard work and self-restraint a man may attain to a very high character. It is not denied that this can be done. But what is denied is that this is growth, and that this process is Christianity. The fact that you can account for it proves that it is not growth. For growth is mysterious; the peculiarity of it is that you cannot account for it. Mysteriousness, as Mozley has well observed, is "the test of spiritual birth." And this was Christ's test. "The wind bloweth where it listeth. Thou hearest the sound thereof, but canst not tell whence it cometh or whither it goeth, *so is every one that is born of the Spirit.*" The test of spirituality is that you cannot tell whence it cometh or whither it goeth. If you can tell, if you can account for it on philosophical principles, on the doctrine of influence, on strength of will, on a favorable environment, it is not growth. It may be so far a success, it may be a perfectly honest, even remarkable, and praiseworthy imitation, but it is not the real thing. The fruits are wax, the flowers artificial—you can tell whence it cometh and whither it goeth.

The conclusion is, then, that the Christian is a unique phenomenon. You cannot account for him. And if you could he would not be a Christian. Mozley has drawn the two characters for us in graphic words: "Take an ordinary man of the world—what he thinks and what he does, his whole standard of duty is taken from the society in which he lives. It is a borrowed standard: he is as good as other people are; he does, in the way of duty, what is generally considered proper and becoming among those with whom his lot is thrown. He reflects established opinion on such points. He follows its lead. His aims and objects in life again are taken from the world around him, and from its dictation. What it considers honorable, worth having, advantageous and good, he thinks so too and pursues it. His motives all come from a visible quarter. It would be absurd to say that there is any mystery in such a character as this, because it is formed from a known external influence—the influence of social opinion and the voice of the world. 'Whence such a character cometh' we see; we venture to say that the source and origin of it is open and palpable, and we know it just as we know the physical causes of many common facts."

Then there is the other. "There is a certain character and disposition of mind of which it is true to say that 'thou canst not tell whence it cometh or whither it goeth.' ... There are those who stand out from among the crowd, which reflects merely the atmosphere of feeling and standard of society around it, with an impress upon them which bespeaks a heavenly birth.... Now, when we see one of those characters, it is a question which we ask ourselves. How has the person become possessed of it? Has he caught it from society around him? That cannot be, because it is wholly different from that of the world around him. Has he caught it from the inoculation of crowds and masses, as the mere religious zealot catches his character? That cannot be either, for the type is altogether different from that which masses of men, under enthusiastic impulses, exhibit. There is nothing gregarious in this character; it is the individual's own; it is not borrowed, it is not a reflection of any fashion or tone of the world outside; it rises up from some fount within, and it is a creation of which the text says, We know not whence it cometh."[53]

Now we have all met these two characters—the one eminently respectable, upright, virtuous, a trifle cold perhaps, and generally, when critically examined, revealing somehow the mark of the tool; the other with God's breath still upon it, an inspiration; not more virtuous, but differently virtuous; not more humble, but different, wearing the meek and quiet spirit artlessly as to the manner born. The other-worldliness of such a character is the thing that strikes you; you are not prepared for what it will do or say or become next, for it moves from a far-off center, and in spite of its transparency and sweetness that presence fills you always with awe. A man never feels the discord of his own life, never hears the jar of the machinery by which he tries to manufacture his own good points, till he has stood in the stillness of such a presence. Then he discerns the difference between growth and work. He has considered the lilies, how they grow.

We have now seen that spiritual growth is a process maintained and secured by a spontaneous and mysterious inward principle. It is a spontaneous principle even in its origin, for it bloweth where it listeth; mysterious in its operation, for we can never tell whence it cometh; obscure in its destination, for we cannot tell whence it goeth. The whole process therefore transcends us; we do not work, we are taken in hand—"it is God which worketh in us, both to will and to do of His good pleasure." We do not plan —we are "created in Christ Jesus unto good works, which God hath before ordained that we should walk in them."

There may be an obvious objection to all this. It takes away all conflict from the Christian life? It makes man, does it not, mere clay in the hands of the potter? It crushes the old character to make a new one, and destroys man's responsibility for his own soul?

Now we are not concerned here in once more striking the time-honored "balance between faith and works." We are considering how lilies grow, and in a specific connection, namely, to discover the attitude of mind which the Christian should preserve regarding his spiritual growth. That attitude, primarily, is to be free from care. We are not lodging a plea for inactivity of the spiritual energies, but for the tranquillity of the spiritual mind. Christ's protest is not against work, but against anxious thought; and rather, therefore, than complement the lesson by showing the other side, we take the risk of still further extending the plea in the original direction.

What is the relation, to recur again to analogy, between growth and work in a boy? Consciously, there is no relation at all. The boy never thinks of connecting his work with his growth. Work in fact is one thing and growth another, and it is so in the spiritual life. If it be asked therefore, Is the Christian wrong in these ceaseless and agonizing efforts after growth? the answer is, Yes, he is quite wrong, or at least, he is quite mistaken. When a boy takes a meal or denies himself indigestible things, he does not say, "All this will minister to my growth;" or when he runs a race he does not say, "This will help the next cubit of my stature." It may or it may not be true that these things will help his stature, but, if he thinks of this, his idea of growth is morbid. And this is the point we are dealing with. His anxiety here is altogether irrelevant and superfluous. Nature is far more bountiful than we think. When she gives us energy she asks none of it back to expend on our own growth. She will attend to that. "Give your work," she says, "and your anxiety to others; trust me to add the cubits to your stature." If God is adding to our spiritual stature, unfolding the new nature within us, it is a mistake to keep twitching at the petals with our coarse fingers. We must seek to let the Creative Hand alone. "It is God which giveth the increase." Yet we never know how little we have learned of the fundamental principle of Christianity till we discover how much we are all bent on supplementing God's free grace. If God is spending work upon a Christian, let him be still and know that it is God. And if he wants work, he will find it there—in the being still.

Not that there is no work for him who would grow, to do. There is work, and severe work—work so great that the worker deserves to have himself relieved of all that is superfluous during his task. If the amount of energy lost in trying to grow were spent in fulfilling rather the conditions of growth, we should have many more cubits to show for our stature. It is with these conditions that the personal work of the Christian is chiefly concerned. Observe for a moment what they are, and their exact relation. For its growth the plant needs heat, light, air, and moisture. A man, therefore, must go in search of these, or their spiritual equivalents, and this is his work? By no means. The Christian's work is not yet. Does the plant go in search of its conditions? Nay, the conditions come to the plant. It no more manufactures the heat, light, air, and moisture, than it manufactures its own stem. It finds them all around it in Nature. It simply stands still with its leaves spread out in unconscious prayer, and Nature lavishes upon it these and all other bounties, bathing it in sunshine, pouring the nourishing air over and over it, reviving it graciously with its nightly dew. Grace, too, is as free as the air. The Lord God is a Sun. He is as the Dew to Israel. A man has no more to manufacture these than he has to manufacture his own soul. He stands surrounded by them, bathed in them, beset behind and before by them. He lives and moves and has his being in them. How then shall he go in search of them? Do not they rather go in search of him? Does he not feel how they press themselves upon him? Does he not know how unweariedly they appeal to him? Has he not heard how they are sorrowful when he will not have them? His work, therefore, is not yet. The voice still says, "Be still."

The conditions of growth, then, and the inward principle of growth being both supplied by Nature, the thing man has to do, the little junction left for him to complete, is to apply the one to the other. He manufactures nothing; he earns nothing; he need be anxious for nothing; his one duty is *to be in* these conditions, to abide in them, to allow grace to play over him, to be still therein and know that this is God.

The conflict begins and prevails in all its life-long agony the moment a man forgets this. He struggles to grow himself instead of struggling to get back again into position. He makes the church into a workshop when God meant it to be a beautiful garden. And even in his closet, where only should reign silence—a silence as of the mountains whereon the lilies grow—is heard the roar and tumult of machinery. True, a man will often have to wrestle with his God—but not for growth. The Christian life is a composed life. The Gospel is Peace. Yet the most anxious people in the world are Christians—Christians who misunderstand the nature of growth. Life is a perpetual self-condemning because they are not growing. And the effect is not only the loss of tranquillity to the individual. The energies which are meant to be spent on the work of Christ are consumed in the soul's own fever. So long as the Church's activities are spent on growing there is nothing to spare for the world. A soldier's time is not spent in earning the money to buy his armor, in finding food and raiment, in seeking shelter. His king provides these things that he may be the more at liberty to fight his battles. So, for the soldier of the Cross all is provided. His Government has planned to leave him free for the Kingdom's work.

The problem of the Christian life finally is simplified to this—man has but to preserve the right attitude. To abide in Christ, to be in position, that is all. Much work is done on board a ship crossing the Atlantic. Yet none of it is spent on making the ship go. The sailor but harnesses his vessel to the wind. He puts his sail and rudder in position, and lo, the miracle is wrought. So everywhere God creates, man utilizes. All the work of the world is merely a taking advantage of energies already there.[54] God gives the wind, and the water, and the heat; man but puts himself in the way of the wind, fixes his water-wheel in the way of the river, puts his piston in the way of the steam; and so holding himself in position before God's Spirit, all the energies of Omnipotence course within his soul. He is like a tree planted by a river whose leaf is green and whose fruits fail not. Such is the deeper lesson to be learned from considering the lily. It is the voice of Nature echoing the whole evangel of Jesus, "Come unto Me, and I will give you rest."

DEATH.

> "What could be easier than to form a catena of the most philosophical defenders of Christianity, who have exhausted language in declaring the impotence of the unassisted intellect? Comte has not more explicitly enounced the incapacity of man to deal with the Absolute and the Infinite than the whole series of orthodox writers. Trust your reason, we have been told till we are tired of the phrase, and you will become Atheists or Agnostics. We take you at your word; we become Agnostics."—*Leslie Stephen.*
>
> "To be carnally minded is Death."—*Paul.*
>
> "I do not wonder at what men suffer, but I wonder often at what they lose."—*Ruskin.*

"Death," wrote Faber, "is an unsurveyed land, an unarranged Science." Poetry draws near Death only to hover over it for a moment and withdraw in terror. History knows it simply as a universal fact. Philosophy finds it among the mysteries of being, the one great mystery of being not. All contributions to this dead theme are marked by an essential vagueness, and every avenue of approach seems darkened by impenetrable shadow.

But modern Biology has found it part of its work to push its way into this silent land, and at last the world is confronted with a scientific treatment of Death. Not that much is added to the old conception, or much taken from it. What it is, this certain Death with its uncertain issues, we know as little as before. But we can define more clearly and attach a narrower meaning to the momentous symbol.

The interest of the investigation here lies in the fact that Death is one of the outstanding things in Nature which has an acknowledged spiritual equivalent. The prominence of the word in the vocabulary of Revelation cannot be exaggerated. Next to Life the most pregnant symbol in religion is its antithesis, Death. And from the time that "If thou eatest thereof thou shalt surely die" was heard in Paradise, this solemn word has been linked with human interests of eternal moment.

Notwithstanding the unparalleled emphasis upon this term in the Christian system, there is none more feebly expressive to the ordinary mind. That mystery which surrounds the word in the natural world shrouds only too completely its spiritual import. The reluctance which prevents men from investigating the secrets of the King of Terrors is for a certain length entitled to respect. But it has left theology with only the vaguest materials to construct a doctrine which, intelligently enforced, ought to appeal to all men with convincing power and lend the most effective argument to Christianity. Whatever may have been its influence in the past, its threat is gone for the modern world. The word has grown weak. Ignorance has robbed the Grave of all its terror, and platitude despoiled Death of its sting. Death itself is ethically dead. Which of us, for example, enters fully into the meaning of words like these: "She that liveth in pleasure is *dead* while she liveth?" Who allows adequate weight to the metaphor in the Pauline phrase, "To be carnally minded is *Death*;" or in this, "The wages of sin is *Death*?" Or what theology has translated into the language of human life the terrific practical import of "Dead in trespasses and sins?" To seek to make these phrases once more real and burning; to clothe time-worn formulæ with living truth; to put the deepest ethical meaning into the gravest symbol of Nature, and fill up with its full consequence the darkest threat of Revelation—these are the objects before us now.

What, then, is Death? Is it possible to define it and embody its essential meaning in an intelligible proposition?

The most recent and the most scientific attempt to investigate Death we owe to the biological studies of Mr. Herbert Spencer. In his search for the meaning of Life the word Death crosses his path, and he turns aside for a moment to define it. Of course what Death is depends upon what Life is. Mr. Herbert Spencer's definition of Life, it is well known, has been subjected to serious criticism. While it has shed much light on many of the phenomena of Life, it cannot be affirmed that it has taken its place in science as the final solution of the fundamental problem of biology. No definition of Life, indeed, that has yet appeared can be said to be even approximately correct. Its mysterious quality evades us; and we have to be content with outward characteristics and accompaniments, leaving the thing itself an unsolved riddle. At the same time Mr. Herbert Spencer's masterly elucidation of the chief phenomena of Life has placed philosophy and science under many obligations, and in the paragraphs which follow we shall have to incur a further debt on behalf of religion.

The meaning of Death depending, as has been said, on the meaning of Life, we must first set ourselves to grasp the leading characteristics which distinguish living things. To a physiologist the living organism is distinguished from the not-living by the performance of certain functions. These functions are four in number—Assimilation, Waste, Reproduction, and Growth. Nothing could be a more interesting task than to point out the co-relatives of these in the spiritual sphere, to show in what ways the discharge of these functions represent the true manifestations of spiritual life, and how the failure to perform them constitutes spiritual Death. But it will bring us more directly to the specific subject before us if we follow rather the newer biological lines of Mr. Herbert Spencer. According to his definition, Life is "The definite combination of heterogeneous changes, both simultaneous and successive, in correspondence with external co-existences and sequences,"[55] or more shortly "The continuous adjustment of internal relations to external relations."[56] An example or two will render these important statements at once intelligible.

The essential characteristic of a living organism, according to these definitions, is that it is in vital connection with its general surroundings. A human being, for instance, is in direct contact with the earth and air, with all surrounding things, with the warmth of the sun, with the music of birds, with the countless influences and activities of nature and of his fellow-men. In biological language he is said thus to be "in correspondence with his environment." He is, that is to say, in active and vital connection with them, influencing them possibly, but especially being influenced by them. Now it is in virtue of this correspondence that he is entitled to be called alive. So long as he is in correspondence with any given point of his environment, he lives. To keep up this correspondence is to keep up life. If his environment changes he must instantly adjust himself to the change. And he continues living only as long as he succeeds in adjusting himself to the "simultaneous and successive changes in his environment" as these occur. What is meant by a change in his environment may be understood from an example, which will at the same time define more clearly the intimacy of the relation between environment and organism. Let us take the case of a civil-servant whose environment is a district in India. It is a region subject to occasional and prolonged droughts resulting in periodical famines. When such a period of scarcity arises, he proceeds immediately to adjust himself to this external change. Having the power of locomotion, he may remove himself to a more fertile district, or, possessing the means of purchase, he may add to his old environment by importation the "external relations" necessary to continued life. But if from any cause he fails to adjust himself to the altered circumstances, his body is thrown out of correspondence with his environment, his "internal relations" are no longer adjusted to his "external relations," and his life must cease.

In ordinary circumstances, and in health, the human organism is in thorough correspondence with its surroundings; but when any part of the organism by disease or accident is thrown out of correspondence, it is in that relation dead.

This Death, this want of correspondence, may be either partial or complete. Part of the organism may be dead to a part of the environment, or the whole to the whole. Thus the victim of famine may have a certain number of his correspondences arrested by the change in his environment, but not all. Luxuries which he once enjoyed no longer enter the country, animals which once furnished his table are driven from it. These still exist, but they are beyond the limit of his correspondence. In relation to these things therefore he is dead. In one sense it might be said that it was the environment which played him false; in another, that it was his own organization—that he was unable to adjust himself, or did not. But, however caused, he pays the penalty with partial Death.

Suppose next the case of a man who is thrown out of correspondence with a part of his environment by some physical infirmity. Let it be that by disease or accident he has been deprived of the use of his ears. The deaf man, in virtue of this imperfection, is thrown out of *rapport* with a large and well-defined part of the environment, namely, its sounds. With regard to that "external relation," therefore, he is no longer living. Part of him may truly be held to be insensible or "Dead." A man who is also blind is thrown out of correspondence with another large part of his environment. The beauty of sea and sky, the forms of cloud and mountain, the features and gestures of friends, are to him as if they were not. They are there, solid and real, but not to him; he is still further "Dead." Next, let it be conceived, the subtle finger of cerebral disease lays hold of him. His whole brain is affected, and the sensory nerves, the medium of communication with the environment, cease altogether to acquaint him with what is doing in the outside world. The outside world is still there, but not to him; he is still further "Dead." And so the death of parts goes on. He becomes less and less alive. "Were the animal frame not the complicated machine we have seen it to be, death might come as a simple and gradual dissolution, the 'sans everything' being the last stage of the successive loss of fundamental powers."[57] But finally some important part of the mere animal framework that remains breaks down. The correlation with the other parts is very intimate, and the stoppage of correspondence with one means an interference with the work of the rest. Something central has snapped, and all are thrown out of work. The lungs refuse to correspond with the air, the heart with the blood. There is now no correspondence whatever with environment—the thing, for it is now a thing, is Dead.

This then is Death; "part of the framework breaks down," "something has snapped"—these phrases by which we describe the phases of death yield their full meaning. They are different ways of saying that "correspondence" has ceased. And the scientific meaning of Death now becomes clearly intelligible. Dying is that breakdown in an organism which throws it out of correspondence with some necessary part of the environment. Death is the result produced, the want of correspondence. We do not say that this is all that is involved. But this is the root idea of Death—Failure to adjust internal relations to external relations, failure to repair the broken inward connection sufficiently to enable it to correspond again with the old surroundings. These preliminary statements may be fitly closed with the words of Mr. Herbert Spencer: "Death by natural decay occurs because in old age the relations between assimilation, oxidation, and genesis of force going on in the organism gradually fall out of correspondence with the relations between oxygen and food and absorption of heat by the environment. Death from disease arises either when the organism is congenitally defective in its power to balance the ordinary external actions by the ordinary internal actions, or when there has taken place some unusual external action to which there was no answering internal action. Death by accident implies some neighboring mechanical changes of which the causes are either unnoticed from inattention, or are so intricate that their results cannot be foreseen, and consequently certain relations in the organism are not adjusted to the relations in the environment."[58]

With the help of these plain biological terms we may now proceed to examine the parallel phenomenon of Death in the spiritual world. The factors with which we have to deal are two in number as before—Organism and Environment. The relation between them may once more be denominated by "correspondence." And the truth to be emphasized resolves itself into this, that Spiritual Death is a want of correspondence between the organism and the spiritual environment.

What is the spiritual environment? This term obviously demands some further definition. For Death is a relative term. And before we can define Death in the spiritual world we must first apprehend the particular relation with reference to which the expression is to be employed. We shall best reach the nature of this relation by considering for a moment the subject of environment generally. By the natural environment we mean the entire surroundings of the natural man, the entire external world in which he lives and moves and has his being. It is not involved in the idea that either with all or part of the environment he is in immediate correspondence. Whether he correspond with it or not, it is there. There is in fact a conscious environment and an environment of which he is not conscious; and it must be borne in mind that the conscious environment is not all the environment that is. All that surrounds him, all that environs him, conscious or unconscious, is environment. The moon and stars are part of it, though in the daytime he may not see them. The polar regions are parts of it, though he is seldom aware of their influence. In its widest sense environment simply means all else that is.

Now it will next be manifest that different organisms correspond with this environment in varying degrees of completeness or incompleteness. At the bottom of the biological scale we find organisms which have only the most limited correspondence with their surroundings. A tree, for example, corresponds with the soil about its stem, with the sunlight, and with the air in contact with its leaves. But it is shut off by its comparatively low development from a whole world to which higher forms of life have additional access. The want of locomotion alone circumscribes most seriously its area of correspondence, so that to a large part of surrounding nature it may truly be said to be dead. So far as consciousness is concerned, we should be justified indeed in saying that it was not alive at all. The murmur of the stream which bathes its roots affects it not. The marvelous insect-life beneath its shadow excites in it no wonder. The tender maternity of the bird which has its nest among its leaves stirs no responsive sympathy. It cannot correspond with those things. To stream and insect and bird it is insensible, torpid, dead. For this is Death, this irresponsiveness.

The bird, again, which is higher in the scale of life, corresponds with a wider environment. The stream is real to it, and the insect. It knows what lies behind the hill; it listens to the love-song of its mate. And to much besides beyond the simple world of the tree this higher organism is alive. The bird we should say is more living than the tree; it has a correspondence with a larger area of environment. But this bird-life is not yet the highest life. Even within the immediate bird-environment there is much to which the bird must still be held to be dead. Introduce a higher organism, place man himself within this same environment, and see how much more living he is. A hundred things which the bird never saw in insect, stream, and tree appeal to him. Each single sense has something to correspond with. Each faculty finds an appropriate exercise. Man is a mass of correspondences, and because of these, because he is alive to countless objects and influences to which lower organisms are dead, he is the most living of all creatures.

The relativity of Death will now have become sufficiently obvious. Man being left out of account, all organisms are seen as it were to be partly living and partly dead. The tree, in correspondence with a narrow area of environment, is to that extent alive; to all beyond, to the all but infinite area beyond, it is dead. A still wider portion of this vast area is the possession of the insect and the bird. Their's also, nevertheless, is but a little world, and to an immense further area insect and bird are dead. All organisms likewise are living and dead—living to all within the circumference of their correspondences, dead to all beyond. As we rise in the scale of life, however, it will be observed that the sway of Death is gradually weakened. More and more of the environment becomes accessible as we ascend, and the domain of life in this way slowly extends in ever-widening circles. But until man appears there is no organism to correspond with the whole environment. Till then the outermost circles have no correspondents. To the inhabitants of the innermost spheres they are as if they were not.

Now follows a momentous question. Is man in correspondence with the whole environment? When we reach the highest living organism, is the final blow dealt to the kingdom of Death? Has the last acre of the infinite area been taken in by his finite faculties? Is his conscious environment the whole environment? Or is there, among these outermost circles, one which with his multitudinous correspondences he fails to reach? If so, this is Death. The question of Life or Death to him is the question of the amount of remaining environment he is able to compass. If there be one circle or one segment of a circle which he yet fails to reach, to correspond with, to know, to be influenced by, he is, with regard to that circle or segment, dead.

What then, practically, is the state of the case? Is man in correspondence with the whole environment or is he not? There is but one answer. He is not. Of men generally it cannot be said that they are in living contact with that part of the environment which is called the spiritual world. In introducing this new term spiritual world, observe, we are not interpolating a new factor. This is an essential part of the old idea. We have been following out an ever-widening environment from point to point, and now we reach the outermost zones. The spiritual world is simply the outermost segment, circle, or circles of the natural world. For purposes of convenience we separate the two just as we separate the animal world from the plant. But the animal world and the plant world are the same world. They are different parts of one environment. And the natural and spiritual are likewise one. The inner circles are called the natural, the outer the spiritual. And we call them spiritual simply because they are beyond us or beyond a part of us. What we have correspondence with, that we call natural; what we have little or no correspondence with, that we call spiritual. But when the appropriate corresponding organism appears, the organism, that is, which can freely communicate with these outer circles, the distinction necessarily disappears. The spiritual to it becomes the outer circle of the natural.

Now of the great mass of living organisms, of the great mass of men, is it not to be affirmed that they are out of correspondence with this outer circle? Suppose, to make the final issue more real, we give this outermost circle of environment a name. Suppose we call it God. Suppose also we substitute a word for "correspondence" to express more intimately the personal relation. Let us call it Communion. We can now determine accurately the spiritual relation of different sections of mankind. Those who are in communion with God live, those who are not are dead.

The extent or depth of this communion, the varying degrees of correspondence in different individuals, and the less or more abundant life which these result in, need not concern us for the present. The task we have set ourselves is to investigate the essential nature of Spiritual Death. And we have found it to consist in a want of communion with God. The unspiritual man is he who lives in the circumscribed environment of this present world. "She that liveth in pleasure is Dead while she liveth." "To be carnally minded is Death." To be carnally minded, translated into the language of science, is to be limited in one's correspondences to the environment of the natural man. It is no necessary part of the conception that the mind should be either purposely irreligious, or directly vicious. The mind of the flesh, φρόνημα τῆς σαρκὸς, by its very nature, limited capacity, and time-ward tendency, is θάνατος, Death. This earthly mind may be of noble caliber, enriched by culture, high toned, virtuous and pure. But if it know not God? What though its correspondences reach to the stars of heaven or grasp the magnitudes of Time and Space? The stars of heaven are not heaven. Space is not God. This mind certainly, has life, life up to its level. There is no trace of Death. Possibly, too, it carries its deprivation lightly, and, up to its level, lies content. We do not picture the possessor of this carnal mind as in any sense a monster. We have said he may be high-toned, virtuous, and pure. The plant is not a monster because it is dead to the voice of the bird; nor is he a monster who is dead to the voice of God. The contention at present simply is that he is *Dead*.

We do not need to go to Revelation for the proof of this. That has been rendered unnecessary by the testimony of the Dead themselves. Thousands have uttered themselves upon their relation to the Spiritual World, and from their own lips we have the proclamation of their Death. The language of theology in describing the state of the natural man is often regarded as severe. The Pauline anthropology has been challenged as an insult to human nature. Culture has opposed the doctrine that "The natural man receiveth not the things of the Spirit of God, for they are foolishness unto him: neither can he know them, because they are spiritually discerned." And even some modern theologies have refused to accept the most plain of the aphorisms of Jesus, that "Except a man be born again he cannot see the Kingdom of God." But this stern doctrine of the spiritual deadness of humanity is no mere dogma of a past theology. The history of thought during the present century proves that the world has come round spontaneously to the position of the first. One of the ablest philosophical schools of the day erects a whole antichristian system on this very doctrine. Seeking by means of it to sap the foundation of spiritual religion, it stands unconsciously as the most significant witness for its truth. What is the creed of the Agnostic, but the confession of the spiritual numbness of humanity? The negative doctrine which it reiterates with such sad persistency, what is it but the echo of the oldest of scientific and religious truths? And what are all these gloomy and rebellious infidelities, these touching, and too sincere confessions of universal nescience, but a protest against this ancient law of Death?

The Christian apologist never further misses the mark than when he refuses the testimony of the Agnostic to himself. When the Agnostic tells me he is blind and deaf, dumb, torpid and dead to the spiritual world, I must believe him. Jesus tells me that. Paul tells me that. Science tells me that. He knows nothing of this outermost circle; and we are compelled to trust his sincerity as readily when he deplores it as if, being a man without an ear, he professed to know nothing of a musical world, or being without taste, of a world of art. The nescience of the Agnostic philosophy is the proof from experience that to be carnally minded is Death. Let the theological value of the concession be duly recognized. It brings no solace to the unspiritual man to be told he is mistaken. To say he is self-deceived is neither to compliment him nor Christianity. He builds in all sincerity who raises his altar to the *Unknown* God. He does not know God. With all his marvelous and complex correspondences, he is still one correspondence short.

It is a point worthy of special note that the proclamation of this truth has always come from science rather than from religion. Its general acceptance by thinkers is based upon the universal failure of a universal experiment. The statement, therefore, that the natural man discerneth not the things of the spirit, is never to be charged against the intolerance of theology. There is no point at which theology has been more modest than here. It has left the preaching of a great fundamental truth almost entirely to philosophy and science. And so very moderate has been its tone, so slight has been the emphasis placed upon the paralysis of the natural with regard to the spiritual, that it may seem to some to have been intolerant. No harm certainly could come now, no offence could be given to science, if religion asserted more clearly its right to the spiritual world. Science has paved the way for the reception of one of the most revolutionary doctrines of Christianity; and if Christianity refuses to take advantage of the opening it will manifest a culpable want of confidence in itself. There never was a time when its fundamental doctrines could more boldly be proclaimed, or when they could better secure the respect and arrest the interest of Science.

To all this, and apparently with force, it may, however, be objected that to every man who truly studies Nature there is a God. Call Him by whatever name—a Creator, a Supreme Being, a Great First Cause, a Power that makes for Righteousness—Science has a God; and he who believes in this, in spite of all protest, possesses a theology. "If we will look at things, and not merely at words, we shall soon see that the scientific man has a theology and a God, a most impressive theology, a most awful and glorious God. I say that man believes in a God who feels himself in the presence of a Power which is not himself, and is immeasurably above himself, a Power in the contemplation of which he is absorbed, in the knowledge of which he finds safety and happiness. And such now is Nature to the scientific man." [59] Such now, we humbly submit, is Nature to the very few. Their own confession is against it. That they are "absorbed" in the contemplation we can well believe. That they might "find safety and happiness" in the knowledge of Him is also possible—if they had it. But this is just what they tell us they have not. What they deny is not a God. It is the correspondence. The very confession of the Unknowable is itself the dull recognition of an Environment beyond themselves, and for which they feel they lack the correspondence. It is this want that makes their God the Unknown God. And it is this that makes them *dead*.

We have not said, or implied, that there is not a God of Nature. We have not affirmed that there is no Natural Religion. We are assured there is. We are even assured that without a Religion of Nature Religion is only half complete; that without a God of Nature the God of Revelation is only half intelligible and only partially known. God is not confined to the outermost circle of environment, He lives and moves and has His being in the whole. Those who only seek Him in the further zone can only find a part. The Christian who knows not God in Nature, who does not, that is to say, correspond with the whole environment, most certainly is partially dead. The author of "Ecce Homo" may be partially right when he says: "I think a bystander would say that though Christianity had in it something far higher and deeper and more ennobling, yet the average scientific man worships just at present a more awful, and, as it were, a greater Deity than the average Christian. In so many Christians the idea of God has been degraded by childish and little-minded teaching; the Eternal and the Infinite and the All-embracing has been represented as the head of the clerical interest, as a sort of clergyman, as a sort of schoolmaster, as a sort of philanthropist. But the scientific man knows Him to be eternal; in astronomy, in geology, he becomes familiar with the countless millenniums of His lifetime. The scientific man strains his mind actually to realize God's infinity. As far off as the fixed stars he traces Him, 'distance inexpressible by numbers that have name.' Meanwhile, to the theologian, infinity and eternity are very much of empty words when applied to the object of his worship. He does not realize them in actual facts and definite computations."[60] Let us accept this rebuke. The principle that want of correspondence is Death applies all round. He who knows not God in Nature only partially lives. The converse of this, however, is not true; and that is the point we are insisting on. He who knows God only in Nature lives not. There is no "correspondence" with an Unknown God, no "continuous adjustment" to a fixed First Cause. There is no "assimilation" of Natural Law; no growth in the Image of "the All-embracing." To correspond with the God of Science assuredly is not to live. "This is Life Eternal, to know Thee, *the true God,* and *Jesus Christ* Whom Thou hast sent."

From the service we have tried to make natural science render to our religion, we might be expected possibly to take up the position that the absolute contribution of Science to Revelation was very great. On the contrary, it is very small. The *absolute* contribution, that is, is very small. The contribution on the whole is immense, vaster than we have yet any idea of. But without the aid of the higher Revelation this many-toned and far-reaching voice had been forever dumb. The light of Nature, say the most for it, is dim—how dim we ourselves, with the glare of other Light upon the modern world, can only realize when we seek among the pagan records of the past for the groupings after truth of those whose only light was this. Powerfully significant and touching as these efforts were in their success, they are far more significant and touching in their failure. For they did fail. It requires no philosophy now to speculate on the adequacy or inadequacy of the Religion of Nature. For us who could never weigh it rightly in the scales of Truth it has been tried in the balance of experience and found wanting. Theism is the easiest of all religions to get, but the most difficult to keep. Individuals have kept it, but nations never. Socrates and Aristotle, Cicero and Epictetus had a theistic religion; Greece and Rome had none. And even after getting what seems like a firm place in the minds of men, its unstable equilibrium sooner or later betrays itself. On the one hand theism has always fallen into the wildest polytheism, or on the other into the blankest atheism. "It is an indubitable historical fact that, outside of the sphere of special revelation, man has never obtained such a knowledge of God as a responsible and religious being plainly requires. The wisdom of the heathen world, at its very best, was utterly inadequate to the accomplishment of such a task as creating a due abhorrence of sin, controlling the passions, purifying the heart, and ennobling the conduct."[61]

What is the inference? That this poor rush-light by itself was never meant to lend the ray by which man should read the riddle of the universe. The mystery is too impenetrable and remote for its uncertain flicker to more than make the darkness deeper. What indeed if this were not a light at all, but only part of a light—the carbon point, the fragment of calcium, the reflector in the great Lantern which contains the Light of the World?

This is one inference. But the most important is that the absence of the true Light means moral Death. The darkness of the natural world to the intellect is not all. What history testifies to is, first the partial, and then the total eclipse of virtue that always follows the abandonment of belief in a personal God. It is not, as has been pointed out a hundred times, that morality in the abstract disappears, but the motive and sanction are gone. There is nothing to raise it from the dead. Man's attitude to it is left to himself. Grant that morals have their own base in human life; grant that Nature has a Religion whose creed is Science; there is yet nothing apart from God to save the world from moral Death. Morality has the power to dictate but none to move. Nature directs but cannot control. As was wisely expressed in one of many pregnant utterances during a recent *Symposium*, "Though the decay of religion may leave the institutes of morality intact, it drains off their inward power. The devout faith of men expresses and measures the intensity of their moral nature, and it cannot be lost without a remission of enthusiasm, and under this low pressure, the successful reëntrance of importunate desires and clamorous passions which had been driven back. To believe in an ever-living and perfect Mind, supreme over the universe, is to invest moral distinctions with immensity and eternity, and lift them from the provincial stage of human society to the imperishable theater of all being. When planted thus in the very substance of things, they justify and support the ideal estimates of the conscience; they deepen every guilty shame; they guarantee every righteous hope; and they help the will with a Divine casting-vote in every balance of temptation."[62] That morality has a basis in human society, that Nature has a Religion, surely makes the Death of the soul when left to itself all the more appalling. It means that, between them, Nature and morality provide all for virtue—except the Life to live it.

It is at this point accordingly that our subject comes into intimate contact with Religion. The proposition that "to be carnally minded is Death" even the moralist will assent to. But when it is further announced that "the carnal mind is *enmity against God*" we find ourselves in a different region. And when we find it also stated that "the wages of *sin* is Death," we are in the heart of the profoundest questions of theology. What before was merely "enmity against society" becomes "enmity against God;" and what was "vice" is "sin." The conception of a God gives an altogether new color to worldliness and vice. Worldliness it changes into heathenism, vice into blasphemy. The carnal mind, the mind which is turned away from God, which will not correspond with God—this is not moral only but spiritual Death. And Sin, that which separates from God, which disobeys God, which *can* not in that state correspond with God—this is hell.

To the estrangement of the soul from God the best of theology traces the ultimate cause of sin. Sin is simply apostasy from God, unbelief in God. "Sin is manifest in its true character when the demand of holiness in the conscience, presenting itself to the man as one of loving submission to God, is put from him with aversion. Here sin appears as it really is, a turning away from God; and while the man's guilt is enhanced, there ensues a benumbing of the heart resulting from the crushing of those higher impulses. This is what is meant by the reprobate state of those who reject Christ and will not believe the Gospel, so often spoken of in the New Testament; this unbelief is just the closing of the heart against the highest love."[63] The other view of sin, probably the more popular at present, that sin consists in selfishness, is merely this from another aspect. Obviously if the mind turns away from one part of the environment it will only do so under some temptation to correspond with another. This temptation, at bottom, can only come from one source—the love of self. The irreligious man's correspondences are concentrated upon himself. He worships himself. Self-gratification rather than self-denial; independence rather than submission—these are the rules of life. And this is at once the poorest and the commonest form of idolatry.

But whichever of these views of sin we emphasize, we find both equally connected with Death. If sin is estrangement from God, this very estrangement is Death. It is a want of correspondence. If sin is selfishness, it is conducted at the expense of life. Its wages are Death—"he that loveth his life," said Christ, "shall lose it."

Yet the paralysis of the moral nature apart from God does not only depend for its evidence upon theology or even upon history. From the analogies of Nature one would expect this result as a necessary consequence. The development of any organism in any direction is dependent on its environment. A living cell cut off from air will die. A seed-germ apart from moisture and an appropriate temperature will make the ground its grave for centuries. Human nature, likewise, is subject to similar conditions. It can only develop in presence of its environment. No matter what its possibilities may be, no matter what seeds of thought or virtue, what germs of genius or of art, lie latent in its breast, until the appropriate environment present itself the correspondence is denied, the development discouraged, the most splendid possibilities of life remain unrealized, and thought and virtue, genius and art, are dead. The true environment of the moral life is God. Here conscience wakes. Here kindles love. Duty here becomes heroic; and that righteousness begins to live which alone is to live forever. But if this Atmosphere is not, the dwarfed soul must perish for mere want of its native air. And its Death is a strictly natural Death. It is not an exceptional judgment upon Atheism. In the same circumstances, in the same averted relation to their environment, the poet, the musician, the artist, would alike perish to poetry, to music, and to art. Every environment is a cause. Its effect upon me is exactly proportionate to my correspondence with it. If I correspond with part of it, part of myself is influenced. If I correspond with more, more of myself is influenced; if with all, all is influenced. If I correspond with the world, I become worldly; if with God, I become

Divine. As without correspondence of the scientific man with the natural environment there could be no Science and no action founded on the knowledge of Nature, so without communion with the spiritual Environment there can be no Religion. To refuse to cultivate the religious relation is to deny to the soul its highest right—the right to a further evolution.[64] We have already admitted that he who knows not God may not be a monster; we cannot say he will not be a dwarf. This precisely, and on perfectly natural principles, is what he must be. You can dwarf a soul just as you can dwarf a plant, by depriving it of a full environment. Such a soul for a time may have "a name to live." Its character may betray no sign of atrophy. But its very virtue somehow has the pallor of a flower that is grown in darkness, or as the herb which has never seen the sun, no fragrance breathes from its spirit. To morality, possibly, this organism offers the example of an irreproachable life; but to science it is an instance of arrested development; and to religion it presents the spectacle of a corpse—a living Death. With Ruskin, "I do not wonder at what men suffer, but I wonder often at what they lose."

FOOTNOTES:

[55] "Principles of Biology," vol. i, p. 74.

[56] *Ibid.*

[57] Foster's "Physiology," p. 642.

[58] Op. cit., pp. 88, 89.

[59] "Natural Religion," p. 19.

[60] "Natural Religion," p. 20.

[61] Prof. Flint, "Theism," p. 805.

[62] Martineau. *Vide* the whole Symposium on "The Influences upon Morality of a Decline in Religious Belief."—*Nineteenth Century*, vol. i. pp. 331, 531.

[63] Müller: "Christian Doctrine of Sin." 2d Ed., vol i. p 131.

[64] It would not be difficult to show, were this the immediate subject, that it is not only a right but a duty to exercise the spiritual faculties, a duty demanded not by religion merely, but by science. Upon biological principles man owes his full development to himself, to nature, and to his fellow-men. Thus Mr. Herbert Spencer affirms, "The performance of every function is, in a sense, a moral

obligation. It is usually thought that morality requires us only to restrain such vital activities as, in our present state, are often pushed to excess, or such as conflict with average welfare, special or general: but it also requires us to carry on these vital activities up to their normal limits. All the animal functions, in common with all the higher functions, have, as thus understood, their imperativeness."—"The Data of Ethics," 2d Ed., p. 76.

MORTIFICATION.

"If, by tying its main artery, we stop most of the blood going to a limb, then, for as long as the limb performs its functions, those parts which are called into play must be wasted faster than they are repaired: whence eventual disablement. The relation between due receipt of nutritive matters through its arteries, and due discharge of its duties by the limb, is a part of the physical order. If instead of cutting off the supply to a particular limb, we bleed the patient largely, so drafting away the materials needed for repairing not one limb but all limbs, and not limbs only but viscera, there results both a muscular debility and an enfeeblement of the vital functions. Here, again, cause and effect are necessarily related.... Pass now to those actions more commonly thought of as the occasions for rules of conduct."—*Herbert Spencer.*

"Mortify therefore your members which are upon earth."—*Paul.*

"O Star-eyed Science! hast thou wandered there
To waft us home the message of despair?"—*Campbell.*

The definition of Death which science has given us is this: *A falling out of correspondence with environment.* When, for example, a man loses the sight of his eyes, his correspondence with the environing world is curtailed. His life is limited in an important direction; he is less living than he was before. If, in addition, he loses the senses of touch and hearing, his correspondences are still further limited; he is therefore still further dead. And when all possible correspondences have ceased, when the nerves decline to respond to any stimulus, when the lungs close their gates against the air, when the heart refuses to correspond with the blood by so much as another beat, the insensate corpse is wholly and forever dead. The soul, in like manner, which has no correspondence with the spiritual environment is spiritually dead. It may be that it never possessed the spiritual eye or the spiritual ear, or a heart which throbbed in response to the love of God. If so, having never lived, it cannot be said to have died. But not to have these correspondences is to be in the state of Death. To the spiritual world, to the Divine Environment, it is dead—as a stone which has never lived is dead to the environment of the organic world.

Having already abundantly illustrated this use of the symbol Death, we may proceed to deal with another class of expressions where the same term is employed in an exactly opposite connection. It is a proof of the radical nature of religion that a word so extreme should have to be used again and again in Christian teaching, to define in different directions the true spiritual relations of mankind. Hitherto we have concerned ourselves with the condition of the natural man with regard to the spiritual world. We have now to speak of the relations of the spiritual man with regard to the natural world. Carrying with us the same essential principle—want of correspondence—underlying the meaning of Death, we shall find that the relation of the spiritual man to the natural world, or at least to part of it, is to be that of Death.

When the natural man becomes the spiritual man, the great change is described by Christ as a passing from Death unto Life. Before the transition occurred, the practical difficulty was this, how to get into correspondence with the new Environment? But no sooner is this correspondence established than the problem is reversed. The question now is, how to get out of correspondence with the old environment? The moment the new life is begun there comes a genuine anxiety to break with the old. For the former environment has now become embarrassing. It refuses its dismissal from consciousness. It competes doggedly with the new Environment for a share of the correspondences. And in a hundred ways the former traditions, the memories and passions of the past, the fixed associations and habits of the earlier life, now complicate the new relation. The complex and bewildered soul, in fact, finds itself in correspondence with two environments, each with urgent but yet incompatible claims. It is a dual soul living in a double world, a world whose inhabitants are deadly enemies, and engaged in perpetual civil-war.

The position of things is perplexing. It is clear that no man can attempt to live both lives. To walk both in the flesh and in the spirit is morally impossible. "No man," as Christ so often emphasized, "can serve two masters." And yet, as matter of fact, here is the new-born being in communication with both environments? With sin and purity, light and darkness, time and Eternity, God and Devil, the confused and undecided soul is now in correspondence. What is to be done in such an emergency? How can the New Life deliver itself from the still-persistent past?

A ready solution of the difficulty would be *to die*. Were one to die organically, to die and "go to heaven," all correspondence with the lower environment would be arrested at a stroke. For Physical Death of course simply means the final stoppage of all natural correspondences with this sinful world.

But this alternative, fortunately or unfortunately, is not open. The detention here of body and spirit for a given period is determined for us, and we are morally bound to accept the situation. We must look then for a further alternative.

Actual Death being denied us, we must ask ourselves if there is nothing else resembling it—no artificial relation, no imitation or semblance of Death which would serve our purpose. If we cannot yet die absolutely, surely the next best thing will be to find a temporary substitute. If we cannot die altogether, in short, the most we can do is to die as much as we can. And we now know this is open to us, and how. To die to any environment is to withdraw correspondence with it, to cut ourselves off, so far as possible, from all communication with it. So that the solution of the problem will simply be this, for the spiritual life to reverse continuously the processes of the natural life. The spiritual man having passed from Death unto Life, the natural man must next proceed to pass from Life unto Death. Having opened the new set of correspondences, he must deliberately close up the old. Regeneration in short must be accompanied by Degeneration.

Now it is no surprise to find that this is the process everywhere described and recommended by the founders of the Christian system. Their proposal to the natural man, or rather to the natural part of the spiritual man, with regard to a whole series of inimical relations, is precisely this. If he cannot really die, he must make an adequate approach to it by "reckoning himself dead." Seeing that, until the cycle of his organic life is complete he cannot die physically, he must meantime die morally, reckoning himself morally dead to that environment which, by competing for his correspondences, has now become an obstacle to his spiritual life.

The variety of ways in which the New Testament writers insist upon this somewhat extraordinary method is sufficiently remarkable. And although the idea involved is essentially the same throughout, it will clearly illustrate the nature of the act if we examine separately three different modes of expression employed in the later Scriptures in this connection. The methods by which the spiritual man is to withdraw himself from the old environment—or from that part of it which will directly hinder the spiritual life—are three in number:—

First, Suicide.
Second, Mortification.
Third, Limitation.

It will be found in practice that these different methods are adapted, respectively, to meet three different forms of temptation; so that we possess a sufficient warrant for giving a brief separate treatment to each.

First, Suicide. Stated in undisguised phraseology, the advice of Paul to the Christian, with regard to a part of his nature, is to commit suicide. If the Christian is to "live unto God," he must "die unto sin." If he does not kill sin, sin will inevitably kill him. Recognizing this, he must set himself to reduce the number of his correspondences—retaining and developing those which lead to a fuller life, unconditionally withdrawing those which in any way tend in an opposite direction. This stoppage of correspondences is a voluntary act, a crucifixion of the flesh, a suicide.

Now the least experience of life will make it evident that a large class of sins can only be met, as it were, by Suicide. The peculiar feature of Death by Suicide is that it is not only self-inflicted but sudden. And there are many sins which must either be dealt with suddenly or not at all. Under this category, for instance, are to be included generally all sins of the appetites and passions. Other sins, from their peculiar nature, can only be treated by methods less abrupt, but the sudden operation of the knife is the only successful means of dealing with fleshly sins. For example, the correspondence of the drunkard with his wine is a thing which can be broken off by degrees only in the rarest cases. To attempt it gradually may in an isolated case succeed, but even then the slightly prolonged gratification is no compensation for the slow torture of a gradually diminishing indulgence. "If thine appetite offend thee cut it off," may seem at first but a harsh remedy; but when we contemplate on the one hand the lingering pain of the gradual process, on the other its constant peril, we are compelled to admit that the principle is as kind as it is wise. The expression "total abstinence" in such a case is a strictly biological formula. It implies the sudden destruction of a definite portion of environment by the total withdrawal of all the connecting links. Obviously of course total abstinence ought thus to be allowed a much wider application than to cases of "intemperance." It's the only decisive method of dealing with any sin of the flesh; The very nature of the relations makes it absolutely imperative that every victim of unlawful appetite, in whatever direction, shall totally abstain. Hence Christ's apparently extreme and peremptory language defines the only possible, as well as the only charitable, expedient: "If thy right eye offend thee, pluck it out, and cast it from thee. And if thy right hand offend thee, cut it off, and cast it from thee."

The humanity of what is called "sudden conversion" has never been insisted on as it deserves. In discussing "Biogenesis"[65] it has been already pointed out that while growth is a slow and gradual process, the change from Death to Life alike in the natural and spiritual spheres is the work of a moment. Whatever the conscious hour of the second birth may be—in the case of an adult it is probably defined by the first real victory over sin—it is certain that on biological principles the real turning-point is literally a moment. But on moral and humane grounds this misunderstood, perverted, and therefore despised doctrine is equally capable of defence. Were any reformer, with an adequate knowledge of human life, to sit down and plan a scheme for the salvation of sinful men, he would probably come to the conclusion that the best way after all, perhaps indeed the only way, to turn a sinner from the error of his ways would be to do it suddenly.

Suppose a drunkard were advised to take off one portion from his usual allowance the first week, another the second, and so on! Or suppose at first, he only allowed himself to become intoxicated in the evenings, then every second evening, then only on Saturday nights, and finally only every Christmas? How would a thief be reformed if he slowly reduced the number of his burglaries, or a wife-beater by gradually diminishing the number of his blows? The argument ends with an *ad absurdum*. "Let him that stole *steal no more*," is the only feasible, the only moral, and the only humane way. This may not apply to every case, but when any part of man's sinful life can be dealt with by immediate Suicide, to make him reach the end, even were it possible, by a lingering death, would be a monstrous cruelty. And yet it is this very thing in "sudden conversion," that men object to—the sudden change, the decisive stand, the uncompromising rupture with the past, the precipitate flight from sin as of one escaping for his life. Men surely forget that this is an escaping for one's life. Let the poor prisoner run

—madly and blindly if he like, for the terror of Death is upon him. God knows, when the pause comes, how the chains will gall him still.

It is a peculiarity of the sinful state, that as a general rule men are linked to evil mainly by a single correspondence. Few men break the whole law. Our natures, fortunately, are not large enough to make us guilty of all, and the restraints of circumstances are usually such as to leave a loophole in the life of each individual for only a single habitual sin. But it is very easy to see how this reduction of our intercourse with evil to a single correspondence blinds us to our true position. Our correspondences, as a whole, are not with evil, and in our calculations as to our spiritual condition we emphasize the many negatives rather than the single positive. One little weakness, we are apt to fancy, all men must be allowed, and we even claim a certain indulgence for that apparent necessity of nature which we call our besetting sin. Yet to break with the lower environment at all, to many, is to break at this single point. It is the only important point at which they touch it, circumstances or natural disposition making habitual contact at other places impossible. The sinful environment, in short, to them means a small but well-defined area. Now if contact at this point be not broken off, they are virtually in contact still with the whole environment. There may be only one avenue between the new life and the old, it may be but a small and *subterranean passage,* but this is sufficient to keep the old life in. So long as that remains the victim is not "dead unto sin," and therefore he cannot "live unto God." Hence the reasonableness of the words, "Whatsoever shall keep the whole law, and yet offend at one point, he is guilty of all." In the natural world it only requires a single vital correspondence of the body to be out of order to insure Death. It is not necessary to have consumption, diabetes, and an aneurism to bring the body to the grave if it have heart-disease. He who is fatally diseased in one organ necessarily pays the penalty with his life, though all the others be in perfect health. And such, likewise, are the mysterious unity and correlation of functions in the spiritual organism that the disease of one member may involve the ruin of the whole. The reason, therefore, with which Christ follows up the announcement of His Doctrine of Mutilation, or local Suicide, finds here at once its justification and interpretation: "If thy right eye offend thee, pluck it out, and cast it from thee: *for* it is profitable for thee that *one* of thy members should perish, and not that thy *whole body* should be cast into hell. And if thy right hand offend thee, cut it off, and cast it from thee: *for* it is profitable for thee that *one* of thy members should perish, and not that thy *whole body* should be cast into hell."

Secondly, Mortification. The warrant for the use of this expression is found in the well-known phrases of Paul, "If ye through the Spirit do mortify the deeds of the body ye shall live," and "Mortify therefore your members which are upon earth." The word mortify here is, literally, to make to die. It is used, of course, in no specially technical sense; and to attempt to draw a detailed moral from the pathology of mortification would be equally fantastic and irrelevant. But without in any way straining the meaning it is obvious that we have here a slight addition to our conception of dying to sin. In contrast with Suicide, Mortification implies a gradual rather than a sudden process. The contexts in which the passages occur will make this meaning so clear, and are otherwise so instructive in the general connection, that we may quote them, from the New Version, at length: "They that are after the flesh do mind the things of the flesh; but they that are after the Spirit the things of the Spirit. For the mind of the flesh is death; but the mind of the Spirit is life and peace: because the mind of the flesh is enmity against God; for it is not subject to the law of God, neither indeed can it be: and they that are in the flesh cannot please God. But ye are not in the flesh, but in the Spirit, if so be that the Spirit of God dwell in you. But if any man hath not the Spirit of Christ, he is none of His. And if Christ is in you, the body is dead because of sin; but the Spirit is life because of righteousness. But if the Spirit of Him that raised up Jesus from the dead dwelleth in you, He that raised up Christ Jesus from the dead shall quicken also your mortal bodies through His Spirit that dwelleth in you. So then, brethren, we are debtors not to the flesh, to live after the flesh: for if ye live after the flesh ye must die; but if by the Spirit ye mortify the doings (marg.) of the body, ye shall live."[66]

And again, "If then ye were raised together with Christ, seek the things that are above, where Christ is seated on the right hand of God. Set your mind on the things that are above, not on the things that are upon the earth. For ye died, and your life is hid with Christ in God. When Christ, who is our life, shall be manifested, then shall ye also with Him be manifested in glory. Mortify therefore your members which are upon the earth; fornication, uncleanness, passion, evil desire, and covetousness, the which is idolatry;

for which things' sake cometh the wrath of God upon the sons of disobedience; in the which ye also walked aforetime, when ye lived in these things. But now put ye also away all these; anger, wrath, malice, railing, shameful speaking out of your mouth: lie not one to another; seeing that ye have put off the old man with his doings, and have put on the new man, which is being renewed unto knowledge after the image of Him that created him."[67]

From the nature of the case as here stated it is evident that no sudden process could entirely transfer a man from the old into the new relation. To break altogether, and at every point, with the old environment, is a simple impossibility. So long as the regenerate man is kept in this world, he must find the old environment at many points a severe temptation. Power over very many of the commonest temptations is only to be won by degrees, and however anxious one might be to apply the summary method to every case, he soon finds it impossible in practice. The difficulty in these cases arises from a peculiar feature of the temptation. The difference between a sin of drunkenness, and, let us say, a sin of temper, is that in the former case the victim who would reform has mainly to deal with the environment, but in the latter with the correspondence. The drunkard's temptation is a known and definite quantity. His safety lies in avoiding some external and material substance. Of course, at bottom, he is really dealing with the correspondence every time he resists; he is distinctly controlling appetite. Nevertheless it is less the appetite that absorbs his mind than the environment. And so long as he can keep himself clear of the "external relation," to use Mr. Herbert Spencer's phraseology, he has much less difficulty with the "internal relation." The ill-tempered person, on the other hand, can make very little of his environment. However he may attempt to circumscribe it in certain directions, there will always remain a wide and ever-changing area to stimulate his irascibility. His environment, in short, is an inconstant quantity, and his most elaborate calculations and precautions must often and suddenly fail him.

What he has to deal with, then, mainly is the correspondence, the temper itself. And that, he well knows, involves a long and humiliating discipline. The case now is not at all a surgical but a medical one, and the knife is here of no more use than in a fever. A specific irritant has poisoned his veins. And the acrid humors that are breaking out all over the surface of his life are only to be subdued by a gradual sweetening of the inward spirit. It is now known that the human body acts toward certain fever-germs as a sort of soil. The man whose blood is pure has nothing to fear. So he whose spirit is purified and sweetened becomes proof against these germs of sin. "Anger, wrath, malice and railing" in such a soil can find no root.

The difference between this and the former method of dealing with sin may be illustrated by another analogy. The two processes depend upon two different natural principles. The Mutilation of a member, for instance, finds its analogue in the horticultural operation of *pruning,* where the object is to divert life from a useless into a useful channel. A part of a plant which previously monopolized a large share of the vigor of the total organism, but without yielding any adequate return, is suddenly cut off, so that the vital processes may proceed more actively in some fruitful parts. Christ's use of this figure is well-known: "Every branch in Me that beareth not fruit He purgeth it that it may bring forth more fruit." The strength of the plant, that is, being given to the formation of mere wood, a number of useless correspondences have to be abruptly closed while the useful connections are allowed to remain. The Mortification of a member, again, is based on the Law of Degeneration. The useless member here is not cut off, but simply relieved as much as possible of all exercise. This encourages the gradual decay of the parts, and as it is more and more neglected it ceases to be a channel for life at all. So an organism "mortifies" its members.

Thirdly, Limitation. While a large number of correspondences between man and his environment can be stopped in these ways, there are many more which neither can be reduced by a gradual Mortification nor cut short by sudden Death. One reason for this is that to tamper with these correspondences might involve injury to closely related vital parts. Or, again, there are organs which are really essential to the normal life of the organism, and which therefore the organism cannot afford to lose even though at times they act prejudicially. Not a few correspondences, for instance, are not wrong in themselves but only in their extremes. Up to a certain point they are lawful and necessary; beyond that point they may become not only unnecessary but sinful. The appropriate treatment in these and similar cases consists in a process of Limitation. The performance of this operation, it must be confessed, requires a most delicate hand. It is an art, moreover, which no one can teach another. And yet, if it is not learned by all who are trying to lead the Christian life, it cannot be for want of practice. For, as we shall see, the Christian is called upon to exercise few things more frequently.

An easy illustration of a correspondence which is only wrong when carried to an extreme, is the love of money. The love of money up to a certain point is a necessity; beyond that it may become one of the worst of sins. Christ said: "Ye cannot serve God and Mammon." The two services, at a definite point, become incompatible, and hence correspondence with one must cease. At what point, however, it must cease each man has to determine for himself. And in this consists at once the difficulty and the dignity of Limitation.

There is another class of cases where the adjustments are still more difficult to determine. Innumerable points exist in our surroundings with which it is perfectly legitimate to enjoy, and even to cultivate, correspondence, but which privilege, at the same time, it were better on the whole that we did not use. Circumstances are occasionally such—the demands of others upon us, for example, may be so clamant—that we have voluntarily to reduce the area of legitimate pleasure. Or, instead of it coming from others, the claim may come from a still higher direction. Man's spiritual life consists in the number and fullness of his correspondences with God. In order to develop these he may be constrained to insulate them, to inclose them from the other correspondences, to shut himself in with them. In many ways the limitation of the natural life is the necessary condition of the full enjoyment of the spiritual life.

In this principle lies the true philosophy of self-denial. No man is called to a life of self-denial for its own sake. It is in order to a compensation which, though sometimes difficult to see, is always real and always proportionate. No truth, perhaps, in practical religion is more lost sight of. We cherish somehow a lingering rebellion against the doctrine of self-denial—as if our nature, or our circumstances, or our conscience, dealt with us severely in loading us with the daily cross. But is it not plain after all that the life of self-denial is the more abundant life—more abundant just in proportion to the ampler crucifixion of the narrower life? Is it not a clear case of exchange—an exchange however where the advantage is entirely on our side? We give up a correspondence in which there is a little life to enjoy a correspondence in which there is an abundant life. What though we sacrifice a hundred such correspondences? We make but the more room for the great one that is left. The lesson of self-denial, that is to say of Limitation, is *concentration*. Do not spoil your life, it says, at the outset with unworthy and impoverishing correspondences; and if it is growing truly rich and abundant, be very jealous of ever diluting its high eternal quality with anything of earth. To concentrate upon a few great correspondences, to oppose to the death the perpetual petty larceny of our life by trifles—these are the conditions for the highest and happiest life. It is only Limitation which can secure the Illimitable.

The penalty of evading self-denial also is just that we get the lesser instead of the larger good. The punishment of sin is inseparably bound up with itself. To refuse to deny one's self is just to be left with the self undenied. When the balance of life is struck, the self will be found still there. The discipline of life was meant to destroy this self, but that discipline having been evaded—and we all to some extent have opportunities, and too often exercise them, of taking the narrow path by the shortest cuts—its purpose is balked. But the soul is the loser. In seeking to gain its life it has really lost it. This is what Christ meant when He said: "He that loveth his life shall lose it, and he that hateth his life in this world shall keep it unto life eternal."

Why does Christ say: "Hate Life?" Does He mean that life is a sin? No. Life is not a sin. Still, He says we must hate it. But we must live. Why should we hate what we must do? For this reason: Life is not a sin, but the love of life may be a sin. And the best way not to love life is to hate it. Is it a sin then to love life? Not a sin exactly, but a mistake. It is a sin to love some life, a mistake to love the rest. Because that love is lost. All that is lavished on it is lost. Christ does not say it is wrong to love life. He simply says it is *loss*. Each man has only a certain amount of life, of time, of attention—a definite measurable quantity. If he gives any of it to this life solely it is wasted. Therefore Christ says, Hate life, limit life, lest you steal your love for it from something that deserves it more.

Now this does not apply to all life. It is "life in this world" that is to be hated. For life in this world implies conformity to this world. It may not mean pursuing worldly pleasures, or mixing with worldly sets; but a subtler thing than that—a silent deference to worldly opinion; an almost unconscious lowering of religious tone to the level of the worldly-religious world around; a subdued resistance to the soul's delicate promptings to greater consecration, out of deference to "breadth" or fear of ridicule. These, and such things, are what Christ tells us we must hate. For these things are of the very essence of worldliness. "If any man love the world," even in this sense, "the love of the Father is not in him."

There are two ways of hating life, a true and a false. Some men hate life because it hates them. They have seen through it, and it has turned round upon them. They have drunk it, and come to the dregs; therefore they hate it. This is one of the ways in which the man who loves his life literally loses it. He loves it till he loses it, then he hates it because it has fooled him. The other way is the religious. For religious reasons a man deliberately braces himself to the systematic hating of his life. "No man can serve two masters, for either he must hate the one and love the other, or else he must hold to the one and despise the other." Despising the other—this is hating life, limiting life. It is not misanthropy, but Christianity.

This principle, as has been said, contains the true philosophy of self-denial. It also holds the secret by which self-denial may be most easily borne. A common conception of self-denial is that there are a multitude of things about life which are to be put down with a high hand the moment they make their appearance. They are temptations which are not to be tolerated, but must be instantly crushed out of being with pang and effort.

So life comes to be a constant and sore cutting off of things which we love as our right hand. But now suppose one tried boldly to hate these things? Suppose we deliberately made up our minds as to what things we were henceforth to allow to become our life? Suppose we selected a given area of our environment and determined once for all that our correspondences should go to that alone, fencing in this area all round with a morally impassable wall? True, to others, we should seem to live a poorer life; they would see that our environment was circumscribed, and call us narrow because it was narrow. But, well-chosen, this limited life would be really the fullest life; it would be rich in the highest and worthiest, and poor in the smallest and basest correspondences. The well-defined spiritual life is not only the highest life, but it is also the most easily lived. The whole cross is more easily carried than the half. It is the man who tries to make the best of both worlds who makes nothing of either. And he who seeks to serve two masters misses the benediction of both. But he who has taken his stand, who has drawn a boundary line, sharp and deep about his religious life, who has marked off all beyond as forever forbidden ground to him, finds the yoke easy and the burden light. For this forbidden environment comes to be as if it were not. His faculties falling out of correspondence, slowly lose their sensibilities. And the balm of Death numbing his lower nature releases him for the scarce disturbed communion of a higher life. So even here to die is gain.

FOOTNOTES:

[65] Page 80.

[66] Rom. viii. 5-13.

[67] Col. iii. 1-10.

ETERNAL LIFE.

"Supposing that man, in some form, is permitted to remain on the earth for a long series of years, we merely lengthen out the period, but we cannot escape the final catastrophe. The earth will gradually lose its energy of relation, as well as that of revolution round the sun. The sun himself will wax dim and become useless as a source of energy, until at last the favorable conditions of the present solar system will have quite disappeared.

"But what happens to our system will happen likewise to the whole visible universe, which will, if finite, become a lifeless mass, if indeed it be not doomed to utter dissolution. In fine, it will become old and effete, no less truly than the individual. It is a glorious garment, this visible universe, but not an immortal one. We must look elsewhere if we are to be clothed with immortality as with a garment."—*The Unseen Universe.*

"This is Life Eternal—that they might know Thee, the True God, and Jesus Christ whom Thou hast sent."—*Jesus Christ.*

"Perfect correspondence would be perfect life. Were there no changes in the environment but such as the organism had adapted changes to meet, and were it never to fail in the efficiency with which it met them, there would be eternal existence and eternal knowledge."—*Herbert Spencer.*

One of the most startling achievements of recent science is a definition of Eternal Life. To the religious mind this is a contribution of immense moment. For eighteen hundred years only one definition of Life Eternal was before the world. Now there are two.

Through all these centuries revealed religion had this doctrine to itself. Ethics had a voice, as well as Christianity, on the question of the *summum bonum*; Philosophy ventured to speculate on the Being of a God. But no source outside Christianity contributed anything to the doctrine of Eternal Life. Apart from Revelation, this great truth was unguaranteed. It was the one thing in the Christian system that most needed verification from without, yet none was forthcoming. And never has any further light been thrown upon the question why in its very nature the Christian Life should be Eternal. Christianity itself even upon this point has been obscure. Its decision upon the bare fact is authoritative and specific. But as to what there is in the Spiritual Life necessarily endowing it with the element of Eternity, the maturest theology is all but silent.

It has been reserved for modern biology at once to defend and illuminate this central truth of the Christian faith. And hence in the interests of religion, practical and evidential, this second and scientific definition of Eternal Life is to be hailed as an announcement of commanding interest. Why it should not yet have received the recognition of religious thinkers—for already it has lain some years unnoticed—is not difficult to understand. The belief in Science as an aid to faith is not yet ripe enough to warrant men in searching there for witnesses to the highest Christian truths. The inspiration of Nature, it is thought, extends to the humbler doctrines alone. And yet the reverent inquirer who guides his steps in the right direction may find even now in the still dim twilight of the scientific world much that will illuminate and intensify his sublimest faith. Here, at least, comes, and comes unbidden, the opportunity of testing the most vital point of the Christian system. Hitherto the Christian philosopher has remained content with the scientific evidence against Annihilation. Or, with Butler, he has reasoned from the Metamorphoses of Insects to a future life. Or again, with the authors of "The Unseen Universe," the apologist has constructed elaborate, and certainly impressive, arguments upon the Law of Continuity. But now we may draw nearer. For the first time Science touches Christianity *positively* on the doctrine of Immortality. It confronts us with an actual definition of an Eternal Life, based on a full and rigidly accurate examination of the necessary conditions. Science does not pretend that it can fulfill these conditions. Its votaries make no claim to possess the Eternal Life. It simply postulates the requisite conditions without concerning itself whether any organism should ever appear, or does now exist, which might fulfill them. The claim of religion, on the other hand, is that there are organisms which possess Eternal Life. And the problem for us to solve is this: Do those who profess to possess Eternal Life fulfill the conditions required by Science, or are they different conditions? In a word, Is the Christian conception of Eternal Life scientific?

It may be unnecessary to notice at the outset that the definition of Eternal Life drawn up by Science was framed without reference to religion. It must indeed have been the last thought with the thinker to whom we chiefly owe it, that in unfolding the conception of a Life in its very nature necessarily eternal, he was contributing to Theology.

Mr. Herbert Spencer—for it is to him we owe it—would be the first to admit the impartiality of his definition; and from the connection in which it occurs in his writings, it is obvious that religion was not even present to his mind. He is analyzing with minute care the relations between Environment and Life. He unfolds the principle according to which Life is high or low, long or short. He shows why organisms live and why they die. And finally he defines a condition of things in which an organism would never die—in which it would enjoy a perpetual and perfect Life. This to him is, of course, but a speculation. Life Eternal is a biological conceit. The conditions necessary to an Eternal Life do not exist in the natural world. So that the definition is altogether impartial and independent. A Perfect Life, to Science, is simply a thing which is theoretically possible—like a Perfect Vacuum.

Before giving, in so many words, the definition of Mr. Herbert Spencer, it will render it fully intelligible if we gradually lead up to it by a brief rehearsal of the few and simple biological facts on which it is based. In considering the subject of Death, we have formerly seen that there are degrees of Life. By this is meant that some lives have more and fuller correspondence with Environment than others. The amount of correspondence, again, is determined by the greater or less complexity of the organism. Thus a simple organism like the Amoeba is possessed of very few correspondences. It is a mere sac of transparent structureless jelly for which organization has done almost nothing, and hence it can only communicate with the smallest possible area of Environment. An insect, in virtue of its more complex structure, corresponds with a wider area. Nature has endowed it with special faculties for reaching out to the Environment on many sides; it has more life than the Amoeba. In other words, it is a higher animal. Man again, whose body is still further differentiated, or broken up into different correspondences, finds himself *en rapport* with his surroundings to a further extent. And therefore he is higher still, more living still. And this law, that the degree of Life varies with the degree of correspondence, holds to the minutest detail throughout the entire range of living things. Life becomes fuller and fuller, richer and richer, more and more sensitive and responsive to an ever-widening Environment as we arise in the chain of being.

Now it will speedily appear that a distinct relation exists, and must exist, between complexity and longevity. Death being brought about by the failure of an organism to adjust itself to some change in the Environment, it follows that those organisms which are able to adjust themselves most readily and successfully will live the longest. They will continue time after time to effect the appropriate adjustment, and their power of doing so will be exactly proportionate to their complexity—that is, to the amount of Environment they can control with their correspondences. There are, for example, in the Environment of every animal certain things which are directly or indirectly dangerous to Life. If its equipment of correspondences is not complete enough to enable it to avoid these dangers in all possible circumstances, it must sooner or later succumb. The organism then with the most perfect set of correspondences, that is, the highest and most complex organism, has an obvious advantage over less complex forms. It can adjust itself more perfectly and frequently. But this is just the biological way of saying that it can live the longest. And hence the relation between complexity and longevity may be expressed thus—the most complex organisms are the longest lived.

To state and illustrate the proposition conversely may the point still further clear. The less highly organized an animal is, the less will be its chance of remaining in lengthened correspondence with its Environment. At some time or other in its career circumstances are sure to occur to which the comparatively immobile organism finds itself structurally unable to respond. Thus a *Medusa* tossed ashore by a wave, finds itself so out of correspondence with its new surroundings that its life must pay the forfeit. Had it been able by internal change to adapt itself to external change—to correspond sufficiently with the new environment, as for example to crawl, as an eel would have done, back into that environment with which it had completer correspondence—its life might have been spared. But had this happened it would continue to live henceforth only so long as it could continue in correspondence with all the circumstances in which it might find itself. Even if, however, it became complex enough to resist the ordinary and direct dangers of its environment, it might still be out of correspondence with others. A naturalist for instance, might take advantage of its want of correspondence with particular sights and sounds to capture it for his cabinet, or the sudden dropping of a yacht's anchor or the turn of a screw might cause its untimely death.

Again, in the case of a bird, in virtue of its more complex organization, there is command over a much larger area of environment. It can take precautions such as the *Medusa* could not; it has increased facilities for securing food; its adjustments all round are more complex; and therefore it ought to be able to maintain its Life for a longer period. There is still a large area, however, over which it has no control. Its power of internal change is not complete enough to afford it perfect correspondence with all external changes, and its tenure of Life is to that extent insecure. Its correspondence, moreover, is limited even with regard to those external conditions with which it has been partially established. Thus a bird in ordinary circumstances has no difficulty in adapting itself to changes of temperature, but if these are varied beyond the point at which its capacity of adjustment begins to fail—for example, during an extreme winter—the organism being unable to meet the condition must perish. The human organism, on the other hand, can respond to this external condition, as well as to countless other vicissitudes under which lower forms would inevitably succumb. Man's adjustments are to the largest known area of Environment, and hence he ought to be able furthest to prolong his Life.

It becomes evident, then, that as we ascend in the scale of Life we rise also in the scale of longevity. The lowest organisms are, as a rule, short-lived, and the rate of mortality diminishes more or less regularly as we ascend in the animal scale. So extraordinary indeed is the mortality among lowly-organized forms that in most cases a compensation is actually provided, nature endowing them with a marvelously increased fertility in order to guard against absolute extinction. Almost all lower forms are furnished not only with great reproductive powers, but with different methods of propagation, by which, in various circumstances, and in an incredibly short time, the species can be indefinitely multiplied. Ehrenberg found that by the repeated subdivisions of a single *Paramecium*, no fewer than 268,000,000 similar organisms might be produced in one month. This power steadily decreases as we rise higher in the scale, until forms are reached in which one, two, or at most three, come into being at a birth. It decreases, however, because it is no longer needed. These forms have a much longer lease of

Life. And it may be taken as a rule, although it has exceptions, that complexity in animal organisms is always associated with longevity.

It may be objected that these illustrations are taken merely from morbid conditions. But whether the Life be cut short by accident or by disease the principle is the same. All dissolution is brought about practically in the same way. A certain condition in the Environment fails to be met by a corresponding condition in the organism, and this is death. And conversely the more an organism in virtue of its complexity can adapt itself to all the parts of its Environment, the longer it will live. "It is manifest *a priori*," says Mr. Herbert Spencer, "that since changes in the physical state of the environment, as also those mechanical actions and those variations of available food which occur in it, are liable to stop the processes going on in the organism; and since the adaptive changes in the organism have the effects of directly or indirectly counterbalancing these changes in the environment, it follows that the life of the organism will be short or long, low or high, according to the extent to which changes in the environment are met by corresponding changes in the organism. Allowing a margin for perturbations, the life will continue only while the correspondence continues; the completeness of the life will be proportionate to the completeness of the correspondence; and the life will be perfect only when the correspondence is perfect."[68]

We are now all but in sight of our scientific definitions of Eternal Life. The desideratum is an organism with a correspondence of a very exceptional kind. It must lie beyond the reach of those "mechanical actions" and those "variations of available food," which are "liable to stop the processes going on in the organism." Before we reach an Eternal Life we must pass beyond that point at which all ordinary correspondences inevitably cease. We must find an organism so high and complex, that at some point in its development it shall have added a correspondence which organic death is powerless to arrest. We must in short pass beyond that definite region where the correspondences depend on evanescent and material media, and enter a further region where the Environment corresponded with is itself Eternal. Such an Environment exists. The Environment of the Spiritual world is outside the influence of these "mechanical actions," which sooner or later interrupt the processes going on in all finite organisms. If then we can find an organism which has established a correspondence with the spiritual world, that correspondence will possess the elements of eternity—provided only one other condition be fulfilled.

That condition is that the Environment be perfect. If it is not perfect, if it is not the highest, if it is endowed with the finite quality of change, there can be no guarantee that the Life of its correspondents will be eternal. Some change might occur in it which the correspondents had no adaptive changes to meet, and Life would cease. But grant a spiritual organism in perfect correspondence with a perfect spiritual Environment, and the conditions necessary to Eternal Life are satisfied.

The exact terms of Mr. Herbert Spencer's definition of Eternal Life may now be given. And it will be seen that they include essentially the conditions here laid down. "Perfect correspondence would be perfect life. Were there no changes in the environment but such as the organism had adapted changes to meet, and were it never to fail in the efficiency with which it met them, there would be eternal existence and eternal knowledge."[69] Reserving the question as to the possible fulfillment of these conditions, let us turn for a moment to the definition of Eternal Life laid down by Christ. Let us place it alongside the definition of Science, and mark the points of contact. Uninterrupted correspondence with a perfect Environment is Eternal Life according to Science. "This is Life Eternal," said Christ, "that they may know Thee, the only true God, and Jesus Christ whom Thou hast sent."[70] Life Eternal is to know God. To know God is to "correspond" with God. To correspond with God is to correspond with a Perfect Environment. And the organism which attains to this, in the nature of things must live forever. Here is "eternal existence and eternal knowledge."

The main point of agreement between the scientific and the religious definition is that Life consists in a peculiar and personal relation defined as a "correspondence." This conception, that Life consists in correspondences, has been so abundantly illustrated already that it is now unnecessary to discuss it further. All Life indeed consists essentially in correspondences with various Environments. The artist's life is a correspondence with art; the musician's with music. To cut them off from these Environments is in that relation to cut off their Life. To be cut off from all Environment is death. To find a new Environment again and cultivate relation with it is to find a new

Life. To live is to correspond, and to correspond is to live. So much is true in Science. But it is also true in Religion. And it is of great importance to observe that to Religion also the conception of Life is a correspondence. No truth of Christianity has been more ignorantly or willfully travestied than the doctrine of Immortality. The popular idea, in spite of a hundred protests, is that Eternal Life is to live forever. A single glance at the *locus classicus* might have made this error impossible. There we are told that Life Eternal is not to live. This is Life Eternal—*to know*. And yet—and it is a notorious instance of the fact that men who are opposed to Religion will take their conceptions of its profoundest truths from mere vulgar perversions—this view still represents to many cultivated men the Scriptural doctrine of Eternal Life. From time to time the taunt is thrown at Religion, not unseldom from lips which Science ought to have taught more caution, that the Future Life of Christianity is simply a prolonged existence, an eternal monotony, a blind and indefinite continuance of being. The Bible never could commit itself to any such empty platitudes; nor could Christianity ever offer to the world a hope so colorless. Not that Eternal Life has nothing to do with everlastingness. That is part of the conception. And it is this aspect of the question that first arrests us in the field of Science. But even Science has more in its definition than longevity. It has a correspondence and an Environment; and although it cannot fill up these terms for Religion, it can indicate at least the nature of the relation, the kind of thing that is meant by Life. Science speaks to us indeed of much more than numbers of years. It defines degrees of Life. It explains a widening Environment. It unfolds the relation between a widening Environment and increasing complexity in organisms. And if it has no absolute contribution to the content of Religion, its analogies are not limited to a point. It yields to Immortality, and this is the most that Science can do in any case, the board framework for a doctrine.

The further definition, moreover, of this correspondence as *knowing* is in the highest degree significant. Is not this the precise quality in an Eternal correspondence which the analogies of Science would prepare us to look for? Longevity is associated with complexity. And complexity in organisms is manifested by the successive addition of correspondences, each richer and larger than those which have gone before. The differentiation, therefore, of the spiritual organism ought to be signalized by the addition of the highest possible correspondence. It is not essential to the idea that the correspondence should be altogether novel; it is necessary rather that it should not. An altogether new correspondence appearing suddenly without shadow or prophecy would be a violation of continuity. What we should expect would be something new, and yet something that we were already prepared for. We should look for a further development in harmony with current developments; the extension of the last and highest correspondence in a new and higher direction. And this is exactly what we have. In the world with which biology deals, Evolution culminates in Knowledge.

At whatever point in the zoological scale this correspondence, or set of correspondences, begins, it is certain there is nothing higher. In its stunted infancy merely, when we meet with its rudest beginnings in animal intelligence, it is a thing so wonderful, as to strike every thoughtful and reverent observer with awe. Even among the invertebrates so marvelously are these or kindred powers displayed, that naturalists do not hesitate now, on the ground of intelligence at least, to classify some of the humblest creatures next to man himself.[71] Nothing in nature, indeed, is so unlike the rest of nature, so prophetic of what is beyond it, so supernatural. And as manifested in Man who crowns creation with his all-embracing consciousness, there is but one word to describe his knowledge: it is Divine. If then from this point there is to be any further Evolution, this surely must be the correspondence in which it shall take place? This correspondence is great enough to demand development; and yet it is little enough to need it. The magnificence of what it has achieved relatively, is the pledge of the possibility of more; the insignificance of its conquest absolutely involves the probability of still richer triumphs. If anything, in short, in humanity is to go on it must be this. Other correspondences may continue likewise; others, again, we can well afford to leave behind. But this cannot cease. This correspondence—or this set of correspondences, for it is very complex—is it not that to which men with one consent would attach Eternal Life? Is there anything else to which they would attach it? Is anything better conceivable, anything worthier, fuller, nobler, anything which would represent a higher form of Evolution or offer a more perfect ideal for an Eternal Life?

But these are questions of quality; and the moment we pass from quantity to quality we leave Science behind. In the vocabulary of Science, Eternity is only the fraction of a word. It means mere everlastingness. To Religion, on the other hand, Eternity has little to do with time. To correspond with the God of Science, the Eternal Unknowable, would be everlasting existence; to correspond with "the true God and Jesus Christ," is Eternal Life. The quality of the Eternal Life alone makes the heaven; mere everlastingness might be no boon. Even the brief span of the temporal life is too long for those who spend its years in sorrow. Time itself, let alone Eternity, is all but excruciating to Doubt. And many besides Schopenhauer have secretly regarded consciousness as the hideous mistake and malady of Nature. Therefore we must not only have quantity of years, to speak in the language of the present, but quality of correspondence. When we leave Science behind, this correspondence also receives a higher name. It becomes communion. Other names there are for it, religious and theological. It may be included in a general expression, Faith; or we may call it by a personal and specific term, Love. For the knowing of a Whole so great involves the co-operation of many parts.

Communion with God—can it be demonstrated in terms of Science that this is a correspondence which will never break? We do not appeal to Science for such a testimony. We have asked for its conception of an Eternal Life; and we have received for answer that Eternal Life would consist in a correspondence which should never cease, with an Environment which should never pass away. And yet what would Science demand of a perfect correspondence that is not met by this, *the knowing of God*? There is no other correspondence which could satisfy one at least of the conditions. Not one could be named which would not bear on the face of it the mark and pledge of its mortality. But this, to know God, stands alone. To know God, to be linked with God, to be linked with Eternity—if this is not the "eternal existence" of biology, what can more nearly approach it? And yet we are still a great way off—to establish a communication with the Eternal is not to secure Eternal Life. It must be assumed that the communication could be sustained. And to assume this would be to beg the question. So that we have still to prove Eternal Life. But let it be again repeated, we are not here seeking proofs. We are seeking light. We are merely reconnoitring from the furthest promontory of Science if so be that through the haze we may discern the outline of a distant coast and come to some conclusion as to the possibility of landing.

But, it may be replied, it is not open to any one handling the question of Immortality from the side of Science to remain neutral as to the question of fact. It is not enough to announce that he has no addition to make to the positive argument. This may be permitted with reference to other points of contact between Science and Religion, but not with this. We are told this question is settled—that there is no positive side. Science meets the entire conception of Immortality with a direct negative. In the face of a powerful consensus against even the possibility of a Future Life, to content one's self with saying that Science pretended to no argument in favor of it would be at once impertinent and dishonest. We must therefore devote ourselves for a moment to the question of possibility.

The problem is, with a material body and a mental organization inseparably connected with it, to bridge the grave. Emotion, volition, thought itself, are functions of the brain. When the brain is impaired, they are impaired. When the brain is not, they are not. Everything ceases with the dissolution of the material fabric; muscular activity and mental activity perish alike. With the pronounced positive statements on this point from many departments of modern Science we are all familiar. The fatal verdict is recorded by a hundred hands and with scarcely a shadow of qualification. "Unprejudiced philosophy is compelled to reject the idea of an individual immortality and of a personal continuance after death. With the decay and dissolution of its material substratum, through which alone it has acquired a conscious existence and become a person, and upon which it was dependent, the spirit must cease to exist."[72] To the same effect Vogt: "Physiology decides definitely and categorically against individual immortality, as against any special existence of the soul. The soul does not enter the fœtus like the evil spirit into persons possessed, but is a product of the development of the brain, just as muscular activity is a product of muscular development, and secretion a product of glandular development." After a careful review of the position of recent Science with regard to the whole doctrine, Mr. Graham sums up thus: "Such is the argument of Science, seemingly decisive against a future life. As we listen to her array of syllogisms, our hearts die within us. The hopes of men, placed in one scale to be weighed, seem to fly up against the massive weight of her evidence, placed in the other. It seems as if all our arguments were vain and unsubstantial, as if our future expectations were the foolish dreams of children, as if there could not be any other possible verdict arrived at upon the evidence brought forward."[73]

Can we go on in the teeth of so real an obstruction? Has not our own weapon turned against us, Science abolishing with authoritative hand the very truth we are asking it to define?

What the philosopher has to throw into the other scale can be easily indicated. Generally speaking, he demurs to the dogmatism of the conclusion. That mind and brain react, that the mental and the physiological processes are related, and very intimately related, is beyond controversy. But how they are related, he submits, is still altogether unknown. The correlation of mind and brain do not involve their identity. And not a few authorities accordingly have consistently hesitated to draw any conclusion at all. Even Büchner's statement turns out, on close examination, to be tentative in the extreme. In prefacing his chapter on Personal Continuance, after a single sentence on the dependence of the soul and its manifestations upon a material substratum, he remarks, "Though we are unable to form a definite idea as to the *how* of this connection, we are still by these facts justified in asserting, that the mode of this connection renders it *apparently* impossible that they should continue to exist separately."[74] There is, therefore, a flaw at this point in the argument for materialism. It may not help the spiritualist in the least degree positively. He may be as far as ever from a theory of how consciousness could continue without the material tissue. But his contention secures for him the right of speculation. The path beyond may lie in hopeless gloom; but it is not barred. He may bring forward his theory if he will. And this is something. For a permission to go on is often the most that Science can grant to Religion.

Men have taken advantage of this loophole in various ways. And though it cannot be said that these speculations offer us more than a probability, this is still enough to combine with the deep-seated expectation in the bosom of mankind and give fresh luster to the hope of a future life. Whether we find relief in the theory of a simple dualism; whether with Ulrici we further define the soul as an invisible enswathement of the body, material yet non-atomic; whether, with the "Unseen Universe," we are helped by the spectacle of known forms of matter shading off into an ever-growing subtilty, mobility, and immateriality; or whether, with Wundt, we regard the soul as "the ordered unity of many elements," it is certain that shapes can be given to the conception of a correspondence which shall bridge the grave such as to satisfy minds too much accustomed to weigh evidence to put themselves off with fancies.

But whether the possibilities of physiology or the theories of philosophy do or do not substantially assist us in realizing Immortality, is to Religion, to Religion at least regarded from the present point of view, of inferior moment. The fact of Immortality rests for us on a different basis. Probably, indeed, after all the Christian philosopher never engaged himself in a more superfluous task than in seeking along physiological lines to find room for a soul. The theory of Christianity has only to be fairly stated to make manifest its thorough independence of all the usual speculations on Immortality. The theory is not that thought, volition, or emotion, as such are to survive the grave. The difficulty of holding a doctrine in this form, in spite of what has been advanced to the contrary, in spite of the hopes and wishes of mankind, in spite of all the scientific and philosophical attempts to make it tenable, is still profound. No secular theory of personal continuance, as even Butler acknowledged, does not equally demand the eternity of the brute. No secular theory defines the point in the chain of Evolution at which organisms became endowed with Immortality. No secular theory explains the condition of the endowment, nor indicates its goal. And if we have nothing more to fan hope than the unexplored mystery of the whole region, or the unknown remainders among the potencies of Life, then, as those who have "hope only in this world," we are "of all men the most miserable."

When we turn, on the other hand, to the doctrine as it came from the lips of Christ, we find ourselves in an entirely different region. He makes no attempt to project the material into the immaterial. The old elements, however refined and subtle as to their matter, are not in themselves to inherit the Kingdom of God. That which is flesh is flesh. Instead of attaching Immortality to the natural organism, He introduces a new and original factor which none of the secular, and few even of the theological theories, seem to take sufficiently into account. To Christianity, "he that hath the Son of God hath Life, and he that hath not the Son hath not Life." This, as we take it, defines the correspondence which is to bridge the grave.

This is the clue to the nature of the Life that lies at the back of the spiritual organism. And this is the true solution of the mystery of Eternal Life.

There lies a something at the back of the correspondences of the spiritual organism—just as there lies a something at the back of the natural correspondences. To say that Life is a correspondence is only to express the partial truth. There is something behind. Life manifests itself in correspondences. But what determines them? The organism exhibits a variety of correspondences. What organizes them? As in the natural, so in the spiritual, there is a Principle of Life. We cannot get rid of that term. However clumsy, however provisional, however much a mere cloak for ignorance, Science as yet is unable to dispense with the idea of a Principle of Life. We must work with the word till we get a better. Now that which determines the correspondence of the spiritual organism is a Principle of Spiritual Life. It is a new and Divine Possession. He that hath the Son hath Life; conversely, he that hath Life hath the Son. And this indicates at once the quality and the quantity of the correspondence which is to bridge the grave. He that hath Life hath *the Son*. He possesses the Spirit of a Son. That spirit is, so to speak, organized within him by the Son. It is the manifestation of the new nature—of which more anon. The fact to note at present is that this is not an organic correspondence, but a spiritual correspondence. It comes not from generation, but from regeneration. The relation between the spiritual man and his Environment is, in theological language, a filial relation. With the new Spirit, the filial correspondence, he knows the Father—and this is Life Eternal. This is not only the real relation, but the only possible relation: "Neither knoweth any man the Father save the Son, and he to whomsoever the Son will reveal Him." And this on purely natural grounds. It takes the Divine to know the Divine—but in no more mysterious sense than it takes the human to understand the human. The analogy, indeed, for the whole field here has been finely expressed already by Paul: "What man," he asks, "knoweth the things of a man, save the spirit of man which is in him? even so the things of God knoweth no man, but the Spirit of God. Now we have received, not the spirit of the world, but the Spirit which is of God; that we might know the things that are freely given to us of God."[75]

It were idle, such being the quality of the new relation, to add that this also contains the guarantee of its eternity. Here at last is a correspondence which will never cease. Its powers in bridging the grave have been tried. The correspondence of the spiritual man possesses the supernatural virtues of the Resurrection and the Life. It is known by former experiment to have survived the "changes in the physical state of the environment," and those "mechanical actions" and "variations of available food," which Mr. Herbert Spencer tells us are "liable to stop the processes going on in the organism." In short, this is a correspondence which at once satisfies the demands of Science and Religion. In mere quantity it is different from every other correspondence known. Setting aside everything else in Religion, everything adventitious, local, and provisional; dissecting in to the bone and marrow we find this—a correspondence which can never break with an Environment which can never change. Here is a relation established with Eternity. The passing years lay no limiting hand on it. Corruption injures it not. It survives Death. It, and it only, will stretch beyond the grave and be found inviolate—

> "When the moon is old,
> And the stars are cold,
> And the books of the Judgment-day unfold."

The misgiving which will creep sometimes over the brightest faith has already received its expression and its rebuke: "Who shall separate us from the love of Christ? Shall tribulation, or distress, or persecution, or famine, or nakedness, or peril, or sword?" Shall these "changes in the physical state of the environment" which threaten death to the natural man destroy the spiritual? Shall death, or life, or angels, or principalities, or powers, arrest or tamper with his eternal correspondences? "Nay, in all these things we are more than conquerors through Him that loved us. For I am persuaded that neither death, nor life, nor angels, nor principalities, nor powers, nor things present, nor things to come, nor height, nor depth, nor any other creature, shall be able to separate us from the love of God, which is in Christ Jesus our Lord."[76]

It may seem an objection to some that the "perfect correspondence" should come to man in so extraordinary a way. The earlier stages in the doctrine are promising enough; they are entirely in line with Nature. And if Nature had also furnished the "perfect correspondence" demanded for an Eternal Life the position might be unassailable. But this sudden reference to a something outside the natural Environment destroys the continuity, and discovers a permanent weakness in the whole theory?

To which there is a twofold reply. In the first place, to go outside what we call Nature is not to go outside Environment. Nature, the natural Environment, is only a part of Environment. There is another large part which, though some profess to have no correspondence with it, is not on that account unreal, or even unnatural. The mental and moral world is unknown to the plant. But it is real. It cannot be affirmed either that it is unnatural to the plant; although it might be said that from the point of view of the Vegetable Kingdom it was *supernatural*. Things are natural or supernatural simply according to where one stands. Man is supernatural to the mineral; God is supernatural to the man. When a mineral is seized upon by the living plant and elevated to the organic kingdom, no trespass against Nature is committed. It merely enters a larger Environment, which before was supernatural to it, but which now is entirely natural. When the heart of a man, again, is seized upon by the quickening Spirit of God, no further violence is done to natural law. It is another case of the inorganic, so to speak, passing into the organic.

But in the second place, it is complained as if it were an enormity in itself that the spiritual correspondence should be furnished from the spiritual world. And to this the answer lies in the same direction. Correspondence in any case is the gift of Environment. The natural Environment gives men their natural faculties; the spiritual affords them their spiritual faculties. It is natural for the spiritual Environment to supply the spiritual faculties; it would be quite unnatural for the natural Environment to do it. The natural law of Biogenesis forbids it; the moral fact that the finite cannot comprehend the Infinite is against it; the spiritual principle that flesh and blood cannot inherit the kingdom of God renders it absurd. Not, however, that the spiritual faculties are, as it were, manufactured in the spiritual world and supplied ready-made to the spiritual organism—forced upon it as an external equipment. This certainly is not involved in saying that the spiritual faculties are furnished by the spiritual world. Organisms are not added to by accretion, as in the case of minerals, but by growth. And the spiritual faculties are organized in the spiritual protoplasm of the soul, just as other faculties are organized in the protoplasm of the body. The plant is made of materials which have once been inorganic. An organizing principle not belonging to their kingdom lays hold of them and elaborates them until they have correspondences with the kingdom to which the organizing principle belonged. Their original organizing principle, if it can be called by this name, was Crystallization; so that we have now a distinctly foreign power organizing in totally new and higher directions. In the spiritual world, similarly, we find an organizing principle at work among the materials of the organic kingdom, performing a further miracle, but not a different kind of miracle, producing organizations of a novel kind, but not by a novel method. The second process, in fact, is simply what an enlightened evolutionist would have expected from the first. It marks the natural and legitimate progress of the development. And this in the line of the true Evolution—not the *linear* Evolution, which would look for the development of the natural man through powers already inherent, as if one were to look to Crystallization to accomplish the development of the mineral into the plant—but that larger form of Evolution which includes among its factors the double Law of Biogenesis and the immense further truth that this involves.

What is further included in this complex correspondence we shall have opportunity to illustrate afterward.[77] Meantime let it be noted on what the Christian argument for Immortality really rests. It stands upon the pedestal on which the theologian rests the whole of historical Christianity—the Resurrection of Jesus Christ.

It ought to be placed in the forefront of all Christian teaching that Christ's mission on earth was to give men Life. "I am come," He said, "that ye might have Life, and that ye might have it more abundantly." And that He meant literal Life, literal spiritual and Eternal Life, is clear from the whole course of His teaching and acting. To impose a metaphorical meaning on the commonest word of the New Testament is to violate every canon of interpretation, and at the same time to charge the greatest of teachers with persistently mystifying His hearers by an unusual use of so exact a vehicle for expressing definite thought as the Greek language, and that on the most momentous subject of which He ever spoke to men. It is a canon of interpretation, according to Alford, that "a figurative sense of words is never admissible except when required by the context." The context, in most cases, is not only directly unfavorable to a figurative meaning, but in innumerable instances in Christ's teaching Life is broadly contrasted with Death. In the teaching of the apostles, again, we find that, without exception, they accepted the term in its simple literal sense. Reuss defines the apostolic belief with his usual impartiality when—and the quotation is doubly pertinent here—he discovers in the apostle's conception of Life, first, "the idea of a real existence, an existence such as is proper to God and to the Word; an imperishable existence—that is to say, not subject to the vicissitudes and imperfections of the finite world. This primary idea is repeatedly expressed, at least in a negative form; it leads to a doctrine of immortality, or, to speak more correctly, of life, far surpassing any that had been expressed in the formulas of the current philosophy or theology, and resting upon premises and conceptions altogether different. In fact, it can dispense both with the philosophical thesis of the immateriality or indestructibility of the human soul, and with the theological thesis of a miraculous corporeal reconstruction of our person; theses, the first of which is altogether foreign to the religion of the Bible, and the second absolutely opposed to reason." Second, "the idea of life, as it is conceived in this system, implies the idea of a power, an operation, a communication, since this life no longer remains, so to speak, latent or passive in God and in the Word, but through them reaches the believer. It is not a mental somnolent thing; it is not a plant without fruit; it is a germ which is to find fullest development."[78]

If we are asked to define more clearly what is meant by this mysterious endowment of Life, we again hand over the difficulty to Science. When Science can define the Natural Life and the Physical Force we may hope for further clearness on the nature and action of the Spiritual Powers. The effort to detect the living Spirit must be at least as idle as the attempt to subject protoplasm to microscopic examination in the hope of discovering Life. We are warned, also, not to expect too much. "Thou canst not tell whence it cometh or whither it goeth." This being its quality, when the Spiritual Life is discovered in the laboratory it will possibly be time to give it up altogether. It may say, as Socrates of his soul, "You may bury me—if you can catch me."

Science never corroborates a spiritual truth without illuminating it. The threshold of Eternity is a place where many shadows meet. And the light of Science here, where everything is so dark, is welcome a thousand times. Many men would be religious if they knew where to begin; many would be more religious if they were sure where it would end. It is not indifference that keeps some men from God, but ignorance. "Good Master, what must I do to inherit Eternal Life?" is still the deepest question of the age. What is Religion? What am I to believe? What seek with all my heart and soul and mind?—this is the imperious question sent up to consciousness from the depths of being in all earnest hours; sent down again, alas, with many of us, time after time, unanswered. Into all our thought and work and reading this question pursues us. But the theories are rejected one by one; the great books are returned sadly to their shelves, the years pass, and the problem remains unsolved. The confusion of tongues here is terrible. Every day a new authority announces himself. Poets, philosophers, preachers try their hand on us in turn. New prophets arise, and beseech us for our soul's sake to give ear to them—at last in an hour of inspiration they have discovered the final truth. Yet the doctrine of yesterday is challenged by a fresh philosophy to-day: and the creed of to-day will fall in turn before the criticism of to-morrow. Increase of knowledge increaseth sorrow. And at length the conflicting truths, like the beams of light in the laboratory experiment, combine in the mind to make total darkness.

But here are two outstanding authorities agreed—not men, not philosophers, not creeds. Here is the voice of God and the voice of Nature. I cannot be wrong if I listen to them. Sometimes when uncertain of a voice from its very loudness, we catch the missing syllable in the echo. In God and Nature we have Voice and Echo. When I hear both, I am assured. My sense of hearing does not betray me twice. I recognize the Voice in the Echo, the Echo makes me certain of the Voice; I listen and I know. The question of a Future Life is a biological question. Nature may be silent on other problems of Religion; but here she has a right to speak. The whole confusion around the doctrine of Eternal Life has arisen from making it a question of Philosophy. We shall do ill to refuse a hearing to any speculation of Philosophy; the ethical relations here especially are intimate and real. But in the first instance Eternal Life, as a question of *Life*, is a problem for Biology. The soul is a living organism. And for any question as to the soul's Life we must appeal to Life-science. And what does the Life-science teach? That if I am to inherit Eternal Life, I must cultivate a correspondence with the Eternal. This is a simple proposition, for Nature is always simple. I take this proposition, and, leaving Nature, proceed to fill it in. I search everywhere for a clue to the Eternal. I ransack literature for a definition of a correspondence between man and God. Obviously that can only come from one source. And the analogies of Science permits us to apply to it. All knowledge lies in Environment. When I want to know about minerals I go to minerals. When I want to know about flowers I go to flowers. And they tell me. In their own way they speak to me, each in its own way, and each for itself—not the mineral for the flower, which is impossible, nor the flower for the mineral, which is also impossible. So if I want to know about Man, I go to his part of the Environment. And he tells me about himself, not as the plant or the mineral, for he is neither, but in his own way. And if I want to know about God, I go to His part of the Environment. And He tells me about Himself, not as a Man, for He is not Man, but in His own way. And just as naturally as the flower and the mineral and the Man, each in their own way, tell me about themselves, He tells me about Himself. He very strangely condescends indeed in making things plain to me, actually assuming for a time the Form of a Man that I at my poor level may better see Him. This is my opportunity to know Him. This incarnation is God making Himself accessible to human thought—God opening to man the possibility of correspondence through Jesus Christ. And this correspondence and this Environment are those I seek. He Himself assures me, "This is Life Eternal, that they might know Thee, the only true God, and Jesus Christ whom Thou hast sent."

Do I not now discern the deeper meaning in "*Jesus Christ whom Thou hast sent?*" Do I not better understand with what vision and rapture the profoundest of the disciples exclaims, "The Son of God is come, and hath given us an understanding that we might know Him that is True?"[79]

Having opened correspondence with the Eternal Environment, the subsequent stages are in the line of all other normal development. We have but to continue, to deepen, to extend, and to enrich the correspondence that has been begun. And we shall soon find to our surprise that this is accompanied by another and parallel process. The action is not all upon our side. The Environment also will be found to correspond. The influence of Environment is one of the greatest and most substantial of modern biological doctrines. Of the power of Environment to form or transform organisms, of its ability to develop or suppress function, of its potency in determining growth, and generally of its immense influence in Evolution, there is no need now to speak. But Environment is now acknowledged to be one of the most potent factors in the Evolution of Life. The influence of Environment too seems to increase rather than diminish as we approach the higher forms of being. The highest forms are the most mobile; their capacity of change is the greatest; they are, in short, most easily acted on by Environment. And not only are the highest organisms the most mobile, but the highest part of the highest organisms are more mobile than the lower. Environment can do little, comparatively, in the direction of inducing variation in the body of a child: but how plastic is its mind! How infinitely sensitive is its soul! How infallibly can it be turned to music or to dissonance by the moral harmony or discord of its outward lot! How decisively indeed are we not all formed and moulded, made or unmade, by external circumstance! Might we not all confess with Ulysses—

"I am a part of all that I have met."

Much more, then, shall we look for the influence of Environment on the spiritual nature of him who has opened correspondence with God. Reaching out his eager and quickened faculties to the spiritual world around him, shall he not become spiritual? In vital contact with Holiness, shall he not become holy? Breathing now an atmosphere of ineffable Purity, shall he miss becoming pure? Walking with God from day to day, shall he fail to be taught of God?

Growth in grace is sometimes described as a strange, mystical, and unintelligible process. It is mystical, but neither strange nor unintelligible. It proceeds according to Natural Law, and the leading factor in sanctification is Influence of Environment. The possibility of it depends upon the mobility of the organism; the result, on the extent and frequency of certain correspondences. These facts insensibly lead on to a further suggestion. Is it not possible that these biological truths may carry with them the clue to still profounder philosophy—even that of Regeneration?

Evolutionists tell us that by the influence of environment certain aquatic animals have become adapted to a terrestrial mode of life. Breathing normally by gills, as the result and reward of a continued effort carried on from generation to generation to inspire the air of heaven direct, they have slowly acquired the lung-function. In the young organism, true to the ancestral type, the gill still persists—as in the tadpole of the common frog. But as maturity approaches the true lung appears; the gill gradually transfers its task to the higher organ. It then becomes atrophied and disappears, and finally respiration in the adult is conducted by lungs alone. [80] We may be far, in the meantime, from saying that this is proved. It is for those who accept it to deny the justice of the spiritual analogy. Is religion to them unscientific in its doctrine of Regeneration? Will the evolutionist who admits the regeneration of the frog under the modifying influence of a continued correspondence with a new environment, care to question the possibility of the soul acquiring such a faculty as that of Prayer, the marvelous breathing-function of the new creature, when in contact with the atmosphere of a besetting God? Is the change from the earthly to the heavenly more mysterious than the change from the aquatic to the terrestrial mode of life? Is Evolution to stop with the organic? If it be objected that it has taken ages to perfect the function in the batrachian, the reply is, that it will take ages to perfect the function in the Christian. For every thousand years the natural evolution will allow for the development of its organism, the Higher Biology will grant its product millions. We have indeed spoken of the spiritual correspondence as already perfect—but it is perfect only as the bud is perfect. "It doth not yet appear what it shall be," any more than it appeared a million years ago what the evolving batrachian would be.

But to return. We have been dealing with the scientific aspects of communion with God. Insensibly, from quantity we have been led to speak of quality. And enough has now been advanced to indicate generally the nature of that correspondence with which is necessarily associated Eternal Life. There remain but one or two details to which we must lastly, and very briefly, address ourselves.

The quality of everlastingness belongs, as we have seen, to a single correspondence, or rather to a single set of correspondences. But it is apparent that before this correspondence can take full and final effect a further process is necessary. By some means it must be separated from all the other correspondences of the organism which do not share its peculiar quality. In this life it is restrained by these other correspondences. They may contribute to it, or hinder it; but they are essentially of a different order. They belong not to Eternity but to Time, and to this present world; and, unless some provision is made for dealing with them, they will detain the aspiring organism in this present world till Time is ended. Of course, in a sense, all that belongs to Time belongs also to Eternity; but these lower correspondences are in their nature unfitted for an Eternal Life. Even if they were perfect in their relation to their Environment, they would still not be Eternal. However opposed, apparently, to the scientific definition of Eternal Life, it is yet true that perfect correspondence with Environment is not Eternal Life. A very important word in the complete definition is, in this sentence, omitted. On that word it has not been necessary hitherto, and for obvious reasons, to place any emphasis, but when we come to deal with false pretenders to Immortality we must return to it. Were the definition complete as it stands, it might, with the permission of the psycho-physiologist, guarantee the Immortality of every living thing. In the dog, for instance, the material framework giving way at death might leave the released canine spirit still free to inhabit the old Environment. And so with every creature which had ever established a conscious relation with surrounding things. Now the difficulty in framing a theory of Eternal Life has been to construct one which will exclude the brute creation, drawing the line rigidly at man, or at least, somewhere within the human race. Not that we need object to the Immortality of the dog, or of the whole inferior creation. Nor that we need refuse a place to any intelligible speculation which would people the earth to-day with the invisible forms of all things that have ever lived. Only we still insist that this is not Eternal Life. And why? Because their Environment is not Eternal. Their correspondence, however firmly established, is established with that which shall pass away. An Eternal Life demands an Eternal Environment.

The demand for a perfect Environment as well as for a perfect correspondence is less clear in Mr. Herbert Spencer's definition than it might be. But it is an essential factor. An organism might remain true to its Environment, but what if the Environment played it false? If the organism possessed the power to change, it could adapt itself to successive changes in the Environment. And if this were guaranteed we should also have the conditions for Eternal Life fulfilled. But what if the Environment passed away altogether? What if the earth swept suddenly into the sun? This is a change of Environment against which there could be no precaution and for which there could be as little provision. With a changing Environment even, there must always remain the dread and possibility of a falling out of correspondence. At the best, Life would be uncertain. But with a changeless Environment—such as that possessed by the spiritual organism—the perpetuity of the correspondence, so far as the external relation is concerned, is guaranteed. This quality of permanence in the Environment distinguishes the religious relation from every other. Why should not the musician's life be an Eternal Life? Because, for one thing, the musical world, the Environment with which he corresponds, is not eternal. Even if his correspondence in itself could last, eternally, the environing material things with which he corresponds must pass away. His soul might last forever—but not his violin. So the man of the world might last forever—but not the world. His Environment is not eternal; nor are even his correspondences—the world passeth away *and the lust thereof.*

We find then that man, or the spiritual man, is equipped with two sets of correspondences. One set possesses the quality of everlastingness, the other is temporal. But unless these are separated by some means the temporal will continue to impair and hinder the eternal. The final preparation, therefore, for the inheriting of Eternal Life must consist in the abandonment of the non-eternal elements. These must be unloosed and dissociated from the higher elements. And this is effected by a closing catastrophe—Death.

Death ensues because certain relations in the organism are not adjusted to certain relations in the Environment. There will come a time in each history when the imperfect correspondences of the organism will betray themselves by a failure to compass some necessary adjustment. This is why Death is associated with Imperfection. Death is the necessary result of Imperfection, and the necessary end of it. Imperfect correspondence gives imperfect and uncertain Life. "Perfect correspondence," on the other hand, according to Mr. Herbert Spencer, would be "perfect Life." To abolish Death, therefore, all that would be necessary would be to abolish Imperfection. But it is the claim of Christianity that it can abolish Death. And it is significant to notice that it does so by meeting this very demand of Science—it abolishes Imperfection.

The part of the organism which begins to get out of correspondence with the Organic Environment is the only part which is in vital correspondence with it. Though a fatal disadvantage to the natural man to be thrown out of correspondence with this Environment, it is of inestimable importance to the spiritual man. For so long as it is maintained the way is barred for a further Evolution. And hence the condition necessary for the further Evolution is that the spiritual be released from the natural. That is to say, the condition of the further Evolution is Death. *Mors janua Vitæ*, therefore, becomes a scientific formula. Death, being the final shifting of all the correspondences, is the indispensable factor of the higher Life. In the language of Science, not less than of Scripture, "To die is gain."

The shifting of the correspondences is done by Nature. This is its last and greatest contribution to mankind. Over the mouth of the grave the perfect and the imperfect submit to their final separation. Each goes to its own—earth to earth, ashes to ashes, dust to dust, Spirit to Spirit. "The dust shall return to the earth as it was; and the Spirit shall return unto God who gave it."

ENVIRONMENT.

"When I talked with an ardent missionary and pointed out to him that his creed found no support in my experience, he replied: 'It is not so in your experience, but is so in the other world.' I answered: 'Other world! There is no other world. God is one and omnipresent; here or nowhere is the whole fact.'"—*Emerson.*

"Ye are complete in Him."—*Paul.*

"Whatever amount of power an organism expends in any shape is the correlate and equivalent of a power that was taken into it from without."—*Herbert Spencer.*

Students of Biography will observe that in all well-written Lives attention is concentrated for the first few chapters upon two points. We are first introduced to the family to which the subject of memoir belonged. The grandparents, or even the more remote ancestors, are briefly sketched and their chief characteristics brought prominently into view. Then the parents themselves are photographed in detail. Their appearance and physique, their character, their disposition, their mental qualities, are set before us in a critical analysis. And finally we are asked to observe how much the father and the mother respectively have transmitted of their peculiar nature to their offspring. How faithfully the ancestral lines have met in the latest product, how mysteriously the joint characteristics of body and mind have blended, and how unexpected yet how entirely natural a recombination is the result —these points are elaborated with cumulative effect until we realize at last how little we are dealing with an independent unit, how much with a survival and reorganization of what seemed buried in the grave.

In the second place, we are invited to consider more external influences— schools and schoolmasters, neighbors, home, pecuniary circumstances, scenery, and, by-and-by, the religious and political atmosphere of the time. These also we are assured have played their part in making the individual what he is. We can estimate these early influences in any particular case with but small imagination if we fail to see how powerfully they also have moulded mind and character, and in what subtle ways they have determined the course of the future life.

This twofold relation of the individual, first, to his parents, and second, to his circumstances, is not peculiar to human beings. These two factors are responsible for making all living organisms what they are. When a naturalist attempts to unfold the life-history of any animal, he proceeds precisely on these same lines. Biography is really a branch of Natural History; and the biographer who discusses his hero as the resultant of these two tendencies, follows the scientific method as rigidly as Mr. Darwin in studying "Animals and Plants under Domestication."

Mr. Darwin, following Weismann, long ago pointed out that there are two main factors in all Evolution—the nature of the organism and the nature of the conditions. We have chosen our illustration from the highest or human species in order to define the meaning of these factors in the clearest way; but it must be remembered that the development of man under these directive influences is essentially the same as that of any other organism in the hands of Nature. We are dealing therefore with universal Law. It will still further serve to complete the conception of the general principle if we now substitute for the casual phrases by which the factors have been described the more accurate terminology of Science. Thus what Biography describes as parental influences, Biology would speak of as Heredity; and all that is involved in the second factor—the action of external circumstances and surroundings—the naturalist would include under the single term Environment. These two, Heredity and Environment, are the master-influences of the organic world. These have made all of us what we are. These forces are still ceaselessly playing upon all our lives. And he who truly understands these influences; he who has decided how much to allow to each; he who can regulate new forces as they arise, or adjust them to the old, so directing them as at one moment to make them coöperate, at another to counteract one another, understands the rationale of personal development. To seize continuously the opportunity of more and more perfect adjustment to better and higher conditions, to balance some inward evil with some purer influence acting from without, in a word to make our Environment at the same time that it is making us—these are the secrets of a well-ordered and successful life.

In the spiritual world, also, the subtle influences which form and transform the soul are Heredity and Environment. And here especially where all is invisible, where much that we feel to be real is yet so ill-defined, it becomes of vital practical moment to clarify the atmosphere as far as possible with conceptions borrowed from the natural life. Few things are less understood than the conditions of the spiritual life. The distressing incompetence of which most of us are conscious in trying to work out our spiritual experience is due perhaps less to the diseased will which we commonly blame for it than to imperfect knowledge of the right conditions. It does not occur to us how natural the spiritual is. We still strive for some strange transcendent thing; we seek to promote life by methods as unnatural as they prove unsuccessful; and only the utter incomprehensibility of the whole region prevents us seeing fully—what we already half-suspect—how completely we are missing the road. Living in the spiritual world, nevertheless, is just as simple as living in the natural world; and it is the same kind of simplicity. It is the same kind of simplicity for it is the same kind of world—there are not two kinds of worlds. The conditions of life in the one are the conditions of life in the other. And till these conditions are sensibly grasped, as the conditions of all life, it is impossible that the personal effort after the highest life should be other than a blind struggle carried on in fruitless sorrow and humiliation.

Of these two universal factors, Heredity and Environment, it is unnecessary to balance the relative importance here. The main influence, unquestionably, must be assigned to the former. In practice, however, and for an obvious reason, we are chiefly concerned with the latter. What Heredity has to do for us is determined outside ourselves. No man can select his own parents. But every man to some extent can choose his own Environment. His relation to it, however largely determined by Heredity in the first instance, is always open to alteration. And so great is his control over Environment and so radical its influence over him, that he can so direct it as either to undo, modify, perpetuate or intensify the earlier hereditary influence within certain limits. But the aspects of Environment which we have now to consider do not involve us in questions of such complexity. In what high and mystical sense, also, Heredity applies to the spiritual organism we need not just now inquire. In the simpler relations of the more external factor we shall find a large and fruitful field for study.

The influence of Environment may be investigated in two main aspects. First, one might discuss the modern and very interesting question as to the power of Environment to induce what is known to recent science as

Variation. A change in the surroundings of any animal, it is now well-known, can so react upon it as to cause it to change. By the attempt, conscious or unconscious, to adjust itself to the new conditions, a true physiological change is gradually wrought within the organism. Hunter, for example, in a classical experiment, so changed the Environment of a sea-gull by keeping it in captivity that it could only secure a grain diet. The effect was to modify the stomach of the bird, normally adapted to a fish diet, until in time it came to resemble in structure the gizzard of an ordinary grain-feeder such as the pigeon. Holmgrén again reversed this experiment by feeding pigeons for a lengthened period on a meat-diet, with the result that the gizzard became transformed into the carnivorous stomach. Mr. Alfred Russel Wallace mentions the case of a Brazilian parrot which changes its color from green to red or yellow when fed on the fat of certain fishes. Not only changes of food, however, but changes of climate and of temperature, changes in surrounding organisms, in the case of marine animals even changes of pressure, of ocean currents, of light, and of many other circumstances, are known to exert a powerful modifying influence upon living organisms. These relations are still being worked out in many directions, but the influence of Environment as a prime factor in Variation is now a recognized doctrine of science.[81]

Even the popular mind has been struck with the curious adaptation of nearly all animals to their *habitat*, for example in the matter of color. The sandy hue of the sole and flounder, the white of the polar bear with its suggestion of Arctic snows, the stripes of the Bengal tiger—as if the actual reeds of its native jungle had nature-printed themselves on its hide;—these, and a hundred others which will occur to every one, are marked instances of adaptation to Environment, induced by Natural Selection or otherwise, for the purpose, obviously in these cases at least, of protection.

To continue the investigation of the modifying action of Environment into the moral and spiritual spheres, would be to open a fascinating and suggestive inquiry. One might show how the moral man is acted upon and changed continuously by the influences, secret and open, of his surroundings, by the tone of society, by the company he keeps, by his occupation, by the books he reads, by Nature, by all, in short, that constitutes the habitual atmosphere of his thoughts and the little world of his daily choice. Or one might go deeper still and prove how the spiritual life also is modified from outside sources—its health or disease, its growth or decay, all its changes for better or for worse being determined by the varying and successive circumstances in which the religious habits are cultivated. But we must rather transfer our attention to a second aspect of Environment, not perhaps so fascinating but yet more important.

So much of the modern discussion of Environment revolves round the mere question of Variation that one is apt to overlook a previous question. Environment as a factor in life is not exhausted when we have realized its modifying influence. Its significance is scarcely touched. The great function of Environment is not to modify but to *sustain*. In sustaining life, it is true, it modifies. But the latter influence is incidental, the former essential. Our Environment is that in which we live and move and have our being. Without it we should neither live or move nor have any being. In the organism lies the principle of life; in the Environment are the conditions of life. Without the fulfillment of these conditions, which are wholly supplied by Environment, there can be no life. An organism in itself is but a part; Nature is its complement. Alone, cut off from its surroundings, it is not. Alone, cut off from my surroundings, I am not—physically I am not. I am, only as I am sustained. I continue only as I receive. My Environment may modify me, but it has first to keep me. And all the time its secret transforming power is indirectly moulding body and mind it is directly active in the more open task of ministering to my myriad wants and from hour to hour sustaining life itself.

To understand the sustaining influence of Environment in the animal world, one has only to recall what the biologist terms the extrinsic or subsidiary conditions of vitality. Every living thing normally requires for its development an Environment containing air, light, heat, and water. In addition to these, if vitality is to be prolonged for any length of time, and if it is to be accompanied with growth and the expenditure of energy, there must be a constant supply of food. When we simply remember how indispensable food is to growth and work, and when we further bear in mind that the food-supply is solely contributed by the Environment, we shall realize at once the meaning and the truth of the proposition that without Environment there can be no life. Seventy per cent. at least of the human body is made of pure water, the rest of gases and earth. These have all come from Environment. Through the secret pores of the skin two pounds of water are exhaled daily from every healthy adult. The supply is kept up by Environment. The Environment is really an unappropriated part of ourselves. Definite portions are continuously abstracted from it and added to the organism. And so long as the organism continues to grow, act, think, speak, work, or perform any other function demanding a supply of energy, there is a constant, simultaneous, and proportionate drain upon its surroundings.

This is a truth in the physical, and therefore in the spiritual, world of so great importance that we shall not mis-spend time if we follow it, for further confirmation, into another department of nature. Its significance in Biology is self-evident; let us appeal to Chemistry.

When a piece of coal is thrown on the fire, we say that it will radiate into the room a certain quantity of heat. This heat, in the popular conception, is supposed to reside in the coal and to be set free during the process of combustion. In reality, however, the heat energy is only in part contained in the coal. It is contained just as truly in the coal's Environment—that is to say, in the oxygen of the air. The atoms of carbon which compose the coal have a powerful affinity for the oxygen of the air. Whenever they are made to approach within a certain distance of one another, by the initial application of heat, they rush together with inconceivable velocity. The heat which appears at this moment, comes neither from the carbon alone, nor from the oxygen alone. These two substances are really inconsumable, and continue to exist, after they meet in a combined form, as carbonic acid gas. The heat is due to the energy developed by the chemical embrace, the precipitate rushing together of the molecules of carbon and the molecules of oxygen. It comes, therefore, partly from the coal and partly from the Environment. Coal alone never could produce heat, neither alone could Environment. The two are mutually dependent. And although in nearly all the arts we credit everything to the substance which we can weigh and handle, it is certain that in the most cases the larger debt is due to an invisible Environment.

This is one of those great commonplaces which slip out of general reckoning by reason of their very largeness and simplicity. How profound, nevertheless, are the issues which hang on this elementary truth, we shall discover immediately. Nothing in this age is more needed in every department of knowledge than the rejuvenescence of the commonplace. In the spiritual world especially, he will be wise who courts acquaintance with the most ordinary and transparent facts of Nature; and in laying the foundations for a religious life he will make no unworthy beginning who carries with him an impressive sense of so obvious a truth as that without Environment there can be no life.

For what does this amount to in the spiritual world? Is it not merely the scientific re-statement of the reiterated aphorism of Christ, "Without Me ye can do nothing?" There is in the spiritual organism a principle of life; but that is not self-existent. It requires a second factor, a something in which to live and move and have its being, an Environment. Without this it cannot live or move or have any being. Without Environment the soul is as the carbon without the oxygen, as the fish without the water, as the animal frame without the extrinsic conditions of vitality.

And what is the spiritual Environment? It is God. Without this, therefore, there is no life, no thought, no energy, nothing—"without Me ye can do nothing."

The cardinal error in the religious life is to attempt to live without an Environment. Spiritual experience occupies itself, not too much, but too exclusively, with one factor—the soul. We delight in dissecting this much tortured faculty, from time to time, in search of a certain something which we call our faith—forgetting that faith is but an attitude, an empty hand for grasping an environing Presence. And when we feel the need of a power by which to overcome the world, how often do we not seek to generate it within ourselves by some forced process, some fresh girding of the will, some strained activity which only leaves the soul in further exhaustion? To examine ourselves is good; but useless unless we also examine Environment. To bewail our weakness is right, but not remedial. The cause must be investigated as well as the result. And yet, because we never see the other half of the problem, our failures even fail to instruct us. After each new collapse we begin our life anew, but on the old conditions; and the attempt ends as usual in the repetition—in the circumstances the inevitable repetition—of the old disaster. Not that at times we do not obtain glimpses of the true state of the case. After seasons of much discouragement, with the sore sense upon us of our abject feebleness, we do confer with ourselves, insisting for the thousandth time, "My soul, wait thou only upon God." But the lesson is soon forgotten. The strength supplied we speedily credit to our own achievement; and even the temporary success is mistaken for a symptom of improved inward vitality. Once more we become self-existent. Once more we go on living without an Environment. And once more, after days of wasting without repairing, of spending without replenishing, we begin to perish with hunger, only returning to God again, as a last resort, when we have reached starvation point.

Now why do we do this? Why do we seek to breathe without an atmosphere, to drink without a well? Why this unscientific attempt to sustain life for weeks at a time without an Environment? It is because we have never truly seen the necessity for an Environment. We have not been working with a principle. We are told to "wait only upon God," but we do not know why. It has never been as clear to us that without God the soul will die as that without food the body will perish. In short, we have never comprehended the doctrine of the Persistence of Force. Instead of being content to transform energy we have tried to create it.

The Law of Nature here is as clear as Science can make it. In the words of Mr. Herbert Spencer, "It is a corollary from that primordial truth which, as we have seen, underlies all other truths, that whatever amount of power an organism expends in any shape is the correlate and equivalent of a power that was taken into it from without,"[82] We are dealing here with a simple question of dynamics. Whatever energy the soul expends must first be "taken into it from without." We are not Creators, but creatures; God is our refuge *and strength.* Communion with God, therefore, is a scientific necessity; and nothing will more help the defeated spirit which is struggling in the wreck of its religious life than a common-sense hold of this plain biological principle that without Environment he can do nothing. What he wants is not an occasional view, but a principle—a basal principle like this, broad as the universe, solid as nature. In the natural world we act upon this law unconsciously. We absorb heat, breathe air, draw on Environment all but automatically for meat and drink, for the nourishment of the senses, for mental stimulus, for all that, penetrating us from without, can prolong, enrich, and elevate life. But in the spiritual world we have all this to learn. We are new creatures, and even the bare living has to be acquired.

Now the great point in learning to live is to live naturally. As closely as possible we must follow the broad, clear lines of the natural life. And there are three things especially which it is necessary for us to keep continually in view. The first is that the organism contains within itself only one-half of what is essential to life; the second is that the other half is contained in the Environment; the third, that the condition of receptivity is simple union between the organism and the Environment.

Translated into the language of religion these propositions yield, and place on a scientific basis, truths of immense practical interest. To say, first, that the organism contains within itself only one-half of what is essential to life, is to repeat the evangelical confession, so worn and yet so true to universal experience, of the utter helplessness of man. Who has not come to the conclusion that he is but a part, a fraction of some larger whole? Who does not miss at every turn of his life an absent God? That man is but a part, he knows, for there is room in him for more. That God is the other part, he feels, because at times He satisfies his need. Who does not tremble often under that sicklier symptom of his incompleteness, his want of spiritual energy, his helplessness with sin? But now he understands both—the void in his life, the powerlessness of his will. He understands that, like all other energy, spiritual power is contained in Environment. He finds here at last the true root of all human frailty, emptiness, nothingness, sin. This is why "without Me ye can do nothing." Powerlessness is the normal state not only of this but of every organism—of every organism apart from its Environment.

The entire dependence of the soul upon God is not an exceptional mystery, nor is man's helplessness an arbitrary and unprecedented phenomenon. It is the law of all Nature. The spiritual man is not taxed beyond the natural. He is not purposely handicapped by singular limitations or unusual incapacities. God has not designedly made the religious life as hard as possible. The arrangements for the spiritual life are the same as for the natural life. When in their hours of unbelief men challenge their Creator for placing the obstacle of human frailty in the way of their highest development, their protest is against the order of nature. They object to the sun for being the source of energy and not the engine, to the carbonic acid being in the air and not in the plant. They would equip each organism with a personal atmosphere, each brain with a private store of energy; they would grow corn in the interior of the body, and make bread by a special apparatus in the digestive organs. They must, in short, have the creature transformed into a Creator. The organism must either depend on his environment, or be self-sufficient. But who will not rather approve the arrangement by which man in his creatural life may have unbroken access to an Infinite Power? What soul will seek to remain self-luminous when it knows that "The Lord God is a *Sun*?" Who will not willingly exchange his shallow vessel for Christ's well of living water? Even if the organism, launched into being like a ship putting out to sea, possessed a full equipment, its little store must soon come to an end. But in contact with a large and bounteous Environment its supply is limitless. In every direction its resources are infinite.

There is a modern school which protests against the doctrine of man's inability as the heartless fiction of a past theology. While some forms of that dogma, to any one who knows man, are incapable of defence, there are others which, to any one who knows Nature, are incapable of denial. Those who oppose it, in their jealousy for humanity, credit the organism with the properties of Environment. All true theology, on the other hand, has remained loyal to at least the root-idea in this truth. The New Testament is nowhere more impressive than where it insists on the fact of man's dependence. In its view the first step in religion is for man to feel his helplessness. Christ's first beatitude is to the poor in spirit. The condition of entrance into the spiritual kingdom is to possess the child-spirit—that state of mind combining at once the profoundest helplessness with the most artless feeling of dependence. Substantially the same idea underlies the countless passages in which Christ affirms that He has not come to call the righteous, but sinners to repentance. And in that farewell discourse into which the Great Teacher poured the most burning convictions of His life, He gives to this doctrine an ever increasing emphasis. No words could be more solemn or arresting than the sentence in the last great allegory devoted to this theme, "As the branch cannot bear fruit of itself except it abide in the vine, no more can ye except ye abide in Me." The word here, it will be observed again, is *cannot*. It is the imperative of natural law. Fruit-bearing without Christ is not an improbability, but an impossibility. As well expect the natural fruit to flourish without air and heat, without soil and sunshine. How thoroughly also Paul grasped this truth is apparent from a hundred pregnant passages in which he echoes his Master's teaching. To him life was hid with Christ in God. And that he embraced this not as a theory but as an experimental truth we gather from his constant confession, "When I am weak, then am I strong."

This leads by a natural transition to the second of the three points we are seeking to illustrate. We have seen that the organism contains within itself only one half of what is essential to life. We have next to observe, as the complement of this, how the second half is contained in the Environment.

One result of the due apprehension of our personal helplessness will be that we shall no longer waste our time over the impossible task of manufacturing energy for ourselves. Our science will bring to an abrupt end the long series of severe experiments in which we have indulged in the hope of finding a perpetual motion. And having decided upon this once for all, our first step in seeking a more satisfactory state of things must be to find a new source of energy. Following Nature, only one course is open to us. We must refer to Environment. The natural life owes all to Environment, so must the spiritual. Now the Environment of the spiritual life is God. As Nature therefore forms the complement of the natural life, God is the complement of the spiritual.

The proof of this? That Nature is not more natural to my body than God is to my soul. Every animal and plant has its own Environment. And the further one inquires into the relations of the one to the other, the more one sees the marvelous intricacy and beauty of the adjustments. These wonderful adaptations of each organism to its surroundings—of the fish to the water, of the eagle to the air, of the insect to the forest bed; and of each part of every organism—the fish's swim-bladder, the eagle's eye, the insect's breathing tubes—which the old argument from design brought home to us with such enthusiasm, inspire us still with a sense of the boundless resources and skill of Nature in perfecting her arrangements for each single life. Down to the last detail the world is made for what is in it; and by whatever process things are as they are, all organisms find in surrounding Nature the ample complement of themselves. Man, too, finds in his Environment provision for all capacities, scope for the exercise of every faculty, room for the indulgence of each appetite, a just supply for every want. So the spiritual man at the apex of the pyramid of life finds in the vaster range of his Environment a provision, as much higher, it is true, as he is higher, but as delicately adjusted to his varying needs. And all this is supplied to him just as the lower organisms are ministered to by the lower environment, in the same simple ways, in the same constant sequence, as appropriately and as lavishly. We fail to praise the ceaseless ministry of the great inanimate world around us only because its kindness is unobtrusive. Nature is always noiseless. All her greatest gifts are given in secret. And we forget how truly every good and perfect gift comes from without, and from above, because no pause in her changeless beneficence teaches us the sad lesson of deprivation.

It is not a strange thing, then, for the soul to find its life in God. This is its native air. God as the Environment of the soul has been from the remotest age the doctrine of all the deepest thinkers in religion. How profoundly Hebrew poetry is saturated with this high thought will appear when we try to conceive of it with this left out. True poetry is only science in another form. And long before it was possible for religion to give scientific expression to its greatest truths, men of insight uttered themselves in psalms which could not have been truer to Nature had the most modern light controlled the inspiration. "As the hart panteth after the water-brooks, so panteth my soul after Thee, O God." What fine sense of the analogy of the natural and the spiritual does not underlie these words. As the hart after its Environment, so man after his; as the water-brooks are fitly designed to meet the natural wants, so fitly does God implement the spiritual need of man. It will be noticed that in the Hebrew poets the longing for God never strikes one as morbid, or unnatural to the men who utter it. It is as natural to them to long for God as for the swallow to seek her nest. Throughout all their images no suspicion rises within us that they are exaggerating. We feel how truly they are reading themselves, their deepest selves. No false note occurs in all their aspiration. There is no weariness even in their ceaseless sighing, except the lover's weariness for the absent—if they would fly away, it is only to be at rest. Men who have no soul can only wonder at this. Men who have a soul, but with little faith, can only envy it. How joyous a thing it was to the Hebrews to seek their God! How artlessly they call upon Him to entertain them in His pavilion, to cover them with His feathers, to hide them in His secret place, to hold them in the hollow of His hand or stretch around them the everlasting arms! These men were true children of Nature. As the humming-bird among its own palm-trees, as the ephemera in the sunshine of a summer evening, so they lived their joyous lives. And even the full share of the sadder experience of life which came to all of them but drove them the further into the Secret Place, and led them with more consecration to make, as they expressed it, "the Lord their portion." All that has been said since from Marcus Aurelius to Swedenborg, from Augustine to Schleiermacher of a besetting God as the final complement of humanity is but a repetition of the Hebrew poets' faith. And even the New Testament has nothing higher to offer man than this. The psalmist's "God is our refuge and strength" is only the earlier form, less defined, less practicable, but not less noble, of Christ's "Come unto Me, and I will give you rest."

There is a brief phrase of Paul's which defines the relation with almost scientific accuracy—"Ye are complete in Him." In this is summed up the whole of the Bible anthropology—the completeness of man in God, his incompleteness apart from God.

If it be asked, In what is man incomplete, or, In what does God complete him? the question is a wide one. But it may serve to show at least the direction in which the Divine Environment forms the complement of human life if we ask ourselves once more what it is in life that needs complementing. And to this question we receive the significant answer that it is in the higher departments alone, or mainly, that the incompleteness of our life appears. The lower departments of Nature are already complete enough. The world itself is about as good a world as might be. It has been long in the making, its furniture is all in, its laws are in perfect working order; and although wise men at various times have suggested improvements, there is on the whole a tolerably unanimous vote of confidence in things as they exist. The Divine Environment has little more to do for this planet so far as we can see, and so far as the existing generation is concerned. Then the lower organic life of the world is also so far complete. God, through Evolution or otherwise, may still have finishing touches to add here and there, but already it is "all very good." It is difficult to conceive anything better of its kind than a lily or a cedar, an ant or an ant-eater. These organisms, so far as we can judge, lack nothing. It might be said of them, "they are complete in Nature." Of man also, of man the animal, it may be affirmed that his Environment satisfies him. He has food and drink, and good food and good drink. And there is in him no purely animal want which is not really provided for, and that apparently in the happiest possible way.

But the moment we pass beyond the mere animal life we begin to come upon an incompleteness. The symptoms at first are slight, and betray themselves only by an unexplained restlessness or a dull sense of want. Then the feverishness increases, becomes more defined, and passes slowly into abiding pain. To some come darker moments when the unrest deepens into a mental agony of which all the other woes of earth are mockeries—moments when the forsaken soul can only cry in terror for the Living God. Up to a point the natural Environment supplies man's wants, beyond that it only derides him. How much in man lies beyond that point? Very much—almost all, all that makes man man. The first suspicion of the terrible truth—so for the time let us call it—wakens with the dawn of the intellectual life. It is a solemn moment when the slow-moving mind reaches at length the verge of its mental horizon, and, looking over, sees nothing more. Its straining makes the abyss but more profound. Its cry comes back without an echo. Where is the Environment to complete this rational soul? Men either find one—*One*—or spend the rest of their days in trying to shut their eyes. The alternatives of the intellectual life are Christianity or Agnosticism. The Agnostic is right when he trumpets his incompleteness. He who is not complete in Him must be forever incomplete. Still more grave becomes man's case when he begins further to explore his moral and social nature. The problems of the heart and conscience are infinitely more perplexing than those of the intellect. Has love no future? Has right no triumph? Is the unfinished self to remain unfinished? Again, the alternatives are two, Christianity or Pessimism. But when we ascend the further height of the religious nature, the crisis comes. There, without Environment, the darkness is unutterable. So maddening now becomes the mystery that men are compelled to construct an Environment for themselves. No Environment here is unthinkable. An altar of some sort men must have—God, or Nature, or Law. But the anguish of Atheism is only a negative proof of man's incompleteness. A witness more overwhelming is the prayer of the Christian. What a very strange thing, is it not, for man to pray? It is the symbol at once of his littleness and of his greatness. Here the sense of imperfection, controlled and silenced in the narrower reaches of his being, becomes audible. Now he must utter himself. The sense of need is so real, and the sense of Environment, that he calls out to it, addressing it articulately, and imploring it to satisfy his need. Surely there is nothing more touching in Nature than this? Man could never so expose himself, so break through all constraint, except from a dire necessity. It is the suddenness and unpremeditatedness of Prayer that gives it a unique value as an apologetic.

Man has three questions to put to his Environment, three symbols of his incompleteness. They come from three different centers of his being. The first is the question of the intellect, What is Truth? The natural Environment answers, "Increase of Knowledge increaseth Sorrow," and "much study is a Weariness." Christ replies, "Learn of Me, and ye shall find Rest." Contrast the world's word "Weariness" with Christ's word "Rest." No other teacher since the world began has ever associated "learn" with "Rest." Learn of me, says the philosopher, and you shall find Restlessness. Learn of Me, says Christ, and ye shall find Rest. Thought, which the godless man has cursed, that eternally starved yet ever living specter, finds at last its imperishable glory; Thought is complete in Him. The second question is sent up from the moral nature, Who will show us any good? And again we have a contrast: the world's verdict, "There is none that doeth good, no, not one;" and Christ's, "There is none good but God only." And finally, there is the lonely cry of the spirit, most pathetic and most deep of all, Where is he whom my soul seeketh? And the yearning is met as before, "I looked on my right hand, and beheld, but there was no man that would know me; refuge failed me; no man cared for my soul. I cried unto Thee, O Lord: I said, Thou are my refuge and my portion in the land of the living."[83]

Are these the directions in which men in these days are seeking to complete their lives? The completion of Life is just now a supreme question. It is important to observe how it is being answered. If we ask Science or Philosophy they will refer us to Evolution. The struggle for Life, they assure us, is steadily eliminating imperfect forms, and as the fittest continue to survive we shall have a gradual perfecting of being. That is to say, that completeness is to be sought for in the organism—we are to be complete in Nature and in ourselves. To Evolution, certainly, all men will look for a further perfecting of Life. But it must be an Evolution which includes all the factors. Civilization, it may be said, will deal with the second factor. It will improve the Environment step by step as it improves the organism, or the organism as it improves the Environment. This is well, and it will perfect Life up to a point. But beyond that it cannot carry us. As the possibilities of the natural Life become more defined, its impossibilities will become the more appalling. The most perfect civilization would leave the best part of us still incomplete. Men will have to give up the experiment of attempting to live in half an Environment. Half an Environment will give but half a Life. Half an Environment? He whose correspondences are with this world alone has only a thousandth part, a fraction, the mere rim and shade of an Environment, and only the fraction of a Life. How long will it take Science to believe its own creed, that the material universe we see around us is only a fragment of the universe we do not see? The very retention of the phrase "Material Universe," we are told, is the confession of our unbelief and ignorance; since "matter is the less important half of the material of the physical universe."[84]

The thing to be aimed at is not an organism self-contained and self-sufficient, however high in the scale of being, but an organism complete in the whole Environment. It is open to any one to aim at a self-sufficient Life, but he will find no encouragement in Nature. The Life of the body may complete itself in the physical world; that is its legitimate Environment. The Life of the senses, high and low, may perfect itself in Nature. Even the Life of thought may find a large complement in surrounding things. But the higher thought, and the conscience, and the religious Life, can only perfect themselves in God. To make the influence of Environment stop with the natural world is to doom the spiritual nature to death. For the soul, like the body, can never perfect itself in isolation. The law for both is to be complete in the appropriate Environment. And the perfection to be sought in the spiritual world is a perfection of relation, a perfect adjustment of that which is becoming perfect to that which is perfect.

The third problem, now simplified to a point, finally presents itself. Where do organism and Environment meet? How does that which is becoming perfect avail itself of its perfecting Environment? And the answer is, just as in Nature. The condition is simple receptivity. And yet this is perhaps the least simple of all conditions. It is so simple that we will not act upon it. But there is no other condition. Christ has condensed the whole truth into one memorable sentence, "As the branch cannot bear fruit of itself except it abide in the vine, no more can ye except ye abide in Me." And on the positive side, "He that abideth in Me the same bringeth forth much fruit."

CONFORMITY TO TYPE.

> "'So careful of the type?' but no.
>   From scarpèd cliff and quarried stone
>   She cries, 'A thousand types are gone:
> I care for nothing, all shall go.
>
> 'Thou makest thine appeal to me;
>   I bring to life, I bring to death:
>   The spirit does but mean thy breath:
> I know no more.' And he, shall he,
>
> Man, her last work, who seem'd so fair,
>   Such splendid purpose in his eyes,
>   Who roll'd the psalm to wintry skies,
> Who built him fanes of fruitless prayer,
>
> Who trusted God was love indeed
>   And love Creation's final law—
>   Tho' Nature, red in tooth and claw
> With ravine, shriek'd against his creed—
>
> Who loved, who suffer'd countless ills,
>   Who battled for the True, the Just,
>   Be blown about the desert dust
> Or seal'd within the iron hills?"
>   —*In Memoriam.*

"Until Christ be formed in you."—*Paul.*

"The one end to which, in all living beings, the formative impulse is tending—the one scheme which the Archæus of the old speculators strives to carry out, seems to be to mould the offspring into the likeness of the parent. It is the first great law of reproduction, that the offspring tends to resemble its parent or parents more closely than anything else."—*Huxley.*

If a botanist be asked the difference between an oak, a palm-tree and a lichen, he will declare that they are separated from one another by the broadest line known to classification. Without taking into account the outward differences of size and form, the variety of flower and fruit, the peculiarities of leaf and branch, he sees even in their general architecture types of structure as distinct as Norman, Gothic and Egyptian. But if the first young germs of these three plants are placed before him and he is called upon to define the difference, he finds it impossible. He cannot even say which is which. Examined under the highest powers of the microscope they yield no clue. Analyzed by the chemist with all the appliances of his laboratory they keep their secret.

The same experiment can be tried with the embryos of animals. Take the ovule of the worm, the eagle, the elephant, and of man himself. Let the most skilled observer apply the most searching tests to distinguish one from the other and he will fail. But there is something more surprising still. Compare next the two sets of germs, the vegetable and the animal. And there is still no shade of difference. Oak and palm, worm and man all start in life together. No matter into what strangely different forms they may afterward develop, no matter whether they are to live on sea or land, creep or fly, swim or walk, think or vegetate, in the embryo as it first meets the eye of Science they are indistinguishable. The apple which fell in Newton's garden, Newton's dog Diamond, and Newton himself, began life at the same point.[85]

If we analyze this material point at which all life starts, we shall find it to consist of a clear structureless jelly-like substance resembling albumen or white of egg. It is made of Carbon, Hydrogen, Oxygen and Nitrogen. Its name is protoplasm. And it is not only the structural unit with which all living bodies start in life, but with which they are subsequently built up. "Protoplasm," says Huxley, "simple or nucleated, is the formal basis of all life. It is the clay of the Potter." "Beast and fowl, reptile and fish, mollusk, worm and polype are all composed of structural units of the same character, namely, masses of protoplasm with a nucleus."[86]

What then determines the difference between different animals? What makes one little speck of protoplasm grow into Newton's dog Diamond, and another, exactly the same, into Newton himself? It is a mysterious something which has entered into this protoplasm. No eye can see it. No science can define it. There is a different something for Newton's dog and a different something for Newton; so that though both use the same matter they build it up in these widely different ways. Protoplasm being the clay, this something is the Potter. And as there is only one clay and yet all these curious forms are developed out of it, it follows necessarily that the difference lies in the potters. There must in short be as many potters as there are forms. There is the potter who segments the worm, and the potter who builds up the form of the dog, and the potter who moulds the man. To understand unmistakably that it is really the potter who does the work, let us follow for a moment a description of the process by a trained eye-witness. The observer is Mr. Huxley. Through the tube of his microscope he is watching the development, out of a speck of protoplasm, of one of the commonest animals: "Strange possibilities," he says, "lie dormant in that semi-fluid globule. Let a moderate supply of warmth reach its watery cradle and the plastic matter undergoes changes so rapid and yet so steady and purposelike in their succession that one can only compare them to those operated by a skilled modeler upon a formless lump of clay. As with an invisible trowel the mass is divided and subdivided into smaller and smaller portions, until it is reduced to an aggregation of granules not too large to build withal the finest fabrics of the nascent organism. And, then, it is as if a delicate finger traced out the line to be occupied by the spinal column, and moulded the contour of the body; pinching up the head at one end, the tail at the other, and fashioning flank and limb into due proportions in so artistic a way, that, after watching the process hour by hour, one is almost involuntarily possessed by the notion, that some more subtle aid to vision than an achromatic would show the hidden artist, with his plan before him, striving with skillful manipulation to perfect his work."[87]

Besides the fact, so luminously brought out here, that the artist is distinct from the "semi-fluid globule" of protoplasm in which he works, there is this other essential point to notice, that in all his "skillful manipulation" the artist is not working at random, but according to law. He has "his plan before him." In the zoological laboratory of Nature it is not as in a workshop where a skilled artisan can turn his hand to anything—where the same potter one day moulds a dog, the next a bird, and the next a man. In Nature one potter is set apart to make each. It is a more complete system of division of labor. One artist makes all the dogs, another makes all the birds, a third makes all the men. Moreover, each artist confines himself exclusively to working out his own plan. He appears to have his own plan somehow stamped upon himself, and his work is rigidly to reproduce himself.

The Scientific Law by which this takes place is the Law of Conformity to Type. It is contained, to a large extent, in the ordinary Law of Inheritance; or it may be considered as simply another way of stating what Darwin calls the Laws of Unity of Type. Darwin defines it thus: "By Unity of Type is meant that fundamental agreement in structure which we see in organic beings of the same class, and which is quite independent of their habits of life."[88] According to this law every living thing that comes into the world is compelled to stamp upon its offspring the image of itself. The dog, according to its type, produces a dog; the bird a bird.

The artist who operates upon matter in this subtle way and carries out this law is Life. There are a great many different kinds of Life. If one might give the broader meaning to the words of the apostle: "All life is not the same life. There is one kind of life of men, another life of beasts, another of fishes, and another of birds." There is the Life, or the Artist, or the Potter who segments the worm, the potter who forms the dog, the potter who moulds the man.[89]

What goes on then in the animal kingdom is this—the Bird-Life seizes upon the bird-germ and builds it up into a bird, the image of itself. The Reptile Life seizes upon another germinal speck, assimilates surrounding matter, and fashions it into a reptile. The Reptile-Life thus simply makes an incarnation of itself. The visible bird is simply an incarnation of the invisible Bird-Life.

Now we are nearing the point where the spiritual analogy appears. It is a very wonderful analogy, so wonderful that one almost hesitates to put it into words. Yet Nature is reverent; and it is her voice to which we listen. These lower phenomena of life, she says, are but an allegory. There is another kind of Life of which Science as yet has taken little cognizance. It obeys the same laws. It builds up an organism into its own form. It is the Christ-Life. As the Bird-Life builds up a bird, the image of itself, so the Christ-Life builds up a Christ, the image of Himself, in the inward nature of man. When a man becomes a Christian the natural process is this: The Living Christ enters into his soul. Development begins. The quickening Life seizes upon the soul, assimilates surrounding elements, and begins to fashion it. According to the great Law of Conformity to Type this fashioning takes a specific form. It is that of the Artist who fashions. And all through Life this wonderful, mystical, glorious, yet perfectly definite process, goes on "until Christ be formed" in it.

The Christian Life is not a vague effort after righteousness—an ill-defined pointless struggle for an ill-defined pointless end. Religion is no dishevelled mass of aspiration, prayer, and faith. There is no more mystery in Religion as to its processes than in Biology. There is much mystery in Biology. We know all but nothing of Life yet, nothing of development. There is the same mystery in the spiritual Life. But the great lines are the same, as decided, as luminous; and the laws of natural and spiritual are the same, as unerring, as simple. Will everything else in the natural world unfold its order, and yield to Science more and more a vision of harmony, and Religion, which should complement and perfect all, remain a chaos? From the standpoint of Revelation no truth is more obscure than Conformity to Type. If Science can furnish a companion phenomenon from an every-day process of the natural life, it may at least throw this most mystical doctrine of Christianity into thinkable form. Is there any fallacy in speaking of the Embryology of the New Life? Is the analogy invalid? Are there not vital processes in the Spiritual as well as in the Natural world? The Bird being an incarnation of the Bird-Life, may not the Christian be a spiritual incarnation of the Christ-Life? And is here not a real justification in the processes of the New-Birth for such a parallel?

Let us appeal to the record of these processes.

In what terms does the New Testament describe them? The answer is sufficiently striking. It uses everywhere the language of Biology. It is impossible that the New Testament writers should have been familiar with these biological facts. It is impossible that their views of this great truth should have been as clear as Science can make them now. But they had no alternative. There was no other way of expressing this truth. It was a biological question. So they struck out unhesitatingly into the new fields of words, and, with an originality which commands both reverence and surprise, stated their truth with such light, or darkness, as they had. They did not mean to be scientific, only to be accurate, and their fearless accuracy has made them scientific.

What could be more original, for instance, than the Apostle's reiteration that the Christian was a new creature, a new man, a babe?[90] Or that this new man was "begotten of God," God's workmanship?[91] And what could be a more accurate expression of the law of Conformity to Type than this: "Put on the new man, which is renewed in knowledge after the image of Him that created him?"[92] Or this, "We are changed into the same image from glory to glory?"[93] And elsewhere we are expressly told by the same writer that this Conformity is the end and goal of the Christian life. To work this Type in us is the whole purpose of God for man. "Whom He did foreknow He also did predestinate to be conformed to the image of His Son."[94]

One must confess that the originality of this entire New Testament conception is most startling. Even for the nineteenth century it is the most startling. But when one remembers that such an idea took form in the first, one cannot fail to be impressed with a deepening wonder at the system which begat and cherished it. Men seek the origin of Christianity among philosophies of that age. Scholars contrast it still with these philosophies, and scheme to fit it in to those of later growth. Has it never occurred to them how much more it is than a philosophy, that it includes a science, a Biology pure and simple? As well might naturalists contrast zoology with chemistry, or seek to incorporate geology with botany—the living with the dead—as try to explain the spiritual life in terms of mind alone. When will it be seen that the characteristic of the Christian Religion is its Life, that a true theology must begin with a Biology? Theology is the Science of God. Why will men treat God as inorganic?

If this analogy is capable of being worked out, we should expect answers to at least three questions.

First: What corresponds to the protoplasm in the spiritual sphere?

Second: What is the Life, the Hidden Artist who fashions it?

Third: What do we know of the process and the plan?

First: The Protoplasm.

We should be forsaking the lines of nature were we to imagine for a moment that the new creature was to be found out of nothing. *Ex nihilo nihil*—nothing can be made out of nothing. Matter is uncreatable and indestructible; Nature and man can only form and transform. Hence when a new animal is made, no new clay is made. Life merely enters into already existing matter, assimilates more of the same sort and re-builds it. The spiritual Artist works in the same way. He must have a peculiar kind of protoplasm, a basis of life, and that must be already existing.

Now we find this in the materials of character with which the natural man is previously provided. Mind and character, the will and the affections, the moral nature—these form the bases of spiritual life. To look in this direction for the protoplasm of the spiritual life is consistent with all analogy. The lowest or mineral world mainly supplies the material—and this is true even for insectivorous species—for the vegetable kingdom. The vegetable supplies the material for the animal. Next in turn, the animal furnishes material for the mental, and lastly the mental for the spiritual. Each member of the series is complete only when the steps below it are complete; the highest demands all. It is not necessary for the immediate purpose to go so far into the psychology either of the new creature or of the old as to define more clearly what these moral bases are. It is enough to discover that in this womb the new creature is to be born, fashioned out of the mental and moral parts, substance, or essence of the natural man. The only thing to be insisted upon is that in the natural man this mental and moral substance or basis is spiritually lifeless. However active the intellectual or moral life may be, from the point of view of this other Life it is dead. That which is flesh is flesh. It wants, that is to say, the kind of Life which constitutes the difference between the Christian and the not-a-Christian. It has not yet been "born of the Spirit."

To show further that this protoplasm possesses the necessary properties of a normal protoplasm it will be necessary to examine in passing what these properties are. They are two in number, the capacity for life and plasticity. Consider first the capacity for life. It is not enough to find an adequate supply of material. That must be of the right kind. For all kinds of matter have not the power to be the vehicle of life—all kinds of matter are not even fitted to be the vehicle of electricity. What peculiarity there is in Carbon, Hydrogen, Oxygen, and Nitrogen, when combined in a certain way, to receive life, we cannot tell. We only know that life is always associated in Nature with this particular physical basis and never with any other. But we are not in the same darkness with regard to the moral protoplasm. When we look at this complex combination which we have predicted as the basis of spiritual life, we do find something which gives it a peculiar qualification for being the protoplasm of the Christ-Life. We discover one strong reason at least, not only why this kind of life should be associated with this kind of protoplasm, but why it should never be associated with other kinds which seem to resemble it—why, for instance, this spiritual life should not be engrafted upon the intelligence of a dog or the instincts of an ant.

The protoplasm in man has a something in addition to its instincts or its habits. It has a capacity for God. In this capacity for God lies its receptivity; it is the very protoplasm that was necessary. The chamber is not only ready to receive the new Life, but the Guest is expected, and, till He comes, is missed. Till then the soul longs and yearns, wastes and pines, waving its tentacles piteously in the empty air, feeling after God if so be that it may find Him. This is not peculiar to the protoplasm of the Christian's soul. In every land and in every age there have been altars to the Known or Unknown God. It is now agreed as a mere question of anthropology that the universal language of the human soul has always been "I perish with hunger." This is what fits it for Christ. There is a grandeur in this cry from the depths which makes its very unhappiness sublime.

The other quality we are to look for in the soul is mouldableness, plasticity. Conformity demands conformability. Now plasticity is not only a marked characteristic of all forms of life, but in a special sense of the highest forms. It increases steadily as we rise in the scale. The inorganic world, to begin with, is rigid. A crystal of silica dissolved and redissolved a thousand times will never assume any other form than the hexagonal. The plant next, though plastic in its elements, is comparatively insusceptible of change. The very fixity of its sphere, the imprisonment for life in a single spot of earth, is the symbol of a certain degradation. The animal in all parts is mobile, sensitive, free; the highest animal, man, is the most mobile, the most at leisure from routine, the most impressionable, the most open for change. And when we reach the mind and soul, this mobility is found in its most developed form. Whether we regard its susceptibility to impressions, its lightning-like response even to influences the most impalpable and subtle, its power of instantaneous adjustment, or whether we regard the delicacy and variety of its moods, or its vast powers of growth, we are forced to recognize in this the most perfect capacity for change. This marvellous plasticity of mind contains at once the possibility and prophecy of its transformation. The soul, in a word, is made to be *converted*.

Second: The Life.

The main reason for giving the Life, the agent of this change, a separate treatment, is to emphasize the distinction between it and the natural man on the one hand, and the spiritual man on the other. The natural man is its basis, the spiritual man is its product, the Life itself is something different. Just as in an organism we have these three things—formative matter, formed matter, and the forming principle or life; so in the soul we have the old nature, the renewed nature, and the transforming Life.

This being made evident, little remains here to be added. No man has ever seen this Life. It cannot be analyzed, or weighed, or traced in its essential nature. But this is just what we expected. This invisibility is the same property which we found to be peculiar to the natural life. We saw no life in the first embryos, in oak, in palm, or in bird. In the adult it likewise escapes us. We shall not wonder if we cannot see it in the Christian. We shall not expect to see it. *A fortiori* we shall not expect to see it, for we are further removed from the coarser matter—moving now among ethereal and spiritual things. It is because it conforms to the law of this analogy so well that men, not seeing it, have denied its being. Is it hopeless to point out that one of the most recognizable characteristics of life is its unrecognizableness, and that the very token of its spiritual nature lies in its being beyond the grossness of our eyes?

We do not pretend that Science can define this Life to be Christ. It has no definition to give even of its own life, much less of this. But there are converging lines which point, at least, in the direction that it is Christ. There was One whom history acknowledges to have been the Truth. One of His claims was this, "I am the Life." According to the doctrine of Biogenesis, life can only come from life. It was His additional claim that His function in the world was to give men Life. "I am come that ye might have Life, and that ye might have it more abundantly." This could not refer to the natural life, for men had that already. He that hath the Son hath another Life. "Know ye not your own selves how that Jesus Christ is in you."

Again, there are men whose characters assume a strange resemblance to Him who was the Life. When we see the bird-character appear in an organism we assume that the Bird-Life has been there at work. And when we behold Conformity to Type in a Christian, and know moreover that the type-organization can be produced by the type-life alone does this not lend support to the hypothesis that the Type-Life also has been here at work? If every effect demands a cause, what other cause is there for the Christian? When we have a cause, and an adequate cause, and no other adequate cause; when we have the express statement of that Cause that he is that cause, what more is possible? Let not Science, knowing nothing of its own life, go further than to say it knows nothing of this Life. We shall not dissent from its silence. But till it tells us what it is, we wait for evidence that it is not this.

Third: The Process.

It is impossible to enter at length into any details of the great miracle by which this protoplasm is to be conformed to the Image of the Son. We enter that province now only so far as this Law of Conformity compels us. Nor is it so much the nature of the process we have to consider as its general direction and results. We are dealing with a question of morphology rather than of physiology.

It must occur to one on reaching this point, that a new element here comes in which compels us, for the moment, to part company with zoology. That element is the conscious power of choice. The animal in following the type is blind. It does not only follow the type involuntarily and compulsorily, but does not know that it is following it. We might certainly have been made to conform to the Type in the higher sphere with no more knowledge or power of choice than animals or automata. But then we should not have been men. It is a possible case, but not possible to the kind of protoplasm with which men are furnished. Owing to the peculiar characteristics of this protoplasm an additional and exceptional provision is essential.

The first demand is that being conscious and having this power of choice, the mind should have an adequate knowledge of what it is to choose. Some revelation of the Type, that is to say, is necessary. And as that revelation can only come from the Type, we must look there for it.

We are confronted at once with the Incarnation. There we find how the Christ-Life has clothed Himself with matter, taken literal flesh, and dwelt among us. The Incarnation is the Life revealing the Type. Men are long since agreed that this is the end of the Incarnation—the revealing of God. But why should God be revealed? Why, indeed, but for man? Why but that "beholding as in a glass the glory of the only begotten we should be changed into the same image?"

To meet the power of choice, however, something more was necessary than the mere revelation of the Type—it was necessary that the Type should be the highest conceivable Type. In other words, the Type must be an Ideal. For all true human growth, effort, and achievement, an ideal is acknowledged to be indispensable. And all men accordingly whose lives are based on principle, have set themselves an ideal, more or less perfect. It is this which first deflects the will from what is based, and turns the wayward life to what is holy. So much is true as mere philosophy. But philosophy failed to present men with their ideal. It has never been suggested that Christianity has failed. Believers and unbelievers have been compelled to acknowledge that Christianity holds up to the world the missing Type, the Perfect Man.

The recognition of the Ideal is the first step in the direction of Conformity. But let it be clearly observed that it is but a step. There is no vital connection between merely seeing the Ideal and being conformed to it. Thousands admire Christ who never become Christians.

But the great question still remains, How is the Christian to be conformed to the Type, or as we should now say, dealing with consciousness, to the Ideal? The mere knowledge of the Ideal is no more than a motive. How is the process to be practically accomplished? Who is to do it? Where, when, how? This is the test question of Christianity. It is here that all theories of Christianity, all attempts to explain it on natural principles, all reductions of it to philosophy, inevitably break down. It is here that all imitations of Christianity perish. It is here, also, that personal religion finds its most fatal obstacle. Men are all quite clear about the Ideal. We are all convinced of the duty of mankind regarding it. But how to secure that willing men shall attain it—that is the problem of religion. It is the failure to understand the dynamics of Christianity that has most seriously and most pitifully hindered its growth both in the individual and in the race.

From the standpoint of biology this practical difficulty vanishes in a moment. It is probably the very simplicity of the law regarding it that has made men stumble. For nothing is so invisible to most men as transparency. The law here is the same biological law that exists in the natural world. For centuries men have striven to find out ways and means to conform themselves to this type. Impressive motives have been pictured, the proper circumstances arranged, the direction of effort defined, and men have toiled, struggled, and agonized to conform themselves to the Image of the Son. Can the protoplasm *conform itself* to its type? Can the embryo *fashion itself*? Is Conformity to Type produced by the matter *or by the life*, by the protoplasm or by the Type? Is organization the cause of life or the effect of it? It is the effect of it. Conformity to Type, therefore, is secured by the type. Christ makes the Christian.

Men need only reflect on the automatic processes of their natural body to discover that this is the universal law of Life. What does any man consciously do, for instance, in the matter of breathing? What part does he take in circulating the blood, in keeping up the rhythm of his heart? What control has he over growth? What man by taking thought can add a cubit to his stature? What part voluntarily does man take in secretion, in digestion, in the reflex actions? In point of fact is he not after all the veriest automaton, every organ of his body given him, every function arranged for him, brain and nerve, thought and sensation, will and conscience, all provided for him ready made? And yet he turns upon his soul and wishes to organize that himself! O preposterous and vain man, thou who couldest not make a finger-nail of thy body, thinkest thou to fashion this wonderful, mysterious, subtle soul of thine after the ineffable Image? Wilt thou ever permit thyself *to be* conformed to the Image of the Son? Wilt thou, who canst not add a cubit to thy stature, submit *to be* raised by the Type-Life within thee to the perfect stature of Christ?

This is a humbling conclusion. And therefore men will resent it. Men will still experiment "by works of righteousness which they have done" to earn the Ideal life. The doctrine of Human Inability, as the Church calls it, has always been objectionable to men who do not know themselves. The doctrine itself, perhaps, has been partly to blame. While it has been often affirmed in such language as rightly to humble men, it has also been stated and cast in their teeth with words which could only insult them. Merely to assert dogmatically that man has no power to move hand or foot to help himself toward Christ, carries no real conviction. The weight of human authority is always powerless, and ought to be, where the intelligence is denied a rationale. In the light of modern science when men seek a reason for every thought of God or man, this old doctrine with its severe and almost inhuman aspect—till rightly understood—must presently have succumbed. But to the biologist it cannot die. It stands to him on the solid ground of Nature. It has a reason in the laws of life which must resuscitate it and give it another lease of years. Bird-Life makes the Bird. Christ-Life makes the Christian. No man by taking thought can add a cubit to his stature.

So much for the scientific evidence. Here is the corresponding statement of the truth from Scripture. Observe the passive voice in these sentences: "*Begotten* of God;" "The new man which *is renewed* in knowledge after the Image of Him that created him;" or this, "We *are changed* into the same Image;" or this, "Predestinate *to be conformed* to the Image of His Son;" or again, "Until Christ *be formed* in you;" or "Except a man *be born again* he cannot see the Kingdom of God;" "Except a man *be born* of water and of the Spirit he cannot enter the Kingdom of God." There is one outstanding verse which seems at first sight on the other side: "Work out your own salvation with fear and trembling;" but as one reads on he finds, as if the writer dreaded the very misconception, the complement, "For it is God which worketh in you both to will and to do of His good pleasure."

It will be noticed in these passages, and in others which might be named, that the process of transformation is referred indifferently to the agency of each Person of the Trinity in turn. We are not concerned to take up this question of detail. It is sufficient that the transformation is wrought. Theologians, however, distinguish thus: the indirect agent is Christ, the direct influence is the Holy Spirit. In other words, Christ by his Spirit renews the souls of men.

Is man, then, out of the arena altogether? Is he mere clay in the hands of the potter, a machine, a tool, an automaton? Yes and No. If he were a tool he would not be a man. If he were a man he would have something to do. One need not seek to balance what God does here, and what man does. But we shall attain to a sufficient measure of truth on a most delicate problem if we make a final appeal to the natural life. We find that in maintaining this natural life Nature has a share and man has a share. By far the larger part is done for us—the breathing, the secreting, the circulating of the blood, the building up of the organism. And although the part which man plays is a minor part, yet, strange to say, it is not less essential to the well being, and even to the being, of the whole. For instance, man has to take food. He has nothing to do with it after he has once taken it, for the moment it passes his lips it is taken in hand by reflex actions and handed on from one organ to another, his control over it, in the natural course of things, being completely lost. But the initial act was his. And without that nothing could have been done. Now whether there be an exact analogy between the voluntary and involuntary functions in the body, and the corresponding processes in the soul, we do not at present inquire. But this will indicate, at least, that man has his own part to play. Let him choose Life; let him daily nourish his soul; let him forever starve the old life; let him abide continuously as a living branch in the Vine, and the True-Vine Life will flow into his soul, assimilating, renewing, conforming to Type, till Christ, pledged by His own law, be formed in him.

We have been dealing with Christianity at its most mystical point. Mark here once more its absolute naturalness. The pursuit of the Type is just what all Nature is engaged in. Plant and insect, fish and reptile, bird and mammal—these in their several spheres are striving after the Type. To prevent its extinction, to ennoble it, to people earth and sea and sky with it; this is the meaning of the Struggle for Life. And this is our life—to pursue the Type, to populate the world with it.

Our religion is not all a mistake. We are not visionaries. We are not "unpractical," as men pronounce us, when we worship. To try to follow Christ is not to be "righteous overmuch." True men are not rhapsodizing when they preach; nor do those waste their lives who waste themselves in striving to extend the Kingdom of God on earth. This is what life is for. The Christian in his life-aim is in strict line with Nature. What men call his supernatural is quite natural.

Mark well also the splendor of this idea of salvation. It is not merely final "safety," to be forgiven sin, to evade the curse. It is not, vaguely, "to get to heaven." It is to be conformed to the Image of the Son. It is for these poor elements to attain to the Supreme Beauty. The organizing Life being Eternal, so must this Beauty be immortal. Its progress toward the Immaculate is already guaranteed. And more than all there is here fulfilled the sublimest of all prophecies; not Beauty alone but Unity is secured by the Type—Unity of man and man, God and man, God and Christ and man till "all shall be one."

Could Science in its most brilliant anticipations for the future of its highest organism ever have foreshadowed a development like this? Now that the revelation is made to it, it surely recognizes it as the missing point in Evolution, the climax to which all Creation tends. Hitherto Evolution had no future. It was a pillar with marvelous carving, growing richer and finer toward the top, but without a capital; a pyramid, the vast base buried in the inorganic, towering higher and higher, tier above tier, life above life, mind above mind, ever more perfect in its workmanship, more noble in its symmetry, and yet withal so much the more mysterious in its aspiration. The most curious eye, following it upward, saw nothing. The cloud fell and covered it. Just what men wanted to see was hid. The work of the ages had no apex. But the work begun by Nature is finished by the Supernatural—as we are wont to call the higher natural. And as the veil is lifted by Christianity it strikes men dumb with wonder. For the goal of Evolution is Jesus Christ.

The Christian life is the only life that will ever be completed. Apart from Christ the life of man is a broken pillar, the race of men an unfinished pyramid. One by one in sight of Eternity all human Ideals fall short, one by one before the open grave all human hopes dissolve. The Laureate sees a moment's light in Nature's jealousy for the Type; but that too vanishes.

> "'So careful of the type?' but no.
>   From scarpèd cliff and quarried stone
>   She cries, 'A thousand types are gone:
> I care for nothing, all shall go.'"

All shall go? No, one Type remains. "Whom He did foreknow He also did predestinate to be conformed to the Image of His Son." And "when Christ who is our life shall appear, then shall ye also appear with Him in glory."

SEMI-PARASITISM.

> "The Situation that has not its Duty, its Ideal, was never yet occupied by man. Yes, here, in this poor, miserable, hampered, despicable Actual, wherein thou even now standest, here or nowhere is thy Ideal: work it out therefrom; and working, believe, live, be free."—*Carlyle.*
>
> "Work out your own salvation."—*Paul.*
>
> "Any new set of conditions occurring to an animal which render its food and safety very easily attained, seem to lead as a rule to degeneration."—*E. Ray Lankester.*

Parasites are the paupers of Nature. They are forms of life which will not take the trouble to find their own food, but borrow or steal it from the more industrious. So deep-rooted is this tendency in Nature, that plants may become parasitic—it is an acquired habit—as well as animals; and both are found in every state of beggary, some doing a little for themselves, while others, more abject, refuse even to prepare their own food.

There are certain plants—the Dodder, for instance—which begin life with the best intentions, strike true roots into the soil, and really appear as if they meant to be independent for life. But after supporting themselves for a brief period they fix curious sucking discs into the stem and branches of adjacent plants. And after a little experimenting, the epiphyte finally ceases to do anything for its own support, thenceforth drawing all its supplies ready-made from the sap of its host. In this parasitic state it has no need for organs of nutrition of its own, and Nature therefore takes them away. Henceforth, to the botanist, the adult Dodder presents the degraded spectacle of a plant without a root, without a twig, without a leaf, and having a stem so useless as to be inadequate to bear its own weight.

In the Mistletoe the parasitic habit has reached a stage in some respects lower still. It has persisted in the downward course for so many generations that the young forms even have acquired the habit and usually begin life at once as parasites. The Mistletoe berries, which contain the seed of the future plant, are developed especially to minister to this degeneracy, for they glue themselves to the branches of some neighboring oak or apple, and there the young Mistletoe starts as a dependent from the first.

Among animals these *lazzaroni* are more largely represented still. Almost every animal is a living poor-house, and harbors one or more species of *epizoa* or *entozoa*, supplying them gratis, not only with a permanent home, but with all the necessaries and luxuries of life.

Why does the naturalist think hardly of the parasites? Why does he speak of them as degraded, and despise them as the most ignoble creatures in Nature? What more can an animal do than eat, drink, and die to-morrow? If under the fostering care and protection of a higher organism it can eat better, drink more easily, live more merrily, and die, perhaps, not till the day after, why should it not do so? Is parasitism, after all, not a somewhat clever *ruse*? Is it not an ingenious way of securing the benefits of life while evading its responsibilities? And although this mode of livelihood is selfish, and possibly undignified, can it be said that it is immoral?

The naturalist's reply to this is brief. Parasitism, he will say, is one of the gravest crimes in Nature. It is a breach of the law of Evolution. Thou shalt evolve, thou shalt develop all thy faculties to the full, thou shalt attain to the highest conceivable perfection of thy race—and so perfect thy race—this is the first and greatest commandment of nature. But the parasite has no thought for its race, or for perfection in any shape or form. It wants two things—food and shelter. How it gets them is of no moment. Each member lives exclusively on its own account, an isolated, indolent, selfish, and backsliding life.

The remarkable thing is that Nature permits the community to be taxed in this way apparently without protest. For the parasite is a consumer pure and simple. And the "Perfect Economy of Nature" is surely for once at fault when it encourages species numbered by thousands which produce nothing for their own or for the general good, but live, and live luxuriously, at the expense of others?

Now when we look into the matter, we very soon perceive that instead of secretly countenancing this ingenious device by which parasitic animals and plants evade the great law of the Struggle for Life, Nature sets her face most sternly against it. And, instead of allowing the transgressors to slip through her fingers, as one might at first suppose, she visits upon them the most severe and terrible penalties. The parasite, she argues, not only injures itself, but wrongs others. It disobeys the fundamental law of its own being, and taxes the innocent to contribute to its disgrace. So that if Nature is just, if Nature has an avenging hand, if she holds one vial of wrath more full and bitter than another, it shall surely be poured out upon those who are guilty of this double sin. Let us see what form this punishment takes.

Observant visitors to the sea-side, or let us say to an aquarium, are familiar with those curious little creatures known as Hermit-crabs. The peculiarity of the Hermits is that they take up their abode in the cast-off shell of some other animal, not unusually the whelk; and here, like Diogenes in his tub, the creature lives a solitary, but by no means an inactive life.

The *Pagurus*, however, is not a parasite. And yet although in no sense of the word a parasite, this way of inhabiting throughout life a house built by another animal approaches so closely the parasitic habit, that we shall find it instructive as a preliminary illustration, to consider the effect of this free-house policy on the occupant. There is no doubt, to begin with, that, as has been already indicated, the habit is an acquired one. In its general anatomy the Hermit is essentially a crab. Now the crab is an animal which, from the nature of its environment, has to lead a somewhat rough and perilous life. Its days are spent among jagged rocks and boulders. Dashed about by every wave, attacked on every side by monsters of the deep, the crustacean has to protect itself by developing a strong and serviceable coat of mail.

How best to protect themselves has been the problem to which the whole crab family have addressed themselves; and, in considering the matter, the ancestors of the Hermit-crab hit on the happy device of re-utilizing the habitations of the molluscs which lay around them in plenty, well-built, and ready for immediate occupation. For generations and generations accordingly, the Hermit-crab has ceased to exercise itself upon questions of safety, and dwells in its little shell as proudly and securely as if its second-hand house were a fortress erected especially for its private use.

Wherein, then, has the Hermit suffered for this cheap, but real solution of a practical difficulty? Whether its laziness costs it any moral qualms, or whether its cleverness becomes to it a source of congratulation, we do not know; but judged from the appearance the animal makes under the searching gaze of the zoologist, its expedient is certainly not one to be commended. To the eye of Science its sin is written in the plainest characters on its very organization. It has suffered in its own anatomical structure just by as much as it has borrowed from an external source. Instead of being a perfect crustacean it has allowed certain important parts of its body to deteriorate. And several vital organs are partially or wholly atrophied.

Its sphere of life also is now seriously limited; and by a cheap expedient to secure safety, it has fatally lost its independence. It is plain from its anatomy that the Hermit-crab was not always a Hermit-crab. It was meant for higher things. Its ancestors doubtless were more or less perfect crustaceans, though what exact stage of development was reached before the hermit habit became fixed in the species we cannot tell. But from the moment the creature took to relying on an external source, it began to fall. It slowly lost in its own person all that it now draws from external aid.

As an important item in the day's work, namely, the securing of safety and shelter, was now guaranteed to it, one of the chief inducements to a life of high and vigilant effort was at the same time withdrawn. A number of functions, in fact, struck work. The whole of the parts, therefore, of the complex organism which ministered to these functions, from lack of exercise, or total disuse, became gradually feeble; and ultimately, by the stern law that an unused organ must suffer a slow but inevitable atrophy, the creature not only lost all power of motion in these parts, but lost the parts themselves, and otherwise sank into a relatively degenerate condition.

Every normal crustacean, on the other hand, has the abdominal region of the body covered by a thick chitinous shell. In the Hermits this is represented only by a thin and delicate membrane—of which the sorry figure the creature cuts when drawn from its foreign hiding-place is sufficient evidence. Any one who now examines further this half-naked and woe-begone object, will perceive also that the fourth and fifth pair of limbs are either so small and wasted as to be quite useless or altogether rudimentary; and, although certainly the additional development of the extremity of the tail into an organ for holding on to its extemporized retreat may be regarded as a slight compensation, it is clear from the whole structure of the animal that it has allowed itself to undergo severe Degeneration.

In dealing with the Hermit-crab, in short, we are dealing with a case of physiological backsliding. That the creature has lost anything by this process from a practical point of view is not now argued. It might fairly be shown, as already indicated, that its freedom is impaired by its cumbrous exoskeleton, and that, in contrast with other crabs, who lead a free and roving life, its independence generally is greatly limited. But from the physiological standpoint, there is no question that the Hermit tribe have neither discharged their responsibilities to Nature nor to themselves. If the end of life is merely to escape death, and serve themselves, possibly they have done well; but if it is to attain an ever increasing perfection, then are they backsliders indeed.

A zoologist's verdict would be that by this act they have forfeited to some extent their place in the animal scale. An animal is classed as a low or high according as it is adapted to less or more complex conditions of life. This is the true standpoint from which to judge all living organisms. Were perfection merely a matter of continual eating and drinking, the Amœba— the lowest known organism—might take rank with the highest, Man, for the one nourishes itself and saves its skin almost as completely as the other. But judged by the higher standard of Complexity, that is, by greater or lesser adaption to more or less complex conditions, the gulf between them is infinite.

We have now received a preliminary idea, although not from the study of a true parasite, of the essential principles involved in parasitism. And we may proceed to point out the correlative in the moral and spiritual spheres. We confine ourselves for the present to one point. The difference between the Hermit-crab and a true parasite is, that the former has acquired a semi-parasitic habit only with reference to *safety*. It may be that the Hermit devours as a preliminary the accommodating mollusc whose tenement it covets; but it would become a real parasite only on the supposition that the whelk was of such size as to keep providing for it throughout life, and that the external and internal organs of the crab should disappear, while it lived henceforth, by simple imbibition, upon the elaborated juices of its host. All the mollusc provides, however, for the crustacean in this instance is safety, and, accordingly in the meantime we limit our application to this. The true parasite presents us with an organism so much more degraded in all its parts, that its lessons may well be reserved until we have paved the way to understand the deeper bearings of the subject.

The spiritual principle to be illustrated in the meantime stands thus: *Any principle which secures the safety of the individual without personal effort or the vital exercise of faculty is disastrous to moral character.* We do not begin by attempting to define words. Were we to define truly what is meant by safety or salvation, we should be spared further elaboration, and the law would stand out as a sententious common-place. But we have to deal with the ideas of safety as these are popularly held, and the chief purpose at this stage is to expose what may be called the Parasitic Doctrine of Salvation. The phases of religious experience about to be described may be unknown to many. It remains for those who are familiar with the religious conceptions of the masses to determine whether or not we are wasting words.

What is meant by the Parasitic Doctrine of Salvation one may, perhaps, best explain by sketching two of its leading types. The first is the doctrine of the Church of Rome; the second, that represented by the narrower Evangelical Religion. We take these religions, however, not in their ideal form, with which possibly we should have little quarrel, but in their practical working, or in the form in which they are held especially by the rank and file of those who belong respectively to these communions. For the strength or weakness of any religious system is best judged from the form in which it presents itself to, and influences the common mind.

No more perfect or more sad example of semi-parasitism exists than in the case of those illiterate thousands who, scattered everywhere throughout the habitable globe, swell the lower ranks of the Church of Rome. Had an organization been specially designed, indeed, to induce the parasitic habit in the souls of men, nothing better fitted to its disastrous end could be established than the system of Roman Catholicism. Roman Catholicism offers to the masses a molluscan shell. They have simply to shelter themselves within its pale, and they are "safe." But what is this "safe?" It is an external safety—the safety of an institution. It is a salvation recommended to men by all that appeals to the motives in most common use with the vulgar and the superstitious, but which has as little vital connection with the individual soul as the dead whelk's shell with the living Hermit. Salvation is a relation at once vital, personal, and spiritual. This is mechanical and purely external. And this is of course the final secret of its marvelous success and world-wide power. A cheap religion is the desideratum of the human heart; and an assurance of salvation at the smallest possible cost forms the tempting bait held out to a conscience-stricken world by the Romish Church. Thousands, therefore, who have never been taught to use their faculties in "working out their own salvation," thousands who will not exercise themselves religiously, and who yet cannot be without the exercise of religion, intrust themselves in idle faith to that venerable house of refuge which for centuries has stood between God and man. A Church which has harbored generations of the elect, whose archives enshrine the names of saints whose foundations are consecrated with martyrs' blood—shall it not afford a sure asylum still for any soul which would make its peace with God? So, as the Hermit into the molluscan shell, creeps the poor soul within the pale of Rome, seeking, like Adam in the garden, to hide its nakedness from God.

Why does the true lover of men restrain not his lips in warning his fellows against this and all other priestly religions? It is not because he fails to see the prodigious energy of the Papal See, or to appreciate the many noble types of Christian manhood nurtured within its pale. Nor is it because its teachers are often corrupt and its system of doctrine inadequate as a representation of the Truth—charges which have to be made more or less against all religions. But it is because it ministers falsely to the deepest need of man, reduces the end of religion to selfishness, and offers safety without spirituality. That these, theoretically, are its pretensions, we do not affirm; but that its practical working is to induce in man, and in its worst forms, the parasitic habit, is testified by results. No one who has studied the religion of the Continent upon the spot, has failed to be impressed with the appalling spectacle of tens of thousands of unregenerated men sheltering themselves, as they conceive it for Eternity, behind the Sacraments of Rome.

There is no stronger evidence of the inborn parasitic tendency in man in things religious than the absolute complacency with which even cultured men will hand over their eternal interests to the care of a Church. We can never dismiss from memory the sadness with which we once listened to the confession of a certain foreign professor: "I used to be concerned about religion," he said in substance, "but religion is a great subject. I was very busy; there was little time to settle it for myself. A protestant, my attention was called to the Roman Catholic religion. It suited my case. And instead of dabbling in religion for myself I put myself in its hands. Once a year," he concluded, "I go to mass." These were the words of one whose work will live in the history of his country, one, too, who knew all about parasitism. Yet, though he thought it not, this is parasitism in its worst and most degrading form. Nor, in spite of its intellectual, not to say moral sin, is this an extreme or exceptional case. It is a case, which is being duplicated every day in our own country, only here the confessing is expressed with a candor which is rare in company with actions betraying so signally the want of it.

The form of parasitism exhibited by a certain section of the narrower Evangelical school is altogether different from that of the Church of Rome. The parasite in this case seeks its shelter, not in a Church, but in a Doctrine or a Creed. Let it be observed again that we are not dealing with the Evangelical Religion, but only with one of its parasitic forms—a form which will at once be recognized by all who know the popular Protestantism of this country. We confine ourselves also at present to that form which finds its encouragement in a single doctrine, that doctrine being the Doctrine of the Atonement—let us say, rather, a perverted form of this central truth.

The perverted Doctrine of the Atonement, which tends to beget the parasitic habit, may be defined in a single sentence—it is very much because it can be defined in a single sentence that it is a perversion. Let us state it in a concrete form. It is put to the individual in the following syllogism: "You believe Christ died for sinners; you are a sinner; therefore Christ died for you; *and hence you are saved.*" Now what is this but another species of molluscan shell? Could any trap for a benighted soul be more ingeniously planned? It is not superstition that is appealed to this time; it is reason. The agitated soul is invited to creep into the convolutions of a syllogism, and entrench itself behind a Doctrine more venerable even than the Church. But words are mere chitin. Doctrines may have no more vital contact with the soul than priest or sacrament, no further influence on life and character than stone and lime. And yet the apostles of parasitism pick a blackguard from the streets, pass him through this plausible formula, and turn him out a convert in the space of as many minutes as it takes to tell it.

The zeal of these men, assuredly, is not to be questioned: their instincts are right, and their work is often not in vain. It is possible, too, up to a certain point, to defend this Salvation by Formula. Are these not the very words of Scripture? Did not Christ Himself say, "It is finished?" And is it not written, "By grace are ye saved through faith," "Not of works, lest any man should boast," and "He that believeth on the Son hath everlasting life?" To which, however, one might also answer in the words of Scripture, "The Devils also believe," and "Except a man be born again he cannot see the Kingdom of God." But without seeming to make text refute text, let us ask rather what the supposed convert possesses at the end of the process. That Christ saves sinners, even blackguards from the streets, is a great fact; and that the simple words of the street evangelist do sometimes bring this home to man with convincing power is also a fact. But in ordinary circumstances, when the inquirer's mind is rapidly urged through the various stages of the above piece of logic, he is left to face the future and blot out the past with a formula of words.

To be sure these words may already convey a germ of truth, they may yet be filled in with a wealth of meaning and become a life-long power. But we would state the case against Salvation by Formula with ignorant and unwarranted clemency did we for a moment convey the idea that this is always the actual result. The doctrine plays too well into the hands of the parasitic tendency to make it possible that in more than a minority of cases the result is anything but disastrous. And it is disastrous not in that, sooner or later, after losing half their lives, those who rely on the naked syllogism come to see their mistake, but in that thousands never come to see it all. Are there not men who can prove to you and to the world, by the irresistible logic of texts, that they are saved, whom you know to be not only unworthy of the Kingdom of God—which we all are—but absolutely incapable of entering it? The condition of membership in the Kingdom of God is well known; who fulfill this condition and who do not, is not well known. And yet the moral test, in spite of the difficulty of its applications, will always, and rightly, be preferred by the world to the theological. Nevertheless, in spite of the world's verdict, the parasite is content. He is "safe." Years ago his mind worked through a certain chain of phrases in which the words "believe" and "saved" were the conspicuous terms. And from that moment, by all Scriptures, by all logic, and by all theology, his future was guaranteed. He took out, in short, an insurance policy, by which he was infallibly secured eternal life at death. This is not a matter to make light of. We wish we were caricaturing instead of representing things as they are. But we carry with us all who intimately know the spiritual condition of the Narrow Church in asserting that in some cases at least its members have nothing more to show for their religion than a formula, a syllogism, a cant phrase or an experience of some kind which happened long ago, and which men told them at the time was called Salvation. Need we proceed to formulate objections to the parasitism of Evangelicism? Between it and the Religion of the Church of Rome there is an affinity as real as it is unsuspected. For one thing these religions are spiritually disastrous as well as theologically erroneous in propagating a false conception of Christianity. The fundamental idea alike of the extreme Roman Catholic and extreme Evangelical Religions is Escape. Man's chief end is to "get off." And all factors in religion, the highest and most sacred, are degraded to this level. God, for example, is a Great Lawyer. Or He is the Almighty Enemy; it is from Him we have to "get off." Jesus Christ is the One who gets us off—a theological figure who contrives so to adjust matters federally that the way is clear. The Church in the one instance is a kind of conveyancing office where the transaction is duly concluded, each party accepting the others' terms; in the other case, a species of sheep-pen where the flock awaits impatiently and indolently the final consummation. Generally, the means are mistaken for the end, and the opening-up of the possibility of spiritual growth becomes the signal to stop growing.

Second, these being cheap religions, are inevitably accompanied by a cheap life. Safety being guaranteed from the first, there remains nothing else to be done. The mechanical way in which the transaction is effected, leaves the soul without stimulus, and the character remains untouched by the moral aspects of the sacrifice of Christ. He who is unjust is unjust still; he who is unholy is unholy still. Thus the whole scheme ministers to the Degeneration of Organs. For here, again, by just as much as the organism borrows mechanically from an external source, by so much exactly does it lose in its own organization. Whatever rest is provided by Christianity for the children of God, it is certainly never contemplated that it should supersede personal effort. And any rest which ministers to indifference is immoral and unreal—it makes parasites and not men. Just because God worketh in him, as the evidence and triumph of it, the true child of God works out his own salvation—works it out having really received it—not as a light thing, a superfluous labor, but with fear and trembling as a reasonable and indispensable service.

If it be asked, then, shall the parasite be saved or shall he not, the answer is that the idea of salvation conveyed by the question makes a reply all but hopeless. But if by salvation is meant, a trusting in Christ *in order to likeness to Christ,* in order to that *holiness* without which no man shall see the Lord, the reply is that the parasite's hope is absolutely vain. So far from ministering to growth, parasitism ministers to decay. So far from ministering to holiness, that is to *wholeness,* parasitism ministers to exactly the opposite. One by one the spiritual faculties droop and die, one by one from lack of exercise the muscles of the soul grow weak and flaccid, one by one the moral activities cease. So from him that hath not, is taken away that which he hath, and after a few years of parasitism there is nothing left to save.

If our meaning up to this point has been sufficiently obscure to make the objection now possible that this protest against Parasitism is opposed to the doctrines of Free Grace, we cannot hope in a closing sentence to free the argument from a suspicion so ill-judged. The adjustment between Faith and Works does not fall within our province now. Salvation truly is the free gift of God, but he who really knows how much this means knows—and just because it means so much—how much of consequent action it involves. With the central doctrines of grace the whole scientific argument is in too wonderful harmony to be found wanting here. The natural life, not less than the eternal, is the gift of God. But life in either case is the beginning of growth and not the end of grace. To pause where we should begin, to retrograde where we should advance, to seek a mechanical security that we may cover inertia and find a wholesale salvation in which there is no personal sanctification—this is Parasitism.

PARASITISM.

> "And so I live, you see,
> Go through the world, try, prove, reject,
> Prefer, still struggling to effect
> My warfare; happy that I can
> Be crossed and thwarted as a man,
> Not left in God's contempt apart,
> With ghastly smooth life, dead at heart,
> Tame in earth's paddock as her prize.
>
> ::
>
> Thank God, no paradise stands barred
> To entry, and I find it hard
> To be a Christian, as I said."—*Browning.*

"Work out your own salvation."—*Paul.*

"Be no longer a chaos, but a World, or even Worldkin. Produce! Produce! Were it but the pitifullest infinitesimal fraction of a Product, produce it, in God's name!"—*Carlyle.*

From a study of the habits and organization of the family of Hermit-crabs we have already gained some insight into the nature and effects of parasitism. But the Hermit-crab, be it remembered, is in no real sense a parasite. And before we can apply the general principle further we must address ourselves briefly to the examination of a true case of parasitism.

We have not far to seek. Within the body of the Hermit-crab a minute organism may frequently be discovered resembling, when magnified, a miniature kidney-bean. A bunch of root-like processes hangs from one side, and the extremities of these are seen to ramify in delicate films through the living tissues of the crab. This simple organism is known to the naturalist as a Sacculina; and though a full-grown animal, it consists of no more parts than those just named. Not a trace of structure is to be detected within this rude and all but inanimate frame; it possesses neither legs, nor eyes, nor mouth, nor throat, nor stomach, nor any other organs, external or internal. This Sacculina is a typical parasite. By means of its twining and theftuous roots it imbibes automatically its nourishment ready-prepared from the body of the crab. It boards indeed entirely at the expense of its host, who supplies it liberally with food and shelter and everything else it wants. So far as the result to itself is concerned this arrangement may seem at first sight satisfactory enough; but when we inquire into the life history of this small creature we unearth a career of degeneracy all but unparalleled in nature.

The most certain clue to what nature meant any animal to become is to be learned from its embryology. Let us, therefore, examine for a moment the earliest positive stage in the development of the Sacculina. When the embryo first makes its appearance it bears not the remotest resemblance to the adult animal. A different name even is given to it by the biologist, who knows it at this period as a Nauplius. This minute organism has an oval body, supplied with six well-jointed feet by means of which it paddles briskly through the water. For a time it leads an active and independent life, industriously securing its own food and escaping enemies by its own gallantry. But soon a change takes place. The hereditary taint of parasitism is in its blood, and it proceeds to adapt itself to the pauper habits of its race. The tiny body first doubles in upon itself, and from the two front limbs elongated filaments protrude. Its four hind limbs entirely disappear, and twelve short-forked swimming organs temporarily take their place. Thus strangely metamorphosed the Sacculina sets out in search of a suitable host, and in an evil hour, by that fate which is always ready to accommodate the transgressor, is thrown into the company of the Hermit-crab. With its two filamentary processes—which afterward develop into the root-like organs—it penetrates the body; the sac-like form is gradually assumed; the whole of the swimming feet drop off—they will never be needed again—and the animal settles down for the rest of its life as a parasite.

One reason which makes a zoologist certain that the Sacculina is a degenerate type is, that in almost all other instances of animals which begin life in the Nauplius-form—and there are several—the Nauplius develops through higher and higher stages, and arrives finally at the high perfection displayed by the shrimp, lobster, crab, and other crustaceans. But instead of rising to its opportunities, the sacculine Nauplius having reached a certain point turned back. It shrunk from the struggle for life, and beginning probably by seeking shelter from its host went on to demand its food; and so falling from bad to worse, became in time an entire dependant.

In the eyes of Nature this was a twofold crime. It was first a disregard of evolution, and second, which is practically the same thing, an evasion of the great law of work. And the revenge of Nature was therefore necessary. It could not help punishing the Sacculina for violated law, and the punishment, according to the strange and noteworthy way in which Nature usually punishes, was meted but by natural processes, carried on within its own organization. Its punishment was simply that it was a Sacculina—that it was a Sacculina when it might have been a Crustacean. Instead of being a free and independent organism high in structure, original in action, vital with energy, it deteriorated into a torpid and all but amorphous sac confined to perpetual imprisonment and doomed to a living death. "Any new set of conditions," says Ray Lankester, "occurring to an animal which render its food and safety very easily attained, seem to lead as a rule to degeneration; just as an active healthy man sometimes degenerates when he becomes suddenly possessed of a fortune; or as Rome degenerated when possessed of the riches of the ancient world. The habit of parasitism clearly acts upon animal organization in this way. Let the parasitic life once be secured, and away go legs, jaws, eyes, and ears; the active, highly-gifted crab, insect or annelid may become a mere sac, absorbing nourishment and laying eggs." [95]

There could be no more impressive illustration than this of what with entire appropriateness one might call "the physiology of backsliding." We fail to appreciate the meaning of spiritual degeneration or detect the terrible nature of the consequences only because they evade the eye of sense. But could we investigate the spirit as a living organism, or study the soul of the backslider on principles of comparative anatomy, we should have a revelation of the organic effects of sin, even of the mere sin of carelessness as to growth and work, which must revolutionize our ideas of practical religion. There is no room for the doubt even that what goes on in the body does not with equal certainty take place in the spirit under the corresponding conditions.

The penalty of backsliding is not something unreal and vague, some unknown quantity which may be measured out to us disproportionately, or which perchance, since God is good, we may altogether evade. The consequences are already marked within the structure of the soul. So to speak, they are physiological. The thing affected by our indifference or by our indulgence is not the book of final judgment but the present fabric of the soul. The punishment of degeneration is simply degeneration—the loss of functions, the decay of organs, the atrophy of the spiritual nature. It is well known that the recovery of the backslider is one of the hardest problems in spiritual work. To reinvigorate an old organ seems more difficult and hopeless than to develop a new one; and the backslider's terrible lot is to have to retrace with enfeebled feet each step of the way along which he strayed; to make up inch by inch the lee-way he has lost, carrying with him a dead-weight of acquired reluctance, and scarce knowing whether to be stimulated or discouraged by the oppressive memory of the previous fall.

We are not, however, to discuss at present the physiology of backsliding. Nor need we point out at greater length that parasitism is always and indissolubly accompanied by degeneration. We wish rather to examine one or two leading tendencies of the modern religious life which directly or indirectly induce the parasitic habit and bring upon thousands of unsuspecting victims such secret and appalling penalties as have been named.

Two main causes are known to the biologist as tending to induce the parasitic habit. These are, first, the temptation to secure safety without the vital exercise of faculties, and, second, the disposition to find food without earning it. The first, which we have formally considered, is probably the preliminary stage in most cases. The animal, seeking shelter, finds unexpectedly that it can also thereby gain a certain measure of food. Compelled in the first instance, perhaps by stress of circumstances, to rob its host of a meal or perish, it gradually acquires the habit of drawing all its supplies from the same source, and thus becomes in time a confirmed parasite. Whatever be its origin, however, it is certain that the main evil of parasitism is connected with the further question of food. Mere safety with Nature is a secondary, though by no means an insignificant, consideration. And while the organism forfeits a part of its organization by any method of evading enemies which demands no personal effort, the most entire degeneration of the whole system follows the neglect or abuse of the functions of nutrition.

The direction in which we have to seek the wider application of the subject will now appear. We have to look into those cases in the moral and spiritual sphere in which the functions of nutrition are either neglected or abused. To sustain life, physical, mental, moral, or spiritual, some sort of food is essential. To secure an adequate supply each organism also is provided with special and appropriate faculties. But the final gain to the organism does not depend so much on the actual amount of food procured as on the exercise required to obtain it. In one sense the exercise is only a means to an end, namely, the finding food; but in another and equally real sense, the exercise is the end, the food the means to attain that. Neither is of permanent use without the other, but the correlation between them is so intimate that it were idle to say that one is more necessary than the other. Without food exercise is impossible, but without exercise food is useless.

Thus exercise is in order to food, and food is in order to exercise—in order especially to that further progress and maturity which only ceaseless activity can promote. Now food too easily acquired means food without that accompaniment of discipline which is infinitely more valuable than the food itself. It means the possibility of a life which is a mere existence. It leaves the organism *in statu quo,* undeveloped, immature, low in the scale of organization and with a growing tendency to pass from the state of equilibrium to that of increasing degeneration. What an organism is depends upon what it does; its activities make it. And if the stimulus to the exercise of all the innumerable faculties concerned in nutrition be withdrawn by the conditions and circumstances of life becoming, or being made to become, too easy, there is first an arrest of development, and finally a loss of the parts themselves. If, in short, an organism does nothing, in that relation it is nothing.

We may, therefore, formulate the general principle thus: *Any principle which secures food to the individual without the expenditure of work is injurious, and accompanied by the degeneration and loss of parts.*

The social and political analogies of this law, which have been casually referred to already, are sufficiently familiar to render any further development in these directions superfluous. After the eloquent preaching of the Gospel of Work by Thomas Carlyle, this century at least can never plead that one of the most important moral bearings of the subject has not been duly impressed upon it. All that can be said of idleness generally might be fitly urged in support of this great practical truth. All nations which have prematurely passed away, buried in graves dug by their own effeminacy; all those individuals who have secured a hasty wealth by the chances of speculation; all children of fortune; all victims of inheritance; all social sponges; all satellites of the court; all beggars of the market-place—all these are living and unlying witness to the unalterable retributions of the law of parasitism. But it is when we come to study the working of the principle in the religious sphere there we discover the full extent of the ravages which the parasitic habit can make on the souls of men. We can only hope to indicate here one or two of the things in modern Christianity which minister most subtly and widely to this as yet all but unnamed sin.

We begin in what may seem a somewhat unlooked-for quarter. One of the things in the religious world which tends most strongly to induce the parasitic habit is *Going to Church*. Church-going itself every Christian will rightly consider an invaluable aid to the ripe development of the spiritual life. Public worship has a place in the national religious life so firmly established that nothing is ever likely to shake its influence. So supreme indeed, is the ecclesiastical system in all Christian countries that with thousands the religion of the Church and the religion of the individual are one. But just because of its high and unique place in religious regard, does it become men from time to time to inquire how far the Church is really ministering to the spiritual health of the immense religious community which looks to it as its foster-mother. And if it falls to us here reluctantly to expose some secret abuses of this venerable system, let it be well understood that these are abuses, and not that the sacred institution itself is being violated by the attack of an impious hand.

The danger of church-going largely depends on the form of worship, but it may be affirmed that even the most perfect Church affords to all worshipers a greater or less temptation to parasitism. It consists essentially in the deputy-work or deputy-worship inseparable from the church or chapel ministrations. One man is set apart to prepare a certain amount of spiritual truth for the rest. He, if he is a true man, gets all the benefits of original work. He finds the truth, digests it, is nourished and enriched by it before he offers it to his flock. To a large extent it will nourish and enrich in turn a number of his hearers. But still they will lack something. The faculty of selecting truth at first hand and appropriating it for one's self is a lawful possession to every Christian. Rightly exercised it conveys to him truth in its freshest form; it offers him the opportunity of verifying doctrines for himself; it makes religion personal; it deepens and intensifies the only convictions that are worth deepening, those, namely, which are honest; and it supplies the mind with a basis of certainty in religion. But if all one's truth is derived by imbibition from the Church, the faculties for receiving truth are not only undeveloped but one's whole view of truth becomes distorted. He who abandons the personal search for truth, under whatever pretext, abandons truth. The very word truth, by becoming the limited possession of a guild, ceases to have any meaning; and faith, which can only be founded on truth, gives way to credulity, resting on mere opinion.

In those churches especially where all parts of the worship are subordinated to the sermon, this species of parasitism is peculiarly encouraged. What is meant to be a stimulus to thought becomes the substitute for it. The hearer never really learns, he only listens. And while truth and knowledge seem to increase, life and character are left in arrear. Such truth, of course, and such knowledge, are a mere seeming. Having cost nothing, they come to nothing. The organism acquires a growing immobility, and finally exists in a state of entire intellectual helplessness and inertia. So the parasitic Church-member, the literal "adherent," comes not merely to live only within the circle of ideas of his minister, but to be content that his minister has these ideas—like the literary parasite who fancies he knows everything because he has a good library.

Where the worship, again, is largely liturgical the danger assumes an even more serious form, and it acts in some such way as this. Every sincere man who sets out in the Christian race begins by attempting to exercise the spiritual faculties for himself. The young life throbs in his veins, and he sets himself to the further progress with earnest purpose and resolute will. For a time he bids fair to attain a high and original development. But the temptation to relax the always difficult effort at spirituality is greater than he knows. The "carnal mind" itself is "enmity against God," and the antipathy, or the deadlier apathy within, is unexpectedly encouraged from that very outside source from which he anticipates the greatest help. Connecting himself with a Church he is no less interested than surprised to find how rich is the provision there for every part of his spiritual nature. Each service satisfies or surfeits. Twice, or even three times a week, this feast is spread for him. The thoughts are deeper than his own, the faith keener, the worship loftier, the whole ritual more reverent and splendid. What more natural than that he should gradually exchange his personal religion for that of the congregation? What more likely than that a public religion should by insensible stages supplant his individual faith? What more simple than to content himself with the warmth of another's soul. What more tempting than to give up private prayer for the easier worship of the liturgy or of the church? What, in short, more natural than for the independent, free-moving, growing Sacculina to degenerate into the listless, useless, pampered parasite of the pew? The very means he takes to nurse his personal religion often come in time to wean him from it. Hanging admiringly, or even enthusiastically, on the lips of eloquence, his senses now stirred by ceremony, now soothed by music, the parasite of the pew enjoys his weekly worship—his character untouched, his will unbraced, his crude soul unquickened and unimproved. Thus, instead of ministering to the growth of individual members, and very often just in proportion to the superior excellence of the provision made for them by another, does this gigantic system of deputy-nutrition tend to destroy development and arrest the genuine culture of the soul. Our churches overflow with members who are mere consumers. Their interest in religion is purely parasitic. Their only spiritual exercise is the automatic one of imbibition, the clergyman being the faithful Hermit-crab who is to be depended on every Sunday for at least a week's supply.

A physiologist would describe the organism resulting from such a progress as a case of "arrested development." Instead of having learned to pray, the ecclesiastical parasite becomes satisfied with being prayed for. His transactions with the Eternal are effected by commission. His work for Christ is done by a paid deputy. His whole life is a prolonged indulgence in the bounties of the Church; and surely—in some cases at least the crowning irony—he sends for the minister when he lies down to die.

Other signs and consequences of this species of parasitism soon become very apparent. The first symptom is idleness. When a Church is off its true diet it is off its true work. Hence one explanation of the hundreds of large and influential congregations ministered to from week to week by men of eminent learning and earnestness, which yet do little or nothing in the line of these special activities for which all churches exist. An outstanding man at the head of a huge, useless and torpid congregation is always a puzzle.

But is the reason not this, that the congregation gets too good food too cheap? Providence has mercifully delivered the Church from too many great men in her pulpits, but there are enough in every country-side to play the host disastrously to a large circle of otherwise able-bodied Christian people, who, thrown on their own resources, might fatten themselves and help others. There are compensations to a flock for a poor minister after all. Where the fare is indifferent those who are really hungry will exert themselves to procure their own supply.

That the Church has indispensable functions to discharge to the individual is not denied; but taking into consideration the universal tendency to parasitism in the human soul it is a grave question whether in some cases it does not really effect more harm than good. A dead church certainly, a church having no reaction on the community, a church without propagative power in the world, cannot be other than a calamity to all within its borders. Such a church is an institution, first for making, then for screening parasites; and instead of representing to the world the Kingdom of God on earth, it is despised alike by godly and by godless men as the refuge for fear and formalism and the nursery of superstition.

And this suggests a second and not less practical evil of a parasitic piety—that it presents to the world a false conception of the religion of Christ. One notices with a frequency which may well excite alarm that the children of church-going parents often break away as they grow in intelligence, not only from church-connection but from the whole system of family religion. In some cases this is doubtless due to natural perversity, but in others it certainly arises from the hollowness of the outward forms which pass current in society and at home for vital Christianity. These spurious forms, fortunately or unfortunately, soon betray themselves. How little there is in them becomes gradually apparent. And rather than indulge in a sham the budding sceptic, as the first step, parts with the form and in nine cases out of ten concerns himself no further to find a substitute. Quite deliberately, quite honestly, sometimes with real regret and even at personal sacrifice he takes up his position, and to his parent's sorrow and his church's dishonor forsakes forever the faith and religion of his fathers. Who will deny that this is a true account of the natural history of much modern scepticism? A formal religion can never hold its own in the nineteenth century. It is better that it should not. We must either be real or cease to be. We must either give up our Parasitism or our sons.

Any one who will take the trouble to investigate a number of cases where whole families of outwardly godly parents have gone astray, will probably find that the household religion had either some palpable defect, or belonged essentially to the parasitic order. The popular belief that the sons of clergymen turn out worse than those of the laity is, of course, without foundation; but it may also probably be verified that in the instances where clergymen's sons notoriously discredit their father's ministry, that ministry in a majority of cases, will be found to be professional and theological rather than human and spiritual. Sequences in the moral and spiritual world follow more closely than we yet discern the great law of Heredity. The Parasite begets the Parasite—only in the second generation the offspring are sometimes sufficiently wise to make the discovery, and honest enough to proclaim it.

We now pass on to the consideration of another form of Parasitism which though closely related to that just discussed, is of sufficient importance to justify a separate reference. Appealing to a somewhat smaller circle, but affecting it not less disastrously, is the Parasitism induced by certain abuses of *Systems of Theology*.

In its own place, of course, Theology is no more to be dispensed with than the Church. In every perfect religious system three great departments must always be represented—criticism, dogmatism, and evangelism. Without the first there is no guarantee of truth, without the second no defence of truth, and without the third no propagation of truth. But when these departments become mixed up, when their separate functions are forgotten, when one is made to do duty for another, or where either is developed by the church or the individual at the expense of the rest, the result is fatal. The particular abuse, however, of which we have now to speak, concerns the tendency in orthodox communities, first to exalt orthodoxy above all other elements in religion, and secondly to make the possession of sound beliefs equivalent to the possession of truth.

Doctrinal preaching, fortunately, as a constant practice is less in vogue than in a former age, but there are still large numbers whose only contact with religion is through theological forms. The method is supported by a plausible defence. What is doctrine but a compressed form of truth, systematized by able and pious men, and sanctioned by the imprimatur of the Church? If the greatest minds of the Church's past, having exercised themselves profoundly upon the problems of religion, formulated as with one voice a system of doctrine, why should the humble inquirer not gratefully accept it? Why go over the ground again? Why with his dim light should he betake himself afresh to Bible study and with so great a body of divinity already compiled, presume himself to be still a seeker after truth? Does not Theology give him Bible truth in reliable, convenient, and moreover, in logical propositions? There it lies extended to the last detail in the tomes of the Fathers, or abridged in a hundred modern compendia, ready-made to his hand, all cut and dry, guaranteed sound and wholesome, why not use it?

Just because it is all cut and dry. Just because it is ready-made. Just because it lies there in reliable, convenient and logical propositions. The moment you appropriate truth in such a shape you appropriate a form. You cannot cut and dry truth. You cannot accept truth ready-made without it ceasing to nourish the soul as the truth. You cannot live on theological forms without becoming a Parasite and ceasing to be a man.

There is no worse enemy to a living Church than a propositional theology, with the latter controlling the former by traditional authority. For one does not then receive the truth for himself, he accepts it bodily. He begins the Christian life set up by his Church with a stock-in-trade which has cost him nothing, and which, though it may serve him all his life, is just exactly worth as much his belief in his Church. This possession of truth, moreover, thus lightly won, is given to him as infallible. It is a system. There is nothing to add to it. At his peril let him question or take from it. To start a convert in life with such a principle is unspeakably degrading. All through life instead of working toward truth he must work from it. An infallible standard is a temptation to a mechanical faith. Infallibility always paralyzes. It gives rest; but it is the rest of stagnation. Men perform one great act of faith at the beginning of their life, then have done with it forever. All moral, intellectual and spiritual effort is over; and a cheap theology ends in a cheap life.

The same thing that makes men take refuge in the Church of Rome makes them take refuge in a set of dogmas. Infallibility meets the deepest desire of man, but meets it in the most fatal form. Men deal with the hunger after truth in two ways. First by Unbelief—which crushes it by blind force; or, secondly, by resorting to some external source credited with Infallibility—which lulls it to sleep by blind faith. The effect of a doctrinal theology is the effect of Infallibility. And the wholesale belief in such a system, however accurate it may be—grant even that it were infallible—is not Faith though it always gets that name. It is mere Credulity. It is a complacent and idle rest upon authority, not a hard-earned, self-obtained, personal possession. The moral responsibility here, besides, is reduced to nothing. Those who framed the Thirty-nine Articles or the Westminster Confession are responsible. And anything which destroys responsibility, or transfers it, cannot be other than injurious in its moral tendency and useless in itself.

It may be objected perhaps that this statement of the paralysis spiritual and mental induced by Infallibility applies also to the Bible. The answer is that though the Bible is infallible, the Infallibility is not in such a form as to become a temptation. There is the widest possible difference between the form of truth in the Bible and the form in theology.

In theology truth is propositional—tied up in neat parcels, systematized, and arranged in logical order. The Trinity is an intricate doctrinal problem. The Supreme Being is discussed in terms of philosophy. The Atonement is a formula which is to be demonstrated like a proposition in Euclid. And Justification is to be worked out as a question of jurisprudence. There is no necessary connection between these doctrines and the life of him who holds them. They make him orthodox, not necessarily righteous. They satisfy the intellect but need not touch the heart. It does not, in short, take a religious man to be a theologian. It simply takes a man with fair reasoning powers. This man happens to apply these powers to theological subjects—but in no other sense than he might apply them to astronomy or physics. But truth in the Bible is a fountain. It is a diffused nutriment, so diffused that no one can put himself off with the form. It is reached not by thinking, but by doing. It is seen, discerned, not demonstrated. It cannot be bolted whole, but must be slowly absorbed into the system. Its vagueness to the mere intellect, its refusal to be packed into portable phrases, its satisfying unsatisfyingness, its vast atmosphere, its finding of us, its mystical hold of us, these are the tokens of its infinity.

Nature never provides for man's wants in any direction, bodily, mental, or spiritual, in such a form as that he can simply accept her gifts automatically. She puts all the mechanical powers at his disposal—but he must make his lever. She gives him corn, but he must grind it. She elaborates coal, but he must dig for it. Corn is perfect, all the products of Nature are perfect, but he has everything to do to them before he can use them. So with truth; it is perfect, infallible. But he cannot use it as it stands. He must work, think, separate, dissolve, absorb, digest; and most of these he must do for himself and within himself. If it be replied that this is exactly what theology does, we answer it is exactly what it does not. It simply does what the greengrocer does when he arranges his apples and plums in his shop window. He may tell me a magnum bonum from a Victoria, or a Baldwin from a Newtown Pippin. But he does not help me to eat it. His information is useful, and for scientific horticulture essential. Should a sceptical pomologist deny that there was such a thing as a Baldwin, or mistake it for a Newtown Pippin, we should be glad to refer to him; but if we were hungry, and an orchard were handy, we should not trouble him. Truth in the Bible is an orchard rather than a museum. Dogmatism will be very valuable to us when scientific necessity makes us go to the museum. Criticism will be very useful in seeing that only fruit-bearers grow in the orchard. But truth in the doctrinal form is not natural, proper, assimilable food for the soul of man.

Is this a plea then for doubt? Yes, for that philosophic doubt which is the evidence of a faculty doing its own work. It is more necessary for us to be active than to be orthodox. To be orthodox is what we wish to be, but we can only truly reach it by being honest, by being original, by seeing with our own eyes, by believing with our own heart. "An idle life," says Goethe, "is death anticipated." Better far be burned at the stake of Public Opinion than die the living death of Parasitism. Better an aberrant theology than a suppressed organization. Better a little faith dearly won, better launched alone on the infinite bewilderment of Truth, than perish on the splendid plenty of the richest creeds. Such Doubt is no self-willed presumption. Nor, truly exercised, will it prove itself, as much doubt does, the synonym for sorrow. It aims at a life-long learning, prepared for any sacrifice of will yet for none of independence; at that high progressive education which yields rest in work and work in rest, and the development of immortal faculties in both; at that deeper faith which believes in the vastness and variety of the revelations of God, and their accessibility to all obedient hearts.

FOOTNOTES:

[95] "Degeneration," by E. Ray Lankester, p. 33.

www.ingramcontent.com/pod-product-compliance
Lightning Source LLC
Chambersburg PA
CBHW081109080526
44587CB00021B/3512